A Passion

for the

Great
Commission

A
Passion
for the
Great
Commission

Essays in Honor of Alvin L. Reid

LARRY STEVEN MCDONALD
AND
MATT QUEEN

Published by Towering Oaks Books
Greer, South Carolina
ToweringOaksBooks@gmail.com

Library of Congress Control Number: 2014931050

Unless otherwise noted, Scripture is taken from the Holman Christian Standard Bible ® Copyright © 2003, 2002, 2000, 1999 by Holman Bible Publishers. All rights reserved.

Printed in the United States of America.

Any people depicted in stock imagery provided by Thinkstock are models, and such images are being used for illustrative purposes only.

Certain stock imagery © Thinkstock.

Prepared for publishing by Colter & Co. Design, Fort Worth, Texas
www.colterco.com

COLTER & Co.

Table of Contents

Strategies for the Great Commission

The Challenge

Appendices

Preface

For almost a quarter of a century now, Southern Baptist evangelism and discipleship professors have published *festschrifts* in honor of their former evangelism professors. Dr. Thom Rainer began this tradition by editing and contributing to a *festschrift* in honor of Dr. Lewis A. Drummond. Drs. Alvin Reid and Timothy Beougher followed by honoring Dr. Roy J. Fish with a *festschrift*. Most recently, Dr. J. Chris Schofield published a *festschrift* in honor of Dr. Delos Miles. In order to continue this tradition, we present this volume to honor the life and ministry of our former evangelism professor, Dr. Alvin Reid.

A native of Alabama, Dr. Alvin Reid professed his faith in Jesus Christ as an eleven-year-old in 1970 during the Jesus Movement. He met his wife, Michelle, at Samford University in Birmingham, Alabama, where he began his ministry studies. Dr. Reid completed both his MDiv and his PhD in evangelism at Southwestern Baptist Theological Seminary in Fort Worth, Texas. He served as pastor, state evangelism director, music minister, and youth evangelist before beginning his teaching career at Houston Baptist University in Houston, Texas. In 1995 he and his family moved to Wake Forest, North Carolina, where he currently serves as Professor of Evangelism and Student Ministry and occupies the Bailey Smith Chair of Evangelism at Southeastern Baptist Theological Seminary.

A varied group of Dr. Reid's friends, colleagues, and former students have contributed essays to this festschrift. Despite some diversity among the contributors, these authors unite together in this volume to express their sincere gratitude for the ways that God has used Dr. Alvin Reid as a catalyst to ignite a burning passion in believers for the Great Commission. Each author explores topics related to Dr. Reid's personal ministry interests in relation to the Great Commission of our Lord. The essays comprising this volume form four sections arranged according to the areas of Great Commission leadership, history, strategies, and vision. A fifth section of the book presents a bibliography of Dr. Reid's works, some of which are annotated.

We are grateful to each of the contributors for their involvement in this project. We offer special thanks to President James Epting and Vice President J. Samuel Isgett of North Greenville University, as well as President Paige Patterson and Dean Keith Eitel of Southwestern Baptist Theological Seminary, for their support throughout the publication process. We extend sincere thanks to two graduate assistants of Southwestern Baptist Theological Seminary, who researched and assembled this book's Indexes. John Sun, an evangelism and church vitalization PhD student, composed the Scripture Index. Grace Morris, graduate assistant to international PhD students, compiled both the Subject and Person Indexes. Larry expresses sincere appreciation to his wife, Tina for her encouragement and support, to his children, Ben, Lori, ReBecca, and Jessica and to his granddaughter, Brenna Michelle, for the joy and inspiration they provide, and to Charlotte Lovett and Curtis and Debbie White for the writing retreat at the "Amazing Grace Cabin." Matt expresses sincere appreciation to his wife, Hope, and his two daughters, Madison and Matia, for their encouragement to him at all times. Finally, we thank Dr. Alvin Reid for his investment in the lives and ministries of all his students throughout the years, including us.

—LARRY STEVEN MCDONALD
Professor of Christian Spirituality
Dean and Director of Doctor of Ministry Studies
T. Walter Brashier Graduate School of Christian Ministry
North Greenville University
Greenville, South Carolina

—MATT QUEEN
Assistant Professor of Evangelism
Associate Dean for Doctoral Programs
Roy Fish School of Evangelism and Missions
Southwestern Baptist Theological Seminary
Fort Worth, Texas

Foreword

I have written the foreword for two or three books in the past, and it was a hit or miss situation. I had no pattern and not much plan. Thus, when asked to write a foreword for the *festschrift* honoring Alvin Reid, I thought I would check some books in my library and see how others did it. The first thing I discovered was that most books do not have a foreword. Out of over twenty books I checked, only three had one. The rest had a preview or recognition of common judgments.

In this case, I would not want to miss the opportunity of making some type of contribution to this book dedicated to one of the finest scholars. I count it a real privilege to write the foreword of this book. I came to know Alvin well when he was a doctoral student. I recall in the first seminar, when each student introduced himself, Alvin, in telling us a small bit about himself, expressed his desire to be a good writer. After authoring over one hundred published articles and a dozen or so books, plus chapters in a number of others, it appears he is well on the way to achieving his desire.

A *festschrift* is usually dedicated to a professor and is usually composed of essays written by friends, colleagues, and former students. The essays in this book are concerned with a passion for a great commission resurgence. The theme of the book is of critical importance: Never in recent history has the need of revival been so great. A vital part of this theme is a passion for obedience to the Great Commission. There are four major sections of this book. The first deals with leading a Great Commission resurgence and the second with spiritual resurgence from a historical standpoint. The third is concerned with strategy and the last with the present challenge. The authors are some of our finest pastors, professors, and students.

Alvin is a superlative professor. He is touching hundreds of lives and is a credit to his Lord, his seminary, and his denomination. It is a privilege to be the author of the foreword to a book dedicated to him.

—ROY J. FISH
Distinguished Professor Emeritus of Evangelism
L.R. Scarborough Chair of Evangelism ("Chair of Fire")
Southwestern Baptist Theological Seminary
Fort Worth, Texas

Section One

*Leadership for the
Great Commission*

CHAPTER ONE

Integrity And The Great Commission
Doug Munton, Ph.D.

Author's Note

My wife and I were brand new seminary students in Fort Worth, Texas. We knew almost no one in the state having just arrived from the frozen northland of Illinois. We settled into our new home—the luxurious apartments (perhaps my memory is tricky here!) of Seminary Village as it was named.

One January day we were out on the balcony of the apartments—still amazed that we could be out on a balcony in January. There we met a couple with funny accents. It was a boisterous young man and a quiet young woman from Alabama named Alvin and Michelle Reid. They seemed like nice people—despite their curious interest in grits—and so we became friends.

A few years later, Alvin and I began our Ph.D. program in Evangelism together. We toiled under the hot sun of massive papers and ponderous research. I discovered that the southern boy was quite the capable scholar. His sharp mind and hard work soon demonstrated outstanding ability.

Not long afterwards, Alvin came to serve with me at the small church where I served, First Baptist Church of Corinth, Texas. I was the pastor and Alvin became the "Minister of Everything Else." He led the worship services, directed our Sunday School, and befriended everyone in the church. I soon discovered he was more than a scholar of evangelism; he was also a tremendous and committed practitioner.

Together, Alvin and I made visits, shared the gospel and watched that small church grow and grow despite our inexperience and mistakes. Our families ate together, prayed together, and shared life together. We solved most of the problems in Christendom and quite a few of those of the world at large. What fun and life we shared!

Here is what we learned in those exciting, idealistic years of school and ministry. Integrity and the great commission go together. I gladly testify that Alvin Reid has shown decades of commitment to both.

Introduction

The person participating in the great commission is as important as the program of participation in the Great Commission. We can never entirely separate who we are from what we do.

Evangelicals in general and Southern Baptists in particular, often speak of the work of the Great Commission. This is natural and good. But we err if we forget the work of the Lord of the Great Commission in our own lives. In other words, integrity matters in the fulfillment of the Lord's task.

If we lose our commitment to integrity we will, ultimately, lose our commitment to the great commission. If our commitment to our

Lord's commands concerning morality is ignored we will find that our commitment to the Lord's commands concerning evangelism and missions will also be ignored.

The premise of this chapter is that our personal integrity and our commitment to evangelism and missions go together. If we are to have a Great Commission resurgence we need a great holiness resurgence.

I heard a preacher tell this story once. He told of a doctor who was doing emergency surgery. He asked an assistant for a scalpel. "Which one?" he was asked. The preacher told of this simple reply from the surgeon. "It doesn't matter as long as it's clean." The preacher who told that story was Dr. Alvin Reid. The truth behind that story is the story of integrity and the great commission.

Part One: Whatever Happened to Holiness?
The Great Commission Resurgence
and the Call to Holiness

The connection of holiness to the work of the great commission is the connection of God's blessing to His mandate. A godly lifestyle is a necessary ingredient to a godly life of service and effectiveness.

Great Commission work without a holy life is empty. Holiness without obedience to the Lord of holiness is contradictory.

The Neglected Doctrine: Holiness and Love

"Holy, holy, holy is the Lord of Hosts; His glory fills the whole earth" (HCSB). That was the cry of the angels as recorded in Isaiah 6. Whatever happened to that designation of the character of God?

I feel confident that the primary description of God in my community (and in most communities of this country) would be different in this generation. This generation would describe God as love if asked to give a one word description. There is nothing wrong with that. God is love and to describe him as love is to describe accurately one of his characteristics.

It is my opinion, based on my study of the faith history of our country that God would have been described differently in earlier times. In the days of Jonathan Edwards, Charles Wesley, Charles Finney, and D.L. Moody the most common description of God would be that He is holy.[1]

Both descriptions of God are true. God is love and God is holy. But to focus on one aspect while ignoring the other is to miss the full truth of God's nature. To note God's holiness while missing His love is to be in danger of a cold, harsh faith. To see only his love without His holiness is to be in danger of a shallow, superficial faith.

This shallow, superficial faith which rejoices in God's love but forgets God's holiness has become common place in our country and culture. "Why bother too much with obedience to God when we know God is love and forgiveness is easy?" it reasons. Obedience to the great commission (or other difficult commands) becomes a burden too heavy to bear for such weak faith. Besides, disobedience to a god of all love and no holiness carries no real consequences.

The doctrine of holiness must be recaptured in the church. The church of today needs a rediscovery of God's holiness and the ramifications of this truth. Once again the church must join the angels in crying "Holy, holy, holy is the Lord of Hosts."

May I say it more directly? The doctrine of the holiness must be recaptured by you. You and I need a renewed understanding of God's holiness and

---

[1] For additional information on these men and others and their views on holiness and revival see Malcolm McDow & Alvin Reid, *Firefall: How God Has Shaped History Through Revivals* (Nashville: Broadman & Holman, 1997).

the call to holiness we have. We must raise our own voices in the cry of recognition, "Holy, holy, holy is the Lord of Hosts."

Unless and until Christians come to grips with this essential doctrine we will not know the power of God in fulfilling the great commission. We will ignore it or compromise it or rebel against it. But we cannot ignore God's command when we truly know God's character.

The Issue of Lordship

Believers who are serious about faith must ultimately deal with the issue of the lordship of Christ. Jesus begins the section we know as the great commission with the words "All authority has been given to me in heaven and on earth" (Matt 28:18, HCSB).

Jesus is the possessor of all authority. He is, the Bible states to us repeatedly, Lord. Upon the lordship of Christ rests our obedience to his Great Commission. Verses 19–20 of Matthew 28 tell us the work of the Great Commission. Verse 18 tells us the authority of the Great Commission. We are to "Go" because of the "therefore." Verse 18 is the "therefore" of the Great Commission.

If Jesus is my Lord, obedience is my natural response. I obey his mandates and his requirements because He is my Lord. Out of his authority in my life comes my response to make disciples of all nations. The work of the Great Commission becomes an act of my obedience to the Lord of the Great Commission.

Jesus said, "Why do you call Me Lord, Lord and don't do the things I say?" (Luke 6:46, HCSB). If we call Him Lord, we should obey his sayings. Lordship becomes the foundation for our obedience to the work of the great commission.

I am something of a coward. Okay, I have admitted it in public now! I can be something of a coward when it comes to sharing my faith with others. I can be something of a coward when it comes to sacrificial missions giving. And, I might not be the only one.

You may join me in being fearful when it comes to witnessing. Perhaps you have a fear of being willing to follow God anywhere in the world or being willing to give everything to God's work of redemption. Fear is where the "tire" of lordship hits the "road" of obedience for me. I can be cowardly when it comes to witnessing but my obedience to my Lord compels me to witness anyway. I can be nervous about a radical commitment to missions but my obedience to the Lord urges me to be radical anyway. In many ways, lordship is the critical issue for me when it comes to my work in the Great Commission.

Part Two: What Am I to Do?
The Great Commission and Incarnational Ministry

Our commitment to holiness, integrity and the lordship of Christ leads us to obedience to the Great Commission. That obedience becomes a part of the fiber of our ministry and service. The Great Commission is lived out in our actions because it is spoken into our being.

Two major themes permeate the Great Commission: evangelism and discipleship. They go together as two parts of one song or two strands of one cord.

I was told once of a prominent leader who made a terrible appeal. He called on the church to correct a lack of discipleship by having a moratorium on evangelism. What a tragic thought! Would we obey God in His clear teaching on discipleship by disobeying Him on His clear teaching on evangelism?

Better to wed these two friends together than to promote one by ceasing the other. Both evangelism and discipleship are best accomplished by allowing them to become part of the very fabric of our teaching and preaching.

Evangelism and discipleship happen best when they are part of the fabric of our ministries. They are best seen as being part of what we do because they are part of who we are. Perhaps the best word we can use to describe this concept is the word "incarnation."

The word incarnation describes the very nature of Christ. He is God who became man. God "lived out" the truth of the divine in human form. We are to "live out" the great commission. The truths of Christ's command are fleshed out in our work of evangelism and discipleship.

Incarnational Evangelism

Evangelism is the sharing of the gospel with lost people. The Great Commission uses the participle "going" with imperatival force so that it is most often translated "go." The idea is that we are to be involved in the sharing of the message of the gospel with those who are lost.

I am for all evangelism which is done with integrity. Different programs, methods, and styles matter not to me so long as they are done without compromise to the message and to righteousness. But it does seem to me that evangelism must be demonstrated by the life of the evangelist more now than ever.

I recently led an adult woman to Christ who had heard me preach several times. She had heard me do the best I can to tell the message of the gospel through public proclamation. But it was not until I spoke directly with her and her husband that she really heard the nature of the truth. When I preached, it was to them. When I witnessed directly, it was to her.

Perhaps never has there been a time in our history when evangelism needed to be more connected to the lifestyle of the witness. Servant evangelism has never been more effective for that very reason. People are convinced by the life of the messenger—his or her work which verifies the truth—as much as they are by the proclamation of the message itself.

God has always concerned Himself with the integrity of the messenger. It seems to me that society today cares about the integrity of the messenger as well. "If this is true," they reason, "it will show itself in the life of adherents." Perhaps never before has evangelistic activity so needed to be incarnational in nature.

Incarnational Discipleship

Discipleship is quite obviously a core part of the Great Commission. We are not told to make decisions but to make disciples. We are to help people come to Christ as Savior and then to follow Him as their Lord.

Discipleship is not just worked out; it is lived out. That is, we live out the truth of God's commandments in community. Obedience to all that He teaches is lived out in the home, the school, the office and the church.

A pernicious doctrine has infected many believers. It segments the person's life so that they have a sacred life and a secular life. What they believe about God affects their Sunday morning but has little to do with their Saturday evening or Monday morning.

Genuine disciples are to understand that following Christ is part of the totality of life. His word and His leading are to penetrate our whole life. Every aspect of our life belongs to the Lord and there is no "segmentation" of His lordship.

Part Three: Do I Have Any Help?
The Great Commission Resurgence and Accountability

A sports analogy is instructive here. Many view the faith as they view golf. Golf is, by and large, an individual sport. You can play it by yourself and your effectiveness is determined by you and not by the effectiveness of others. You may join others in playing a round, but it is an individual sport.

Team sports, on the other hand, are much more dependent upon others. While a running back on a football team must use individual effort, his success is partly determined by the success of the offensive linemen laboring in obscurity.

Christianity is both an individual and a team sport. (Okay, I won't push the sports analogy much further, but bear with me.) While we are each individually responsible for our choices concerning Christ we need each other in order to live successfully for Christ.

Herein lays a tragic truth. Many Christians have lost the sense of team.

I spoke recently with a young man with an increasingly common story. He was a Christian and wanted to be committed to Christ. But he did not want to participate in a church.

Aside from the obvious issue of obedience to the Lord (see Hebrews 10:24–25 as an example of our need for church attendance), this young man was missing part of the Christian life. My faith is not just about me. It is not just about what I want or like or what is convenient for me. It is about others and serving and fellowship and community.

Together we fulfill the work of the Great Commission. Together we serve the Lord and serve others. Together we teach and we learn. Together we do evangelism and discipleship. We each use our own gifts and talents and resources, yes. But we ultimately do them together.

This is what our togetherness means. We are accountable to each other. We are accountable for using our gifts, talents and resources.

During my football years (I know I am a cream puff now, but once I was the captain of the mighty Wheaton College football team. Oh, the glory!), we always reviewed our previous games by watching the films. These film sessions could be great "Excellent play, Munton. That was not bad for such a knucklehead!" or they could be bad, "That was terrible, Munton. What kind of an idiot are you?" Leaving aside the question of how many different kinds of idiots there may be, these film sessions had a purpose: accountability.

Accountability is a critical part of the Christian life and of fulfilling the work of the Great Commission. We are each responsible for our work and accountable to others in the body of Christ. The Bible says, "Iron sharpens iron, and one man sharpens another" (Prov 27:17, HCSB).

Integrity and Accountability

One of the greatest benefits of accountability comes in the area of integrity. We can hold each other accountable for our obedience to our Lord and to the issues of personal holiness.

There are some factors which tend to keep ministry leaders from the kind of accountability which would benefit their personal walk with the Lord. I will note several general observations about lack of accountability among ministry leaders.

1. Ministers[2] tend to have many casual friendships but few close friendships. They have many they can talk with about golf or church life but few they can talk with about lust.

2. Ministers often fail to keep long-term friendships. The hard work of keeping up with others for a lifetime is replaced with the easier work of keeping friendships with those who have known us only recently.

3. Ministers may undervalue the benefits of close relationships with other ministers. By focusing on their task at hand they forget the value of their natural allies—other ministers.

4. Ministers can get so busy doing the work of God around them that they forget about the work of God in them.

What would happen if accountability became the norm in our Christian lives? What benefits would ministry leaders discover if they had others whom they talked to and prayed with? At least a few benefits become obvious.

1. Smaller issues can be dealt with before they become bigger issues.

2. Encouragement—and its inherent benefits—is given at critical moments.

3. Prayer becomes specific and powerful.

4. Holiness is exalted to a place of greater prominence in their lives.

Early in my ministry I was in a prayer and accountability group which was exceedingly helpful. We held each other accountable to right living

---

[2] I am using the term "minister" here to refer to pastors, missionaries, church staff members, and denominational leaders rather than the broader definition of all who follow Christ.

and right motives. We prayed together and sought the Lord together. As is often the case, that group eventually fizzled out.

I do not blame anyone for the fizzle of that prayer group but I suppose we undervalued the benefits. Our different personalities and busy schedules kept us, perhaps, from fully seeing the long-term assistance it might give to our lives. And some things last only for a season.

I do know this. Accountability can be a great friend of integrity. Having a friend who will tell you the truth in love is important. Having others who will pray for you is critical. And sharing the faith with other believers is priceless. Perhaps you will be willing, hearing this truth again, to invest in a friendship and to build a relationship for the purpose of accountability.

Faithfulness and Accountability

Our convention has been reminded in recent days of the importance of being focused on the mandate of Christ. Reaching the unreached all over the world has been given a larger emphasis in our denomination and churches. We recognize that we are accountable for our faithfulness to the Great Commission.

Accountability is a helpful force in staying faithful to the task. Our seminaries are accountable to our convention for their part in fulfilling the Great Commission. Our state conventions and local associations are accountable to our churches for their part in the mandate. Our mission agencies are accountable for their faithful efforts. And, our missionaries, pastors, church leaders and church planters are accountable to each other and to the Lord for their work in making disciples of all nations.

We are in the work of ministry together. We serve together, plan together and we should pray together. Churches partner with missionaries. Planters partner with established congregations. Laymen partner with vocational ministers. We are all in this together.

Matthew 28:18 is instructive here. "Then Jesus came near and said to them…." He spoke to "them," plural. We, plural, are in this task together. We, plural, are accountable to our Lord and to each other.

The great sports teams are more together than the sum of their parts. Southern Baptist Convention, evangelical community, Christians at large—we can be more together than the sum of our individual efforts. We can join our heart together to the great task of the great commission. We each do our part and we join together collectively to do more than we could do alone.

It is my prayer that we will have a Great Commission resurgence. This must be more than a restructuring of our programs or more than a redistribution of our resources. It must be a new positioning of our hearts. It must be a new commitment to love, obey and serve the Lord. It must be a resurgence of love for the things of God and the purposes of God. And it must be a task that joins our differing personalities, styles and talents into one unified purpose of making disciples of all nations to the honor and glory of our Savior Jesus Christ.

CHAPTER TWO

Valiant Great Commission Families
John Avant, Ph.D.

W HEN I began to minister thirty years ago I saw the seeds of the collapse of the biblical family. I had great concern that these seeds would be watered by the downpour of a foul cultural flood and might produce a harvest of poisonous fruit that would threaten the very fabric of the church. I have been wrong about a lot of things I believed in the early days of ministry. But I actually may have underestimated the issue that the collapse of the family has become to the church today. Today blended and single families are the norm in the church I pastor. Some of these are wonderful families, but they all represent pain and a departure from God's plan at some point. The price to the next generation is staggering. In everything we do as a church, if we have any desire to be missional at all we have to consider how to do transformational ministry to the thousands of children all around us who have little—if any—model of a healthy family. At the same time we have to equip families in our church to wage war against forces that wish to wreck them, and equip them not just to survive, but also to actually make a kingdom impact in the world. I do not believe there is any more important or more difficult challenge the church faces today.

I certainly do not claim to have all the answers or to present anything but a starting point in this brief article, but I will share some of the things that I believe are helping us begin to turn the tide in our church and that we believe will help any family to follow Jesus together to become what He intended them to be.

To write this in honor of Alvin Reid is fully appropriate. There is not a better husband and father that I know. He is also a man who has prayed for my family personally and faithfully through some of the great joys and pain of our lives. Alvin has been there for me since he was my friend and fellow doctoral student, through major life transitions, through the mighty work of God that has become known as the Brownwood revival, through great answered prayers such as the salvation of my father-in-law for which we prayed for a decade. He has also been a father in ministry to countless students. Alvin is that professor who is cool! He is the guy that draws students like a magnet because they know he loves them. Then he takes them to the lost world and teaches the students how to love them too. It does not get much better than that. May this article be some small help to building more men like Alvin Reid and more families like his own.

To see that happen, we are going to have to become militaristic about defending our families, defeating the enemy who assaults our families, and seeing our families move intentionally and aggressively into living lives of victory instead of defeat. I am not talking here about amping up the culture war. Frankly, we are losing the war inside our churches to such an extent that we do not have the power nor the credibility to impact culture. I am talking about becoming militaristic about the attack on MY family, on YOUR family. I asked a man recently what he would do if he knew that right now a man was breaking into his house to rape and kill his wife and children. He replied that he would fight until his last breath to protect them. I then asked him if he had the same passion to defend his family against a real threat—not a hypothetical killer, but a real one who is even now seeking to violate and destroy his family in the worst way. Would he defend them by leading them spiritually, praying for them, over them, with them, teaching them the truths from God's Word that would protect them? Or would he let his family be assaulted while he devoted his time to correcting that wicked slice on the golf course? I think he was stunned at the analogy. But is not that what we are up against?

It's time to go to war. And it will require valor. That is a word we do not use that much anymore. Here is how I define valor: *"Valor is the decision to risk everything and sacrifice self to win victories that really matter."*

Your family really matters. So it is time for valor. It is time to raise up valiant families.

It was 1916 and Fred Bice was going to war. Since he was only fifteen, he had lied about his name and age, taking the first names of his best friends and combining them to form the name Homer Tommie. That is still the name listed for him in the military records. It's a long way from Alabama to Siberia. That is where he found himself as a part of what has become known as America's forgotten war—the battles that continued in Siberia at the end of World War I to protect American interests and refugees during the brutal Russian civil war. He was a part of the 27th infantry, which during his day was dubbed the "Wolfhounds" because of their fierce fighting and amazing speed with which they traveled across frozen Siberia. The 27th is still known as the Wolfhounds today.

On January 10, 1920, Bice (Tommie) was a part of an operation near the city of Posolskaya to stop a man named Semenoff, one of the most brutal commanders in military history. The operation succeeded but in the process, Bice was stabbed, shot, wounded by shrapnel and run over by a train! His best friend was killed. He was found so close to death that he was placed on a cart with dead bodies, and only a groan saved him from a premature burial.

I am glad he survived since Fred Bice was my grandfather! He lived with the loss of a leg and with other injuries all his life, but went on to live a wonderful life. He was awarded the second highest medal in our nation, the Distinguished Service Cross. My Pop has been gone now for many years, but last year my family surprised me and passed on his medal to me. As we were all sitting around the table at my mother and father's house, looking at the medal, my brother-in-law noticed faint engraving on it. With a magnifying glass we could see the worn words, "For Valor."

I have thought about those words many times since then. I will never live the life my grandfather lived. I will never exhibit his valor on a battlefield. But if I choose to, I can live with valor in the most important war we face—the battle for our families. I can live with valor as a husband and a father. I can teach others to do the same. I have a legacy of valor passed on to me. I want to be worthy of that legacy. I want to be a part of the victory of my family and others. What would that look like? How do we build valiant families?

No one gets married hoping for an average love. No one gets married just hoping to survive. Everyone wants the fairy tale, but few are willing to storm the castle and fight the dragon! That's what we must do if we want to win this war. So, in our church, we are determined to help each other. We are determined to return to the word of God for our families. We are determined to grow, and to raise disciples, not just children. If you've got a marriage problem, it is a discipleship problem. We are determined to disciple families again. It is not going to happen overnight, but we are going after it until Jesus comes back. We are going after "Valiant Families."

Let me elaborate on the definition of valor for just a moment. You will make a choice today to risk everything. It is just a matter of how you want to risk it. For instance, today some of you are trying to decide whether you want to stay in your marriage or not and it's hard. Welcome to the real world. Marriage is tough. It is tough for me. It is tough for my wife Donna particularly! Just because I am a preacher, does not mean marriage is easy. I do not make it easy a lot of the time.

Marriage is hard, so you may be tempted to make a terrible decision— to risk everything good that God's given you and pursue greener grass. Who knows, maybe there is someone out there who will make you think you are "happier," or who might fulfill something that your husband or wife does not, or will not, fulfill. But guess what? I would encourage you to take a look and see how that has worked out for our nation, for our families across this country, and see how it works out in the Word of God. There always will be needs that your spouse can fulfill right now that someone else will never be able fulfill. The greener grass out there will wither away once you are living on it!

So, if you are going to risk everything, why not risk it God's way instead of your own? Maybe you will not be as happy as you would like to be. Maybe everything will not be as you want it to be, but you made a promise. Keep it. Decide, "I am going to stay. I am going to choose God's way." When you do that, you are always choosing the right way. That's what we are going after.

You want to know how to have a valiant marriage? You have got to look in that mirror and decide you are going to sacrifice self every time. As long as it's the other person's fault, it's not going to work. You have got to sacrifice self. Is there any victory that matters more than having a great marriage and what that means in your life and the legacy you leave?

Revelation 2 may seem like a strange passage to turn to for marriage help. What in the world are we going to learn from Revelation about marriage? Everything we need. Here's what we forget: The Word of God is your marriage-counseling guide. This is your guide to a valiant marriage and everything else in your life by the way. Let me show you how it applies perfectly to your marriage. Who is the bride of Christ? The church! Is it an accident that Jesus used the symbol of marriage to address the church? Of course not. The church is His bride. We are the model; marriage is the model for the church. When He speaks to the church, He is speaking truth into your marriage. If you think of it that way, every time you open the Bible and read, there is something here for your marriage because we are the bride and He is speaking to our marriage as well.

Revelation 2:1-7 is a letter to the church, His bride, and His it is word to teach you how to divorce proof your marriage. If you will live out principles of Revelation 2, you will never divorce. If a husband and wife will do these principles, it is impossible to divorce. We only divorce when we go in the other direction.

Listen to what it says:

- *To the angel in the church of Ephesus…*The Greek word for angel does not mean an angelic being much of the time. It often means a messenger. We cannot be sure, but this is probably what it means here. John is probably addressing this to the messenger that would bring the letter to the church.

- *These are the words of him who holds the seven stars…* Commentators believe that this is symbolic of the pastors who led these congregations. As a pastor, I have a sacred responsibility to bring God's Word into the lives of our families.

- *He walks among the seven lampstands…*Since it also applies to our marriage, your marriage is meant to be a light in the darkness. Your marriage is meant to be a lampstand, a beautiful wonderful thing. When it is put out or covered up it is a tragedy.

- *You have forsaken your first love…remember…repent…do the things you did at first. If you do not repent, I will come to you and remove your lampstand.*

God is saying to us in our marriages, "If you really are going to break your word to Me and to your spouse, your lampstand is going out and that is tragic."

This letter is written to all of us because it is the Word of God. It was originally written to the church of Ephesus. I want to tell you about Ephesus. Ephesus was an amazing city, like New York or LA in their day. It is in what we now call Turkey.

Do you remember in the book of Acts what happened there? When the apostle Paul brought the gospel there, the entire city began to change. Businesses began to change. People were so affected there that they stopped buying idols and the people who were making idols rushed Paul in a riot into the amphitheater, the center of entertainment of their day. Can you imagine a city changed so much that the people who were selling the vile idols of the day got mad because so many were flocking to Jesus that they could not make money anymore? It happened right there.

It does not look the way it once did, because it is a ruin now. The place where Paul spoke later became the place of the vilest perversion. They lost their families and they lost their culture.

I have been to see those ruins. The streets are still there with pornographic graffiti carved into the walls from the ancient days. They are ruined, and if we do not change, so will we!

We are at the tipping point. The ball is now rolling downhill to a bad place. We have gone so far that statistically it makes no difference in your marriage to be a follower of Jesus. Now atheists have a lower divorce rate than Christians according to Barna. You are more likely to divorce as a

Christian than if you were an atheist. We must stop and push the ball uphill. It is hard work but we have got to do it. The family was established before God established the church. It is the model of His Love, and the marriage relationship gets us out of self and into another life where we are required to speak the language of someone else. We cannot let it be ruined. We are going after valiant marriages.

Recovering Hope

We have to start by recovering hope! We have to start by saying there is hope for our culture and hope for your marriage. Where is it?

Jesus praised the church at Ephesus for several things. I believe He would praise the church in America for some things. We stand against things such as abortion and homosexual marriage In our community we are starting to stand against other things too like racism and poverty. We are standing up for the right things. But Jesus says we have left our first love. "You have left me behind," Jesus said. Yet there is hope.

In verse seven we learn that if we overcome, Jesus Himself will feed us from the tree of life. He will feed your marriage with the fruit of life! I have seen it in 30 years of being a pastor. I know it can happen for you if you are willing to make the choices of valor.

Revelation 12 is a starting place for recovering your hope. The same word "overcome" is used in a different context. In Revelation 12, the Word teaches us how to overcome the enemy. Of course this is the same one who wants your family destroyed. You have an enemy, the dragon in the tower that wants to keep you from anything resembling a happy ending. He wants to destroy you and your family. In Revelation 12, the Lord uses the same word to tell us how to beat him "...*they overcame him by the Blood of the Lamb and the word of their testimony. They did not love their OWN lives so much as to shrink from death.*"

Here is how you recover hope—cry out to God and say, "I can't do this without Your power. I need the Blood of the Lamb to cover my marriage. I need Your story to enter my mess." If God's story had not entered my mess, I would be lost today. If God's story had not entered our marriage, we would be divorced today. Ask Him to write a new story and be willing to sacrifice self. That's valor. These martyrs did not love their own life so much that they would run away from death. If it took death, they were ready to die.

It Will Take Your Death to Save Your Marriage

You will have to say, "God, kill all of this junk that is me and write Your story on my life. Lead me, I cannot do it alone." If you are willing to do that, you have all kinds of hope flowing into you and out of you, because God promised it!

Let me give you three steps from this passage that have helped my wife and I tremendously and that we are teaching our church families regularly:

1. Remember the Missing Moments

Revelation 2:5—*Remember the height from which you have fallen...* Most husbands and wives have totally forgotten why they fell in love in the first place. Couples are sad, depressed, frustrated, angry, and hurt. You do not even remember those moments that were good. You cannot say you never had any good moments. Every single couple had wonderful moments or they never would have gotten married. No one ever proposed by saying "I could not do worse, would you marry me?" There's a reason you fell in love and married. No one ever asked a father's blessing and said to the father, "I have gotten to know your daughter. I am disgusted by her, but can I spend the rest of my life with her?" Do you feel disgusted now? You did not feel that way once upon a time. Storm the castle, kick the dragon out and remember what you are missing. There are precious moments of life that God gave you and you let them be forgotten. You do not even remember what's at stake. Fight back!

For one hour, sit and talk about nothing but your best memories, best things in your marriage and in your life. Refuse to argue. Particularly the missing moments you've let slip away. You will laugh, hold hands, maybe end the evening well—just try it!

2. Repent Passionately

Revelation 2:4 calls the church, and your marriage, to repentance. Repentance is not a word we like but it ought to be one of our favorites. We are passionate fighters and stingy repenters! It ruins us. If your marriage comes to an end and you were to write down all the things you fought about, you would find one or two big things and the rest would be petty stuff that you let build up.

What does repentance do for you as a follower of Jesus? It washes you clean, restores you, gives you a brand new start, and changes your direction from a bad place to a good place.

Do you need this in your marriage? Then repent passionately. Quit arguing about whose fault everything is and look in the mirror. Change you! You cannot change your spouse. Change yourself!! When you begin to change, it does something to your spouse and they want to be different. Repent passionately and watch what God will do.

Recently I was lifting weights with my son who was home from college. My wife came in and told us that our little Boston Terrier dog, PJ, had cut her foot and was limping. Nothing serious. I absent-mindedly suggested she could give PJ some Tylenol. So she did. About that time my son said, "Dad, I think Tylenol kills dogs." Oops. We looked it up on the computer. Yes, Tylenol kills your dog! My wife and I began to argue about whose fault this was. Why did I give this dumb advice. I wondered why she actually took it! So we argued all night and the next day our dog was stiff as a board. No we did not! I took the dog to the vet and she promptly vomited it all up (a wonderful way to spend an evening by the way). The moral of the story is that if we had fought all night long about who was dumber, one of us would have won but we would have a nice grave to visit instead of a dog to love. Who wants to write, "I was Right," on the tombstone of your marriage? REPENT!

3. Rebuild Romance in Your Life

Romance is not a feeling—it's a bond. Romance is the dance of marriage that God gives you with this other person to be shared with no one else. Restore that dance, that romance. God tells us how to do it. Revelation 2:4, *Do the things you did at first.* What did you do to cause that person to fall in love with you? What did you do that made that man pursue you? Did you send her flowers? Did you write him or her notes? Did you go on dates? Did you pray with her? Do those things again! DO THE FIRST THINGS!!!

George Barna says that most Christian couples just follow their instincts and let the chips fall where they may. We cannot afford that anymore. It is time to get intentional about building strong marriages. That is what we will do if we act in valor, if we want to build valiant families. This journey will not be easy, but it is a journey you can take. And you can arrive at a good destination.

We are changing the way we disciple our children. At each stage of life, we are asking three questions:

1. Do our children have the biblical knowledge appropriate for this age?

2. Are we developing the character and understanding of masculinity or femininity they need at this age?

3. Are we teaching them how to live missionally and as leaders in a way appropriate to their age.

We have just begun this journey, but we are very excited about it. We are committed to it for the rest of our lives. We will shape our ministries around these goals, and in doing, so we believe we can build strong valiant families.

On Christmas Eve last year, I received a text from a soldier—a valiant warrior who had just retired after twenty years of leading men into combat. I have been helping him adjust to a different life. Here are his words:

Brother, I love Christmas! I had some neighbors over last night and one of them asked if I remembered where I was this time last year? It pierced me immediately! I said yes I do. My heart has been aching for the ones who will be in a foxhole in the mountains of Afghanistan or on missions unknown and unreported elsewhere in the world. These are the sheepdogs keeping the wolves at bay. The insurgents will surely attack tonight. They know our customs and will try to take advantage of them, but they will find that our warriors fight harder on Christmas because they think of families sitting by a fire together, eating some great dish that Mom or Grandma made, visiting people they haven't seen in a while, the whole family making it to church together, not having to hide from some dictator or terrorist while they worship. They will fight harder because they will think of families tucking their kids in who are so excited about the next morning. They think of those families in nice comfortable beds. All is good. All is safe. Those thoughts remind a warrior why he does what he does. He longs for his spouse and children. He is cold, tired, dirty, in pain, and lonely. But tonight he will shoot more sure and perform better than on any other day of the year. To protect the sheep who are thousands of miles away so they can be safe—so safe that most don't even know there are wolves who want to take it all away. I thank those sheepdogs and their families that have an empty chair at the table this year. They make this Christmas possible. I thank Jesus—and those who fight tonight. Merry Christmas!

I will never forget those words! Most of our families are not thousands of miles away. They are right here! So let's fight for them. Let us stand in the enemy's way. Let us do anything that it takes to build strong biblical families again. Let us be men and women of valor so we can have valiant families. And let us get started!

It's time to fight! Husbands, wives, and young people help your families not fight so much. Church, it is time to give ourselves away so that our church is full of valiant marriages.

Section Two

*Spiritual Awakenings:
Tracing the Great
Commission in the Past*

CHAPTER THREE

Missional Prayer Patterns From John 17 With Application For Spiritual Awakening
J. Chris Schofield, Ph.D.

A Heartfelt Thanks

I AM grateful for the influence Alvin Reid has had in my life. His heart for the lost is always challenging and his desire for excellence in the classroom is refreshing. I was his first Ph.D. student and I am sure a challenge, but I am grateful for his patience and grace. Thanks Dr. Reid for remaining faithful through the years and for continuing to call the church to be involved in the Great Commission and prayer that leads to revival and spiritual awakening.

Praying Toward the Kingdom

In the early-to-mid-1490s, Jerome Savonarola preached and prayed passionately while at the San Marcos Church in Florence, Italy. His desire was that God would save the lost masses and revive His church. God heard his prayers and because of His spiritual leadership thousands were converted and a spirit of revival was unleashed upon the city for two years.[1]

In Matthew 6:9-10 Jesus teaches His followers to pray toward the coming of His Kingdom and the accomplishment of His will on earth. This happens as people experience the rule and reign of Christ when they trust Him to be their Lord and Savior. This also continues to take place in believers as they grow in Christ. Jesus modeled this kind of Kingdom focused praying in John 17.

Over the next few pages I will examine John 17 and extract several missional prayer patterns. Then I will draw out a few points of application toward the concept of spiritual awakening. It is greatly hoped that through this study we will all be challenged, encouraged, and better equipped to pray toward the coming of God's Kingdom in our world.

John 17: A Brief Intro

Jesus has just finished the second part of his farewell discourse in John 16.[2] His crucifixion and departure was something that his followers did

---

[1] For more on Jerome Savonarola, his ministry and the awakening that transpired in Florence see Malcolm McDow and Alvin Reid, *FireFall: How God Has Shaped History Through Revivals* (Nashville: Broadman and Holman, 1997), 129-138 and Wesley Dewel, *Revival Fire* (Grand Rapids: Zondervan, 1995), 44-48.

[2] These discourses are found in John 13-17 and represent a very intimate time of fellowship and instruction for his closest followers. The material contained in these chapters is not found in the Synoptics, but only in John. Andreas Kostenberger divides the farewell discourses into three parts with John 17 being the third section. Borchert describes the farewell section as a farewell cycle because it includes more than discourse. For more on the farewell discourses see Leon Morris, *The Gospel According to John* in The New International Commentary on the New Testament, F. F. Bruce, ed. (Grand Rapids: Eerdmans, 1971), 610-715, Andreas J. Kostenberger, *Encountering John* in the Encountering Biblical Studies, Walter A. Elwell, general ed. (Grand Rapids: Baker, 1999), 139-173; and Gerald Borchert, *John 12-21* in The New American Commentary, E. Ray Clendenen, general ed., v. 25B (Nashville: Broadman and Holman, 2002), 73-212.

not fully grasp, and from their earthly perspective, probably did not want to hear about or experience. Jesus assured them of His abiding presence, peace, and victory. He also instructed them concerning promises relating to praying in His name (see John 16:16-33).

The "high priestly" prayer of John 17 takes place in Jesus' passion during the last week of His earthly life.[3] Over the next few days Jesus would be betrayed, arrested, beaten, crucified, and resurrected. During this intense time of His life and ministry Jesus could have prayed about many issues that related to the circumstances He was encountering. Yet, despite the circumstances, His prayer was entirely focused on the Father's mission being fulfilled. In a nutshell, Jesus desired to please His Father and fulfill His desire to see His mission completed and His followers prepared for the challenges ahead. The reason—so that the Kingdom of God could be proclaimed and move forward through their witness.

Three Sections—Seven Petitions

Many scholars divide John 17 into three sections.[4] Section 1 (17:1-5) represents Jesus' prayer for His glorification and the completion of His mission. Section 2 (17:6-19) contains Jesus' prayers for His disciples and their character. Section 3 (17:20-26) encompasses Jesus' prayers for His disciples and future followers who believe through their witness.

---

[3] Morris cautions readers that, although the common designation of the prayer as "high priestly" points to the "solemn" nature of the prayer and its focus on the cross and the consummation of His priestly work, a sense of hope, joy, and expectancy are present as Jesus looks toward the cross, the ongoing work of His followers, and those who would believe through their witness (consult Morris, *John*, 716).

[4] Scholars differ some on what verses belong to the three sections although Kostenberger, 168-173, Morris (716), Andrew T. Lincoln, "God's Name, Jesus' Name, and Prayer in the Fourth Gospel," in *Into God's Presence*, Richard N. Longenecker, editor (Grand Rapids: Eerdmans, 2002), 160-163; and M. M. B. Turner, "Prayer in the Gospels and Acts," in *Teach Us To Pray,* D. A. Carson, ed. (Eugene, OR: Wipf and Stock, 2002), 77-80 all support these three categories and verse selection.

Found within these three sections are seven actual petitions:[5] Prayer for the glorification of the Father through the glorification of the Son (v. 1); prayer for the completion of the Christ event in the ascension (v. 5); prayer for Jesus' disciples to be guarded or kept in His name (v. 11); prayer for protection from the Evil One (v. 15); prayer for the setting apart of His followers in the Word (truth) of God (v. 17); prayer for oneness (v. 21); and prayer for His followers to be with Him where He is (v. 24). All are missional in purpose and content and all are focused on seeing the Kingdom move forward in and through Jesus and his followers.

Jesus and His Mission (17:1-5)

Jesus wanted to complete His mission and please His Father. That was the most pressing desire of His heart (see John 8:28). His close intimate relationship with the Father is evident as He begins the prayer in verse 1 with the term "Father."[6] The tendency in prayer is often to treat it as something we just do, making it like a ritual or a task. Prayer is relational and is something we "are." We cannot separate ourselves from our prayers. God answers his followers not just the prayers they pray.[7]

The phrase "the hour has come" points to His understanding of the Father's eternal purposes that are being accomplished through His life. This can also be seen in John 12:27-32 where Jesus surrenders to the Father's hour as He prays. At this point, Jesus knew that the cross, the grave, the resurrection, and ascension were before Him. He now asks

---

[5] Borchert does not include verse 5 as a separate petition but does include verse 25 as a petition. The list I use is supported by Morris, Köstenberger, and Lincoln.

[6] The term "Father" or some form (*e.g.*, "Holy Father") of this intimate address is used 6 times in this chapter: verses, 1, 5, 11, 21, 24, and 25. All Scripture references cited are from the NASB.

[7] See Selwyn Hughes, *Everyday with Jesus* (Nashville: Broadman and Holman, 2004), 15. Also see how the writer of Hebrews demonstrates this relational element in Hebrews 10:19-26.

the Father to complete this work as He prays for His own glorification in verses 1 and 5.[8]

"Glorification" is a rich concept in John and refers to the giving of proper esteem, position and honor. Jesus' desire is that all would recognize who the Father was through His own glorification. The glorification of Jesus is linked to the threefold process of His crucifixion, resurrection and ascension. His act of obedience in surrendering to the cross allows for the completion of the work of the Christ beyond that event.

Tied to the glorification/exaltation of Jesus are the three "lifted up" sayings in John (John 3:16; 8:28; and 12:32). The Father is glorified as the Son is lifted up on the cross, out of the grave, and to the right hand of the Father—where he ever lives to make intercession for those who believe (see Heb 7:25). The Father is thus made known (glorified) as Jesus obeys and is lifted up. As the exaltation (ascension) of Jesus takes place, which Jesus also specifically prays toward in verse 5, the Spirit is sent and begins His work of drawing all people to the Father through the Son (John 12:32). The Holy Spirit also convicts the world concerning its need for the Christ (John 16:8). Thus, eternal life is made possible and given to all who know the Father through the Son (see John 17:2-3). As Jesus is glorified, the lost world is redeemed and the Father is ultimately made known and glorified. This is at the heart of our Savior's prayer! Can the same thing be said of our praying?

His Followers and Their Mission (17:6-19)

Jesus is confident that the Father has heard His petitions regarding the completion of His mission because in verse 6 he transitions into a season of prayer for His disciples. Jesus knew the next few days were going to be difficult for even His most faithful followers. He also seeks to prepare

---

[8] These are not self-centered requests as we would often pray. Central to these petitions is the Father's glorification—the moving forward of the mission through His vicarious suffering and victorious resurrection and ascension.

them through prayer for their task after he is no longer with them. The disciples would soon be eyewitnesses to the Christ and bear witness to a pagan world on His behalf.

Jesus had already assured them of His provision for this time through the promise of the Spirit, His role as the true vine and His instructions regarding praying in His name (John 14-16). He also knew that if they were going to be successful in taking the Gospel to their world they would need to walk with Him through His Father's care and provision. What they needed was Christ-like character. This "character" would ensure adequate representation of Jesus to a lost world. In essence they needed to "be" the Gospel as they were "doing" and "telling" the Gospel.[9]

In verse 11 Jesus prays for His disciples to be kept in His name. The term "keep" refers to the concept of being guarded and relates more in this petition to the idea of being guarded in intimacy through personal relationship than it does to protection from danger from an outside source.[10] This prayer refers to His desire that they be attached to Jesus the "True Vine" so that their hearts are focused personally and corporately on His heart (see John 15).

Jesus' departure is fast approaching and His burden for them to remain in Him and focused on His mission is great. Jesus demonstrates with this prayer the importance of being dependent on the Father for a vibrant, real, and alive Christian witness. This petition also is applied to intimacy and oneness in community. The community must be kept together in His name to be the local expression of Christ to the pagan world they are seeking to reach.

---

[9] Delos Miles expounds on this in his *Introduction to Evangelism* (Nashville: Broadman, 2003), 49.

[10] Although both are applicable, the concept of protection for the sake of character related to intimacy and relationship is more understandable here while the latter idea of being protected from the enemy is addressed with His petition in John 17:17. Also, Borchert relates this "keeping" to the protecting power associated with the name of God which is an Old Testament theme seen in Ps 54:1, 20:1 and Prov 18:10. See Borchert, *John 12-21*, 196-197 for more discussion on this distinction.

Today's culture needs to see genuine Christianity being lived out by Christ followers. This takes place as the Father "keeps" us in Jesus' character and intimacy with Him. When that happens unbelievers are engaged by real Christians who are walking with a real Savior who can deliver them from the domain of darkness (see Col 1:13-14).

In verse 15 Jesus prays for His followers to be kept from the "evil one." He knows that protection from Satan, His deceptions and wiles can only take place through the Father. Jesus is concerned for His witnesses as He will soon be departing. He obviously does not want them to fall into temptation but be delivered from the devil and His evil influences.[11] Satan is a thief and is out to steal and destroy every believer's joy and testimony (see John 10:10).

Jesus understood that His disciples would fail if their ability to overcome evil was dependent on their own wisdom and strength. I am convinced that the mission creeps forward today because many Christians are being taunted, oppressed and deceived by the enemy. Living a godly life in holiness cannot take place apart from the work of God's power as it is experienced through His Spirit. Spiritual warfare is real and prayer is key to a believer's ability to successfully say no to Satan's temptations. This is spiritual warfare prayer that is proactive.[12]

---

[11] It is interesting that Jesus, in response to the disciples question "Lord teach us to pray..." (Luke 11:1), teaches the church to pray for protection from the evil one in Matt. 6:13 and also prays the same thing in John 17:15. This is evidently a very important prayer that believers should faithfully pray for one another. This focus also shows Jesus' urgency in this type of specific prayer that recognizes the spiritual battle we are engaged in daily.

[12] Chuck Lawless correctly comments, "Most of our praying is reactive not proactive; that is, we start praying only after we learn of a losing battle (*e.g.*, a family is in trouble, a young person is wondering, or a church is divided). The devil aims his arrows, hits his target—and then we decide to pray." For more see Chuck Lawless, "Prayer and Spiritual Warfare" in *Give Ourselves to Prayer*, Dan R. Crawford, comp. (Terre Haute, IN: PrayerShop, 2008), 471.

In verse 17 Jesus prays for His followers to be sanctified (set apart) in His word (truth). If His witnesses are to have Christ's character, their lives will need to be shaped and directed by the Word of God. Jesus prays specifically for their personal sanctification. "Truth" in John's Gospel is representative of the "revelation of God in Jesus."[13]

Also, in verse 19 Jesus makes reference to His own sanctification, which He accomplished so that His followers can be sanctified "in the truth."[14] This prayer refers to their life of obedience as they encounter the truth of God in the Christ and in His Word (see John 14:6). When we pray for believers to be sanctified in the truth, we are praying for daily encounters with the living Christ, Who is Truth (John 14:6). Jesus sanctified Himself through obedience and gave us truth in the living and active Word of God. These encounters should lead Christians to a life of radical obedience to the Truth. Turner aptly comments, "the presupposition of the disciples' full consecration is the death and exaltation of Jesus. Only with that, and the gift of the Paraclete to which it leads, can the disciples be kept in the name by which they were saved, and sanctified in the truth which they came to believe."[15] Thus, believers must be different or set apart if the pagan world is to believe that Jesus is the One who can give them eternal life. Intentional proactive prayer is essential if this is to happen.

---

[13] Lincoln, "God's Name," 167.

[14] There is nothing about Jesus and His Character that needs sanctifying because He is perfect, yet His act of pleasing and obeying the Father is central to the act of sanctification. As He is set apart and completes His mission in obedience to the Father, the mission of His disciples to bear witness to the truth can likewise take place as they walk in obedience to being sent. For more on the continuity between the mission of Jesus and their mission as witnesses related to this prayer see Lincoln, 167-168.

[15] Turner, *Teach Us to Pray*, 79.

His Followers, Future Believers and the Moving Forward of the Kingdom (17:20-26)

Jesus now prays for His followers and for those who will believe in Him "through their word" (v. 20). In essence, Jesus is praying for future generations of His followers who will believe through the disciples' witness. He prays specifically for the leaders, and He is preparing the way for the moving forward of the mission through their lives. The impact on the world will be huge.

Two requests are central to this section. The first is for oneness (v. 21). This is oneness that centers on the Father and the Son as they are one. Jesus is praying for unity that is experienced through the work of the Spirit and focuses on intimacy and relationship. This is not unity that centers on temporal ideologies, methodological presuppositions, worship styles, attitudes, or personal preferences. It is rather oneness that centers on the Father's purposes and glory which takes place as believers unite their hearts together in His mission.

This prayer also aims at a oneness with the Father through the Son (John 14:6) and demonstrates the dependence that Christians have on Jesus in order to experience the love of the Father and be involved in His mission (John 15:5).[16] This prayer, according to Turner, "puts the Father's glory at the centre, and spreads out in concentric circles of His will and purpose."[17] The result of this unity is that the mission moves forward as the world believes that the Father sent the Son (v. 21).

The second petition in this section is found in verse 24. Here Jesus prays toward His desire for His followers to be with Him. This is more than just a wish but something that he longs to experience. This petition points toward eschatological notions of the experience of His future Glory.

---

[16] For more on this see Morris, *John*, 733-734 and Turner, *Teach Us to Pray*, 80.

[17] Turner, *Teach Us to Pray*, 80.

One day, when this life is over, Christians will experience the bliss of heaven with Jesus forever. However, one must not allow this prayer to be understood as just relating to the future blessing of heaven. It also relates to the present experience of His followers as they unite with Him in His mission.[18] Eternal life is something believers experience in the present, thus allowing them to participate in the redemptive activity of His present glory at work in their world.[19]

The question the church has to answer today is, "Where is Jesus in your world?" Maybe one reason the gospel is not running rapidly (see 2 Thess 3:2) but creeping forward in North America is due to the fact that the Church is not praying to be with Jesus where He is at work in the lost world.

Missional Prayer Patterns

Out of these discussions arise three missional prayer patterns from Jesus' prayer in John 17 that move the Kingdom forward. The first is a focus on the Father. In this prayer, Jesus consistently points us back to the relationship aspect of Kingdom prayer with the Father, His glory, purposes, and desires (*e.g.*, John 17:1, 24). In addition, our relationship with the Father and the Son as it relates to oneness among believers is lifted up as an essential if the mission is to be successful (see John 17:21–23). Thus, if our prayers are to be missional and move the Kingdom forward they must begin, end and be permeated with a focus on Father, His purposes and desires.

Second is a focus on being the gospel. Jesus prays toward his disciples and their character, protection, and sanctification (*e.g.*, John 17:11, 15

---

[18] Borchert points out that although Jesus uses the phrase "where I am" in this prayer the focus is on experiencing and seeing His glory (Borchert, *John 12-21*, 208). There is also merit in studying the seven "I am" passages in John that precede this prayer as they relate to the element of being with Jesus (I am) wherever He is in this world.

[19] Glory in this context is representative of His manifest presence as it relates to the redemptive work of the Christ.

17). Being the gospel before a lost world makes it thirsty for the Christ we represent. When our Christian talk and walk are not congruent, we confuse the world about the Christ we proclaim to love, know, and serve. Christians are dependent on the Father for protection from the enemy to keep their testimony clean and pure.

The last pattern is a focus on eternal/spiritual things. The result of the glorification of Jesus is eternal life for sinful man. Prayers that move the kingdom forward are those that focus on seeing: the lost saved, believers grow in the Father's grace, and glorification of the Father as His followers join Him in the experience of His redemptive glory (John 17:24). The church is making slow headway penetrating the darkness in North American because much of its praying is earthly, temporal, and often focused on self. This has to change!

Application for Spiritual Awakening[20]

Why make application to the subject of spiritual awakening? Think about the results of Jesus' prayer in John 17 as revealed throughout the ages. The proactive praying that Jesus did in John 17 led to the awakening of a culture to the redemptive plans of God through Jesus Christ. It also ensured that His followers would join those redemptive plans as they were empowered and sent to fulfill their missional calling for generations to come.[21] If there ever was a need for a spiritual awakening in the North American church and culture, it is today.

---

[20] The term "spiritual awakening" is used synonymously with the term "revival" to denote a more comprehensive work of God that includes both a renewing or reviving of God's people and an awakening of the culture at large as the Spirit opens the hearts of the lost to Christ in unprecedented ways.

[21] The Book of Acts bears witness to the expansion of the first century Church and the awakening of the culture to the message of the Christ which took place after the prayer of Jesus in John 17.

J. Edwin Orr says that an awakening is a "movement of the Holy Spirit bringing about a revival of New Testament Christianity in the church of Christ and in its related community."[22] Alvin Reid and Malcolm McDow describe revival as "God's invasion into the lives of one or more of His people in order to awaken them spiritually for Kingdom ministry."[23]

These definitions point to the old adage: as goes the church, so goes the culture. I believe that the spiritual degradation we are facing in North America can in part be attributed to the absence of a Kingdom-mindedness in our praying. The church is hunkering down in the trenches because the culture is growing more and more pagan. Our praying often reflects where our hearts or minds are focused. We also often pursue the things we are praying toward. That is why we need to focus our praying on the Kingdom coming as Jesus did. Spiritual awakening must start with the church being revived to a faithful, biblical Christianity that is passionately praying and taking the gospel to the nations. That is in essence what Jesus prayed toward in John 17.

What would happen in the average church if most of the praying were God centered and largely focused on His purposes, desires, and will being accomplished in the world. The end result of Jesus' praying in John 17:1-5 was the redemption of fallen man through the obedience and glorification of Jesus in the completion of His mission. The result today, if that were the churches prayer focus, would be the redemption of a fallen world through the obedience of the church as it walks in oneness with Jesus. Spiritual awakening has always resulted in a great evangelistic thrust by the church.[24]

---

[22] See J. Edwin Orr, *The Fervent Prayer: The Worldwide Impact of the Great Awakening of 1858* (Chicago: Moody, 1974), vii.

[23] McDow and Reid, *Firefall*, 7.

[24] Ibid., 21. Reid and McDow also show that when the church is renewed and experiences a renewed passion for evangelism the society at large can also experience great benefits. Also see James Burns, *The Laws of Revival,* ed. by Tim Phillips (Wheaton: World Wide Publications, 1993), 13-14.

Spiritual awakening includes a renewing or reviving of the church in its desire to be holy, godly, and in a right relationship with Christ. The lack of a Christ-like character is paralyzing the church in North America. Jesus prayed in John 17:11, 15, 17 for the disciple's character as He prayed for them to be kept (guarded) in His name, protected from the evil one and set apart in His truth. When this happens in a Christian's life it represents a life that is holy, set apart, and intimately related and dependent on Christ. This kind of proactive praying is much better than reactive praying that seeks to restore the integrity of a believer who has succumbed to a temptation because they have failed to walk in intimacy with Christ. Christians everywhere are in need of the "character-focused" prayers that Jesus prayed in 17:11, 15, 17.

A final application is drawn from Jesus' missional prayer focus on eternal things (see John 17:2, 24). In John 17:2, 24 Jesus prays toward the giving and experiencing of eternal life and the continual intimacy of his followers as they are with Him in the mission and beholding His redemptive glory. This type of praying produces spirit-filled living and intimacy with Christ eternally as believers walk with Him in His eternal mission to redeem a fallen world. Wherever the Christ is, His desire is for His followers to be there with Him. That was His prayer in John 17:24 and should be the churches prayer today. Praying for the believer to be on mission with Jesus leads to a revived life—where God's redemptive activity is being experienced by His followers on a continual basis. That is awakening in its purest form![25]

Conclusion

In the previous pages I have identified several missional prayer patterns in John 17. I have also applied these patterns to the subject of spiritual awakening. Admittedly, I have just begun to scrape the surface of what is actually present in John 17. Despite the brevity of this examination, I pray

---

[25] For more on this see Burns, *Laws of Revival*, 29-38.

---

that you have been challenged to examine your personal and corporate prayer experiences by Jesus and His prayer priorities and practices found in John 17.

The need of the hour in North America is spiritual awakening. This will only happen as the church practices heartfelt prayer toward God's Kingdom coming and His will being done on earth as it is in heaven. I believe that if the church were to faithfully give itself to the biblical prayer patterns found in John 17, a Kingdom-mindedness in ministry and a moving forward of the Kingdom in times of spiritual awakening and throughout the ages would take place. In light of the above discussion Stanley Grenz's comments in his work, *Prayer: A Cry for the Kingdom* seem appropriate: "The challenge that we face today is the challenge to pray. Meeting this challenge requires that we cease merely talking about prayer and begin to pray.... Let us, therefore, pray. Let us invoke the in-breaking of the kingdom into the situations of life that we face. Let us cry for the Kingdom!"[26]

---

[26] Stanley J. Grenz, *Prayer: A Cry for the Kingdom*, rev. ed. (Grand Rapids: Eerdmans, 2005), 124.

CHAPTER FOUR

Great Commission Lessons From The Haystack Prayer Revival
Tommy Kiker, Ph.D.

Author's Note

I T was January of 2001 when I took a class on the history of revival movements and they became an inspiration and challenge in my life. The professor in that class was Alvin Reid. Reid had endeared himself to me and countless other students with his enthusiasm and passion for souls exhibited in his Introduction to Evangelism courses. However, it was in the History of Spiritual Awakenings class that God greatly refined my passions and desires to see Him move in a Great Awakening once again. Reid's influence in that class, as my mentor during a subsequent doctorate program, and even today, has been and continues to be a source of tremendous encouragement. I count it all joy to write on one of my favorite subjects in honor of one of my favorite laborers for Christ.

Introduction

The influence of Great Awakenings on the Great Commission can be seen in the study of most any major revival movement. This particular study focuses on the story of what is perceived by many as the birth of foreign missions in America through an event known as the Haystack Prayer Meeting and its leader, Samuel J. Mills, Jr. The Haystack Prayer meeting took place in the midst of what is commonly known as the Second Great Awakening. The turn of the century following the American Revolutionary War was an amazing time of transition, and became an incredible time of spiritual vitality, but such spiritual vitality did not seem likely or even possible just a few short years earlier.

Many works on the Second Great Awakening spend a portion of time describing conditions that preceded the movement.[1] Numerous variables affected the spiritual condition of the newly founded nation. Benjamin Lacy notes five factors for the spiritual bankruptcy over the land prior to the Second Great Awakening. First, the aftermath of war as a rule causes people and lands to suffer spiritually. The vast number of changes that were occurring so quickly left the religious arena in disarray. Second, the migration west broke up families and removed a level of spiritual accountability and support. Third, the migration aided in promoting an increased tendency toward greed and selfishness. Fourth, there was a great indifference to evangelical truth and a shortage of missionaries and evangelists in the newly settled

---

[1] Examples of these are Frank G. Beardsley, *Religious Progress Through Religious Revivals* (New York: ATS, 1943) and Frank G. Beardsley *A History of American Revivals* (New York: American Tract Society, 1912); J. Edwin Orr, *The Eager Feet: Evangelical Awakening, 1790-1830* (Chicago: Moody, 1975); and John Boles, *The Great Revival 1787-1805* (Lexington, University of Kentucky, 1972). Boles spends several chapters going into great detail concerning the spiritual conditions before the onset of revival (12-50).

regions. A fifth factor describing the conditions prior to awakening is the influence of French Deism and infidelity.[2]

The spiritual apathy extended even to the colleges which had begun for the most part as training ground for men entering the ministry. Williams College, where the Haystack prayer meeting would occur, was in the spiritual doldrums as well. Early accounts suggest that infidelity was rampant, and harassment and persecution was the reward for any student who would show a sympathy or interest in Christianity. The college had ninety-three men in the first six classes that graduated. Among all of these classes, there were only seven men professing Christ and in three of the classes, none professed Christ.[3]

In 1799, a growing stream of revival swept up two young William's College students who were at home on vacation. James W. Robbins and James W. Cannon came back to Williams and along with four entering Christian students in 1801, the beginning stages of revival began to take root among the students at Williams. The leadership of this small group of Christians and the hospitality of a lady name Mrs. Bardwell opening up her home for prayer, led to a spiritual awakening during 1805 that stirred the hearts of many at Williams.[4] Hopkins explains that the spiritual tide began to turn greatly in the early part of the century. He writes, "In the year 1805, this blessing began to be realized. It commenced in the spring of that year, and was great through the summer. Professors of religion in college were aroused."[5] Durfree explains, "It was not until the summer

---

[2] Benjamin R. Lacy, Jr., *Revivals in the Midst of the Years* (Richmond: Knox, 1943), 63–66. All of the sources noted above in footnote 1 recognize French Deism and infidelity as a factor of religious decline.

[3] Thomas C. Richards, *Samuel J. Mills, Missionary Pathfinder, Pioneer and Promoter* (Boston: Pilgrim, 1906), 25.

[4] Clarence P. Shedd, *Two Centuries of Student Christian Movements* (New York: Association Press, 1934), 48.

[5] Albert Hopkins, "Revivals at Williams College," *American Quarterly Register* 13 (Feb 1841): 344–345.

---

term of 1806 that the work became deep and general in College. It was now that conversions began to be multiplied, it would seem somewhat early in the term."[6]

Though many a student in the past and maybe more so in the present see college as a hiatus until real life commences, Mills had a specific purpose, to immerse himself in preparation to the task at hand, reaching the heathen with the gospel. Samuel Orcutt exclaims, "While he was a member of college, there was a revival of religion in the institution, of which he was the chief instrument."[7] Spring writes, "As a scholar, he was of respectable standing; but as a youth who 'walked with God,' and whose uniform deportment evinced that he was devoted to interests superior to his own, he shone as a light in the earth."[8] It appears that not only did Mills become involved with the existing revival, but became a leader of its continuance. The leadership of Mills and others led to a spiritual landmark of sorts in the fulfillment of the Great Commission through churches in the newly established United States of America.

The precursors that led to the Haystack prayer meeting and the events that followed make for one of the great testimonies of God's powerful hand in the history of the church. Most accounts of the story give credit to Mills as the leader of the meeting. Thornbury writes, "In this group was the man who, in a large measure, was the real moving spirit behind the modern American missionary movement, Samuel J. Mills."[9] There were five men present at this particular time of prayer, Samuel Mills,

---

[6] Calvin Durfree, *History of Williams College* (Boston: A. Williams & Co., 1860), 116.

[7] Samuel Orcutt, *History of Torrington, Connecticut: From Its First Settlement in 1737, with Biographies and Genealogies*. (Albany: J. Munsell, 1878), 552.

[8] Gardiner Spring, *Memoirs of the Rev. Samuel J. Mills* (New York: New York Evangelical Society, 1820), 10.

[9] J. F. Thornbury, *God Sent Revival: The Story of Asahel Nettleton and the Second Great Awakening* (Grand Rapids: Evangelical Press, 1977), 38.

along with Byram Green, Francis L. Robbins, James Richards, and Harvey Loomis.[10]

As mentioned above, revival had already commenced on the campus at Williams. The impulse and continued result of this outpouring included a group that met twice a week on Wednesdays and Saturdays to pray for the spirit of revival to increase. On Wednesdays they would meet south of the college under some willow trees and on Saturdays they would meet in a grove known as Sloan's Meadow near the college. On one particular Saturday the extremely hot conditions had kept the attendance rather low. As the men had gathered to pray in the grove a dark cloud came up and it began to thunder and lightning, so the men left the grove and went under a haystack to gain some protection from the coming storm. As they sat, the conversation turned to the subject of a recent geography class, Asia. Mills saw an opportunity and suggested that they commit to and pray for the sending of the gospel to heathen lands. In great enthusiasm, Mills declared, "We can do it if we will."[11]

Most accounts of the meeting claim that the men then turned to diligent prayer and that all of them petitioned God for the cause of foreign missions except for Loomis. He felt the time was not ripe and such a movement was premature. If missionaries were sent, they could be murdered, and what was needed was a new crusade before the gospel could be sent to the Turks and Arabs. The opinion of Loomis was a widely held opinion as there had been very little movement towards mission causes beyond the borders of the new nation. Stryker comments, "In these years public opinion was decidedly opposed to the enterprise of these young men. Even good men thought their zeal extravagant and

---

[10] Byram Green, "Letter to President Hopkins," In *Proceedings of the Missionary Jubilee Held at Williams College, August 5, 1856* (Boston: T. R. Marvin & Son, 1856), 8.

[11] Cited in Kenneth Latourette, *These Sought a Country* (New York: Harper, 1950), 46.

expected it soon to subside."[12] The men had to overcome the prevailing thoughts of their time period.

The other four men were united in a desire to spread the gospel to foreign lands. Their response to Loomis and others that might reject their plans: "God was always willing to have his gospel spread throughout the world; that if the Christian public was willing and active, the work would be done."[13] Green states that Mills led the group to put the matter to prayer and closed the prayer time emphatically that "God would strike down the arm with the red artillery of heaven that should be raised against a herald of the cross."[14]

Two important facts about the Haystack not always recognized should be noted here. First, the prayer meeting was a consistent one. The power of the Haystack Prayer Meeting did not take place in a one-time gathering, but rather grew in the time leading up to and following the special event. The Haystack was not a first time event but the continuation of a regularly scheduled time of prayer. The writer of *Proceedings of the Missionary Jubilee* acknowledges the significance of this and explains that many young men gave of their Saturday to

---

[12] Elisabeth G. Stryker, *The Story of One Short Life* (Chicago: Woman's Presbyterian Board of Foreign Missions of the Northwest, 1888), 60.

[13] Byram Green, "Letter to President Hopkins," 8. Unless otherwise noted the details concerning the Haystack Prayer meeting have been gleaned from this letter from Mr. Green, a participant in the prayer meeting, to President Hopkins. The letter was in reference to the prayer meeting, its details, and particularly an inquiry into the exact location of the prayer meeting so that a suitable monument might be erected and the event celebrated. The work containing the letter gives a detailed account of the events of the mission's park dedication in celebration of the Fiftieth Anniversary of the Haystack Prayer Meeting. It was not until 1854 that many of the details and the exact location of the Haystack Prayer meeting became known. (See details in *Proceedings of the Missionary Jubilee*, 21). Green was the only surviving member of the group present during the Haystack Prayer Meeting. Mills died in 1818, Richards in 1822, Loomis in 1825, and Robbins in 1850.

[14] Ibid.

prayer "and it was fitting that, in connection with such devotion, and under the broad canopy of heaven, this great and all-embracing idea should start into life."[15] The Haystack Prayer meeting was the result and continuation of a season of revival that led to a significant movement in the work of the great commission.

Second, the conversation of the Haystack was precipitated by the subject of geography of Asia. The idea that basic academic endeavor could encourage and even facilitate a movement of revival is important to recognize. The hope being that "the assimilative power of an ardent piety and what may be the connection between ordinary studies and Christian enterprise."[16] Basically the ability for normal education to stimulate Christian endeavors was a significant evidence of the Haystack Prayer Meeting.

During this prayer time they would covenant to surrender to take the gospel to the heathen of the nations. The amazing fact about this covenant was that a missionary sending agency had yet to be established in the young America.[17] Kenneth Latourette adds clarity to the significance of the Haystack, "It was from this Haystack meeting that the foreign missionary movement of the churches of the United States had an initial main impulse."[18] The intensity of that Haystack meeting inspired the men to continue in prayer and the forthcoming results were extraordinary and continue to be influential. Samuel Capen expounds, "Though the United States was hardly more than a loose union of feeble states, whose people had but recently won independence...Mills and his companions had courage and faith to believe that they could send the gospel thousands of miles to distant peoples. And what is more significant, in six years the

---

[15] Ibid., 10.

[16] Ibid.

[17] David Howard, "The Road to Urbana and Beyond," *Evangelical Missions Quarterly* 21, no. 1, (1985), 8.

[18] Latourette, *These Sought a Country*, 46.

dream became a reality."[19] Capen spoke of the first missionaries being sent from the subsequently established American Board of Commissioners for Foreign Missions (ABCFM). The American Board was the first mission sending agency in America. Capen concludes, "The power of the sun will be measured with a yardstick sooner than the results of the Haystack Meeting by statistics."[20] Clearly the Haystack remains as a landmark of American foreign missions and signifies the influence of Great Awakenings on the Great Commission.

The Haystack had a great influence on the subsequent years of Williams College and the work of missions as well. Dr. Ed Griffin came to be the president in 1821. His coming marked the beginning of better things in the college life. Griffin declared that he owed his own missionary interest and enthusiasm largely to young Mills, who was at one time a student in his home. Griffin's interest in the college and his willingness to become its president arose largely from a former acquaintance with Samuel J Mills, and his knowledge of the college as the birthplace of American foreign missions.[21]

At his inauguration as the President of Williams College Griffin invoked the history of the Haystack. He was encouraged as he spoke, "A College which has been honored and sanctified by being the scene of such events, which has been so pre-eminently the seat of prayer, which has given so many ministers and missionaries to the church, will not, I trust be suffered to fall."[22]

---

[19] Edward Warren Capen, "Significance of the Haystack Centennial," *Bibliotheca Sacra* 13 (Oct 1906), 707.

[20] Quoted in Thomas Richards, *The Haystack Prayer Meeting* (New York: De Vinne Press, 1906), 29.

[21] Ibid., 67.

[22] Quoted in Samuel J. Mills Sr., "Letter to Editor," *Boston Recorder* 8, no. 8 (Feb 22, 1823): 32.

An article by Edward Capen, written just prior to the centennial celebration of the Haystack, gives several reasons supporting the significance of the Haystack Centennial. First, he recognizes the influence of the haystack as a focal event. Capen writes, "So far is known, it was the occasion of the first definite resolution ever made by Americans to begin for themselves the work of foreign missions; and because it was chiefly due to the resolution then formed that four years later, in 1810, the American board was organized, and that in 1812 missionaries actually sailed from the United States to Asia."[23] The Haystack was then, and for many still, remains a source of inspiration concerning the birth of Foreign Missions in America. Capen concludes, "The achievements and the succeeding century of work abroad, which were the outcome of the haystack meeting and of the influences which had made that possible, constitute the first significance of the Haystack Centennial."[24]

Capen explains that a second reason for the significance of the Haystack Centennial was the principles and methods espoused by the leaders of the movement. The missionary movement encouraged by the faith of the Haystack band ushered in an era of great organization and cooperation among varying Christian denominations. The third significance of the Haystack Centennial as described by Capen, was the spirit of the early missionary movement. The story of the actual carrying out of the vision of a mission sending agency is remarkable. The faith required and the obstacles overcome inspired many that were familiar with the work of the American Board and of Mills. The haystack prayer meeting was a result of the fervor of revival, and led to an astounding fervor for the fulfillment of the Great Commission.

Kenneth Latourette agrees that the events of the Haystack and its subsequent influence began a "golden chain" of events that eventually led to the greatest student mission movement in the history of the church.

---

[23]Capen, "The Significance of the Haystack Centennial," 704.
[24]Ibid., 714.

The typical line of the "golden chain" usually takes the following shape. The Haystack led to the formation of the Society of the Brethren as discussed above. The Brethren's work led to the formation of another group named the "Society of Inquiry on the Subject of Missions." Seven of the nine charter members at Andover, including Mills, were members of the Brethren. These Societies of Inquiry laid the ground work for the establishment of the student led YMCA's on many of the major college campuses in America. [25]

The student led societies eventually came together for a student conference held at D. L. Moody's conference center at Mount Hermon in July of 1886. The Conference at Mount Hermon came about because Luther Wishard, traveling YMCA secretary had knelt beside the Haystack Prayer Meeting Monument in the snow and prayed "Lord, do it again! Where water once flowed, let it flow again!" He then persuaded the great evangelist, Moody, to call the conference.[26] They studied the Bible together for a month and the conference led to a hundred students volunteering for the mission field.[27]

On July 24, 1886, Moody was persuaded to allow ten individuals representing ten nations to appeal to other students to surrender for missionary service. Many of them signed what was known as the "Princeton Declaration" committing surrender to go overseas to the mission field. John Mott was included in those that signed and wrote that the meeting "may occupy as significant a place in history of the Christian Church as the Williams Haystack Prayer Meeting."[28] J. Edwin

---

[25] David Howard, *Student Power in World Missions*, (Downers Grove: InterVarsity, 1979), 82-83.

[26] J. Christy Wilson, "Haystack Harvest," in *The Unfinished Task*, ed. John E. Kyle: Ventura, CA: Regal Books, 1984), 14.

[27] See David L. McKenna, *The Coming Great Awakening*, (Downers Grove: InterVarsity, 1990), 38 –39 and Howard, *Student Power*, 89-93.

[28] John Mott, *Five Decades and a Forward View* (New York: Harper, 1939), 4.

Orr writes that "by 1888 over 3,000 (students) had pledged themselves to the cause of foreign missions. Thus, while God had used the YMCA to mobilize Christian students into campus chapters, the Princeton Foreign Missionary Society grew into the Student Volunteer Movement, which was used to send them into the harvest."[29] Orr continues to share that the movement eventually led to over 20,000 students setting sail for foreign lands over the life of the movement.[30] Howard concludes, "The first links of that 'golden chain' were forged under the haystack in 1806. New links were added during the next eighty years. Then, in 1886, the final links were drawn together to make a mighty chain that was to circle the globe."[31] Neill confirms, "By 1945, at the most conservative estimate, 20,500 students from so-called Christian lands, who had signed the declaration, reached the field, for the most part under the missionary societies and boards of the churches."[32] The slogan, "the evangelization of the world in this generation," became the great battle cry of the SVM. Some misunderstood it as an arrogant proclamation of the salvation of all, but it was rather a declaration of the responsibility that each generation has to reach their generation for Christ.[33]

Mott shares the five-fold purpose of the Student Volunteer Movement. First, their goal was to lead students to a thorough consideration of the

---

[29] J. Edwin Orr, "Why Campus Revivals Spark Missionary Advance." In *Journey to the Nations* (Littleton: The Caleb Project, 1983) n.p. [accessed 16 Feb 2008]. Online: www.calebproject.org/bomm/orr_svm.html.

[30] Ibid.

[31] Howard, *Student Power*, 80.

[32] Ruth Rouse and Stephen C. Neill, *A History of the Ecumenical Movement 1517–1948* (Philadelphia: Westminster, 1967), 328.

[33] See William R. Hogg, *Ecumenical Foundations: A History of the International Missionary Council and Its Nineteenth Century Background* (New York: Harper, 1952), 88 and John Mott, *Christian Students and World Problems: Report of the Ninth International Convention of the Student Volunteer Movement for Foreign Missions, Indianapolis, Indiana, December 28, 1923, to January 1, 1924* (New York, Student Volunteer Movement, 1923), 64.

claims of foreign missions upon them personally as a lifework. Second, they foster this purpose by guiding students who became volunteers in their study and activity for missions until they came under the immediate direction of the Mission Boards. Third, the movement was to unite all volunteers in a common, organized, aggressive movement. Fourth, was to secure a sufficient number of well-qualified volunteers to meet the demands of the various Mission Boards. Finally, the fifth purpose was to create and maintain an intelligent, sympathetic backing of the missionary enterprise by their advocacy, their gifts and their prayers.[34]

The Student Volunteer Movement is credited with providing from one half to two thirds of North American Missionaries sent overseas before 1925.[35] The First World War, the Great Depression, and a shift in theological emphasis greatly depleted the strength of the SVM. What had been a mission focused sending movement became a mix of many different social issues. Though the movement lost its power, its influence, and subsequently the influence of Mills and the Haystack touched numerous lives and institutions.

Latourette writes, "Through it (Student Volunteer Movement) the story of Mills and the Haystack meeting was repeated to tens of thousands of youth and the influence of Mills continued to spread."[36] John Mott, the perennial leader of the Student Volunteer Movement recognized the connection between the two movements. He writes, "We recognize the significance of the student missionary uprising of the closing years of last century. It is well to recall the beginnings." [37] Mott explains that the Haystack Prayer Meeting was the beginning of a chain of events that, "Set in motion influences which resulted within four years in

---

[34] Mott, *Five Decades*, 8.

[35] Nathan Showalter, *The End of a Crusade: The Student Volunteer Movement for Foreign Missions and the Great War* (Lanham, Md.: Scarecrow Press, 1998), 3.

[36] Latourette, *These Sought a Country*, 50.

[37] John Mott, *Five Decades and a Forward View*, 1.

the organization of the American Board of Commissioners of Foreign Missions, the parent American missionary society, which led in turn to the present-day vast and widespread missionary activities of the Churches of North America (Student Volunteer Movement)."[38] Mott suggests that the Student Volunteer Movement is the culmination of the work began by the Haystack and the Society of Brethren at Williams College.

The fervor sparked by the Second Great Awakening for foreign missions is clearly evident in the life and influence of Mills and of the Haystack. It has now been well over 200 years since the Haystack Prayer Revival and the need for Great Awakening and a fervor for the Great Commission is greater than ever. May God once again bring a spirit of revival to His people that would stir us more greatly into the work of taking the Gospel to all the nations and fulfilling the Great Commission. May God grant us the grace and vision that our cry would be the same as Mills and the others sheltered by that Haystack Prayer Revival: "We can do it, IF we will!"

---

[38] Ibid., 1-2.

CHAPTER FIVE

Great Commission Lessons From The Jesus Movement
Bobby R. Lewis, Ph.D.

D URING his childhood in the 1960s, Alvin Reid and his family attended the Centercrest Baptist Church in Birmingham, Alabama. As a new decade began to dawn, rather unusual events occurred in the church which would come to have a profound influence on Reid's life. In his 1991 Ph.D. dissertation for Southwestern Baptist Theological Seminary, Reid recalls, "During that year (1970) a large number of young people who clearly fit the contemporary definition of 'hippie' (i.e., love beads, long hair, bizarre clothing, and headbands) suddenly became Christians and involved in the church. The next two years saw a number of ministries develop at Centercrest such as beach dramas in Florida and a Christian 'night club,' which fit the mold of what has come to be called the Jesus Movement."[1] As Reid witnessed a new spiritual awakening

---

[1] See Alvin Lee Reid, "The Impact of the Jesus Movement on Evangelism Among Southern Baptists" (Ph.D. diss., Southwestern Baptist Theological Seminary, 1991), ii. Although the Jesus Movement has been defined in numerous ways, Reid's rather holistic description employed throughout his dissertation serves

begin to influence many young people around him, he soon made a personal commitment to Jesus Christ.

While the Jesus Movement may not have had the tremendous impact of the great spiritual awakenings of earlier centuries in America, it was still a significant Christian movement as revival fires spread from West-to-East across the continent.[2] Churches of numerous denominations along with various parachurch ministries experienced notable increases in baptisms and overall participation, particularly among young people. College campuses also witnessed many powerful movements of God's Spirit. Consider the flames of awakening which had engulfed a private Methodist college in Kentucky.[3] Beginning with a student named David Perry, scores of Asbury College students stood broken before professors and friends, openly confessing their sins during a chapel service on campus. Jack Taylor vividly describes what happened. He writes:

> In 1970 in the little college town of Wilmore, Kentucky, God moved into a college chapel service in the Power of His Spirit and lengthened the fifty-minute chapel service to one hundred and eighty hours of continuous revival. More than twenty news media personnel were saved as they visited to cover the phenomenon. I visited and preached in that chapel a few months after revival broke

---

well for the purpose of this chapter. He writes, "For the following study the term 'Jesus Movement' is meant to refer to the variety of Christian renewal movements affecting the youth population of the United States in the late sixties and early seventies." Reid, "The Impact of the Jesus Movement," 11.

[2] *Spiritual awakening*s refer to "those divine visitations when there is a new awareness of God, a distinct reality of Christ, deep conviction of sin, a time of refreshing from the presence of the Lord.... It is an epoch when the Holy Spirit is working with greater liberty in the hearts of men or groups." See John Caylor, "From the Pen of John Caylor: A Spiritual Awakening and the Church." *Home Missions* 28 (June 1957), 5. See also Reid, "The Impact of the Jesus Movement," 11–33.

[3] See Alvin Reid, *Introduction to Evangelism* (Nashville: Broadman & Holman, 1998), 78-79.

out. The Presence of the Almighty hovered over that little town with unmistakable glory.[4]

Many other colleges and churches throughout the nation experienced revival as Asbury students shared what God had been doing on their campus. This movement among young people continued to spread from a small Methodist college in Kentucky to one of the largest protestant denominations in the world.

From the birth of a new Convention in May of 1845, Southern Baptists have considered the fulfillment of the Great Commission to be of prime importance. As the Southern Baptist Convention met for the first time in Augusta, Georgia, delegates quickly adopted a resolution which articulated this pressing passion by stating, "...it is proper that this Convention at once proceed to organize a Society for the propagation of the Gospel."[5] In order to measure the overall evangelistic effectiveness of the denomination, the SBC has relied on various quantitative data, particularly total baptisms.

As the Jesus Movement became a recognizable spiritual movement in the late 1960s and early 1970s, SBC baptisms reached an all-time high. The 1976 SBC *Annual* reported, "During 1975, for the fifth consecutive year, the churches of the Convention reported more than 400,000 baptisms.... This has been by far the best five-year period in evangelism our denomination has ever known."[6] In fact, a study of baptismal totals from

---

[4] Jack Taylor, *The Key to Triumphant Living: An Adventure in Personal Discovery* (Nashville: Broadman, 1971), 90.

[5] *Annual of the Southern Baptist Convention, Eighteen Hundred and Forty-Five: First Session, First Year* (Nashville: Executive Committee, Southern Baptist Convention, 1845), 13.

[6] *Annual of the Southern Baptist Convention, Nineteen Hundred and Seventy-Six: One Hundred Nineteenth Session, One Hundred Thirty-First Year* (Nashville: Executive Committee, Southern Baptist Convention, 1976), 128. This writer questions the assertion, "This has been by far the best five-year period in evangelism our denomination has ever known." Baptismal ratios should be considered before accepting this type of sweeping evaluation. For example, throughout much of the

1845-2009 reveals that this is still the *only* five-year period in SBC history when baptisms topped 400,000. The highest number of youth baptisms throughout the Convention was also recorded in the early 1970s.[7]

Could such an increase be traced back to any particular program(s) of the SBC, or could the larger spiritual awakening known as the Jesus Movement provide a more accurate explanation? Consider the following baptismal figures for the SBC :

YEAR	TOTAL BAPTISMS
1970	368, 863
1971	409, 659
1972	445, 725 [74]

Accolades are sure to appear with such notable increases in total SBC baptisms. Don Mabry concludes, "There has been a resurgence in evangelism effectiveness during the years 1971 and 1972."[9]Robert Hamblin adds, "In 1972, the denomination reached a new high of 445,725 baptisms.[10]That record was established after two years of Lay Evangelism Schools. Witness training had contributed significantly to baptisms the

1950s these ratios generally hovered around 1:20. By the late 1960s and early 1970s, ratios had risen to approximately 1:30. See Thom S. Rainer, "A Resurgence Not Yet Realized: Evangelistic Effectiveness in the Southern Baptist Convention Since 1979," *Southern Baptist Journal of Theology* 9 no. 1 (Spring 2005), 57-58.

[7] The highest number of youth baptisms ever recorded by the Southern Baptist Convention was 137,667 in 1972.

[8] "Southern Baptist Summary—1845-1981," Quarterly Review, vol. 49, no. 4 (July, August, September, 1989), 71.

[9] Don F. Mabry, "The Demand for a Dynamic Evangelism." Paper presented at the meeting of the State Evangelism Secretaries (Atlanta, December 3, 1973), 12.

[10]At the time of this writing this is still the highest number of total baptisms for the SBC in any one year period.

way revivals had done earlier."[11] Even Chuck Kelley proposes, "Witness training seemed to accomplish what simultaneous crusades and individual revivals had not done in a decade. The number of baptisms began to increase steadily again."[12] In a later article, however, Kelley astutely notes another possibility for explaining the statistical increases: "The Jesus Movement sweeping the country at that time should also be considered as a significant factor in the statistical gain."[13] This brings us to an important caveat—quantitative data must be considered carefully before causal relationships can be determined, if in fact such relationships exist at all.

In an article related to the topic of his Ph.D. dissertation, Reid offers several comments concerning the impact of Lay Evangelism Schools (also known as WIN schools). His insights are worth noting at length. Reid claims:

> The major reason why baptisms in general rose among Southern Baptists in the early 1970s was the Jesus Movement. Many of the evaluations during the period emphasized the introduction of the WIN approach. This Home Mission Board-sponsored effort taught laity on a large scale for the first time to witness personally. The WIN schools served as an excellent method and spread quickly across the country and doubtless had a large impact. However, the milieu of spiritual renewal paved the way for the success of WIN schools. For example, the evangelism report of the Home Mission Board in 1971 noted obvious "signs of spiritual awakening in our

---

[11] Robert L. Hamblin, "Home Mission Board Influence on Southern Baptist Evangelism," *Baptist History and Heritage* 22 no 1 (1987), 25.

[12] Charles S. Kelley, Jr., "An Investigation of the Changing Role of the Revival Meeting in the Southern Baptist Program of Evangelism, 1947–1980" (Th.D. diss., New Orleans Baptist Theological Seminary, 1983), 106-107.

[13] Kelley, "A Theological-Historical Look at Revivalism in the SBC," *Search* 20 (Spring 1990), 36.

convention, especially among the youth." This same report merely introduced the WIN materials. The materials for WIN were not widely distributed until 1972, while the years of greatest baptismal increases were 1970-72. The first WIN schools were not even taught until April and May of 1971, and then in limited areas only. So, one might argue more forcefully that the spiritual tides during the Jesus Movement aided in the success of the WIN schools, and not vice-versa.[14]

Reid notes the importance of "spiritual renewal" when considering such statistical gains.

While SBC leaders have worked diligently to create and promote innovative programs for personal witness training, many realized that these programs alone were not the answer Southern Baptists needed. One such leader during the time of the Jesus Movement, C. B. Hogue contends, "The need today is for evangelism, dynamic evangelism, to become a ground swell; and for the people of the church, unashamed, bold, articulate, to recover the evangelistic thrust of the first-century Christians and embark afresh on a twentieth-century mission."[15] This same admonition holds true for believers in the twenty-first century.

From the time of C. E. Matthews in the 1950s, it appears that SBC evangelism has relied too heavily on programmatic advances in evangelism. Consider the following insights by Reid: "One must not reduce evangelism to a mere working out of a certain technique.

---

[14] Alvin Reid, "The Effect of the Jesus Movement on Evangelism in the Southern Baptist Convention," *Baptist History and Heritage* 30 no 1 (January 1995), 45-46.

[15] C. B. Hogue, *Love Leaves No Choice: Life-Style Evangelism* (Waco: Word Books, 1976), 21. See also, Bobby Ray Lewis, Jr., "A Critical Investigation of C. B. Hogue's Concepts of Evangelism and an Assessment of His Impact on Evangelism in the Southern Baptist Convention," Ph.D. diss., Southeastern Baptist Theological Seminary, 2009.

The supernatural work of the Holy Spirit must always be a major consideration in examining effective times of evangelistic harvesting."[16] Evangelism programs and strategies certainly have their place, yet Southern Baptists have failed at times to acknowledge the crucial role of the Holy Spirit in effective evangelism.[17]

One important lesson learned in light of the Jesus Movement is that the SBC should rely more on dynamic movements of God's Spirit through prayer and awakening than prepackaged programs or evangelistic methodologies. In an effort to avoid extremes or potential errors in orthodoxy or orthopraxy, it appears that the denomination has often been rather tentative with regard to such movements of the Holy Spirit. For this present writer, it seems that the SBC has attempted to avoid possible errors in theology or extremes in practice that have emerged in the last century among various Pentecostal or charismatic groups; however, in so doing, some Southern Baptists may have allowed the pendulum to swing too far toward dead orthodoxy or dry orthopraxy.

A reemphasis on the role of the Holy Spirit and the power of prayer must be coupled with sound theology and innovative methodology, not only in the area of evangelism, but every facet of Southern Baptist life. In an interview with this writer, John Avant shared the following:

> I think during especially the [19]70s and 80s some of
> our greatest days were utilizing what we consider more

---

[16] Reid, "The Impact of the Jesus Movement," 195-196.

[17] Lewis Drummond notes, "In attempting to evaluate the various SBC training programs in evangelism, it is difficult to fault in any major way any actual program itself. Most of the approaches have grown out of the local churches themselves. The programs have, by and large, not been an 'ivory tower' invention. They really have emerged from the heat of attempting to evangelize effectively on the front lines in local churches. Thus, they have a relevancy and effectiveness that has held them in good stead among the churches that use them." Lewis A. Drummond, "Training for Evangelism in Southern Baptist Life," *Baptist History and Heritage* 22 no 1 (January 1987), 35-36.

traditional approaches to evangelism. We had some of
our highest baptismal years—had our highest baptismal
years in the 70s and some pretty good results in the
80s. I think the concern I have is we seem to always
respond to culture rather than saying, "Lord, You
know what's coming. How do You want us to reach
people today?" Our research showed that most of the
methods that we were using in the 70s and 80s, which I
was a part of all of those [and had] tremendous success,
they're simply not being effective now. We had trouble
finding a methodology that we could point to and say,
"Anywhere you look, there's measurable long-term
success with FAITH or CWT, through EE, through the
NET even." At NAMB, we came to the conclusion that
evangelistic churches had a DNA about them. It was
no longer a programmatic answer. We don't really have
programmatic, evangelistic answers to offer.[18]

Avant had seen firsthand that the SBC would not become
more evangelistically effective simply through the creation and
implementation of innovative evangelism programs or strategies. A
movement of God was absolutely essential. For a denomination so
prone to herald a new program as *the* answer for effective evangelism,
particularly in the latter half of the twentieth century, Avant appears to
understand the challenges faced by the SBC today.[19]

---

[18] John Avant, Telephone interview by author, January 6, 2009, Dobson, NC, CD
Recording and Transcript in the hand of Bobby Lewis.

[19] Thom Rainer maintains, "Evangelism and church growth does benefit from
innovative programs. Research is helpful to grasp possible future paths of
evangelistic strategy. But ultimately evangelism is a matter of the heart between
the believer and a sovereign God. It is truly a spiritual matter. And if we are not
personally and corporately evangelistic, the first response must be confession
and repentance toward the God whose grace is sufficient to give us yet another

In his 2006 monograph, Avant describes how Christians have often understood and practiced evangelism. He writes, "I have done evangelism just about every way possible, but I have to confess that I don't find many evangelistic methods of yesterday to be effective today. We have often turned evangelism into a course to learn. We finish the course and then we go 'hunting' for lost people to use our newfound 'skills' and 'techniques' on."[20] Avant adds, "I have taken all the courses. I have learned much from them, but most of the time I wonder if we aren't missing the Jesus way. Jesus evangelized *as He went*."[21] Avant then articulates his understanding of lifestyle evangelism and the likely results as believers follow this evangelistic pattern established by Christ. He asks:

> What if every follower of Christ viewed evangelism as the normal process of making friends, loving people like Jesus did, and sharing good news only with people who actually wanted to hear it? I believe we would see the Spirit of God sweep through our schools, marketplaces, and neighborhoods. Evangelism would become a wonderful part of the journey, not an assignment to dread.[22]

During his relatively brief tenure over SBC evangelism, Avant recalls, "We constantly said we must seek movements and we must be facilitators of movements of God."[23] These movements, Avant insists, would come through genuine relationships between Christians and non-Christians rather than a series of evangelistic hunting expeditions.

---

opportunity." Thom S. Rainer, "A Resurgence Not Yet Realized: Evangelistic Effectiveness in the Southern Baptist Convention Since 1979," *Southern Baptist Journal of Theology* 9 no. 1 (Spring 2005), 67-68.

[20] John Avant, *Authentic Power: How to Unleash It In Your Life* (Sisters, OR: Multnomah, 2006), 166.

[21] Ibid., 166-67.

[22] Ibid., 168.

[23] Avant, Telephone interview, January 6, 2009.

Another significant, related lesson from the Jesus Movement is that a passion for the Great Commission comes from an authentic love for Christ and desire to see His fame spread rather than a dry duty to complete a given evangelistic task. Reid points out, "Evangelism was a primary focus of the movement overall....Those involved in the movement desired to share their joy in Jesus with others."[24] Rather than participating in evangelistic efforts because of guilt or compulsion, witnessing sprang from a genuine desire to share with others what had been experienced with Christ. Young people by the thousands were coming to know Jesus Christ as their Lord and Savior, and they were being radically changed from the inside. From coffeehouses to communes and Jesus marches to dynamic festivals, the spread of the gospel was not confined to the walls of a church building or through a rote presentation. Much like believers in the first-century church, those touched by the Jesus Movement simply shared Christ as they went and where they went. For Southern Baptists in the twenty-first century we are reminded once again to replace the usual "come and see" mentality with the more biblically faithful mandate to "go and tell."

Evangelistic creativity is yet another important implication from the Jesus Movement. According to Roger Palms, numerous creative methods were used by "The Jesus Kids" to share the gospel.[25] These included, but were certainly not limited to, the rise of contemporary Christian music and youth musicals, clothing with religious messages and/or symbols, newspapers to propagate the message to those outside and inform those who were already within the movement, and numerous types of concerts and Jesus rallies. Southern Baptists would do well to remember that creativity in sharing the gospel certainly has its place, but creativity alone is not sufficient. Only the gospel message of Christ empowered by the Holy Spirit will ultimately change lives. As former SBC Evangelism

---

[24] Reid, "The Impact of the Jesus Movement," 25.

[25] Roger C. Palms, *The Jesus Kids* (Vally Forge, PA: Judson Press, 1971), 36. See also, Reid, "The Impact of the Jesus Movement," 26.

Director C. B. Hogue rightly contends, "Gimmicks and super-energized programs do not bring renewal or rejuvenation...."[26]May we never sacrifice the truth and exclusivity of the gospel on the altar of creativity or evangelistic innovation. Only a mighty outpouring of God's Spirit will transform the evangelistic spirit and effectiveness of the SBC.

The Jesus Movement also serves to remind the modern church of the need to reach young people with the life-changing message of Christ. In his dissertation, Reid notes a "record harvest of youth during the Jesus Movement, followed by years of record seminary enrollments...."[27] Southern Baptists would do well to remember that young people are not merely the church of the future; they can and should be part of the active, vibrant church today. Every young person who has placed his or her faith in Jesus Christ is part of the universal church and should be utilized to reach others with the Gospel through the teaching and encouragement of the local church. Since the time of the Jesus movement and the rise of church youth ministries, Southern Baptists have often lowered the bar when it comes to youth. Instead of challenging our young people to be on mission with God now, we have often placated them with a variety of silly songs, games, and activities. Youth have been led to believe erroneously that their time and place of service is somewhere in the future. A greater depth of theological teaching and an increased awareness of God's generous use of young people throughout history, particularly in times of awakening, would serve our youth well.[28]

---

[26] C. B. Hogue, *I Want My Church to Grow* (Nashville: Broadman, 1977), 18. Hogue understood and affirmed Robert Munger's opinion that, "Evangelism today and tomorrow must seek the enduement of the Holy Spirit and rely upon his power." Robert B. Munger, "Some Guidelines for Evangelism Tomorrow," *Southwestern Journal of Theology* 18 (Spring 1976), 44.

[27] Reid, "The Impact of the Jesus Movement," 204.

[28] See Alvin L. Reid, *Raising the Bar* (Grand Rapids: Kregel, 2004); Alvin L. Reid, *Join the Movement: God is Calling You to Change the World* (Grand Rapids: Kregel, 2007); Alvin L. Reid, *Light the Fire: Raising Up a Generation to Live Radically*

Overall, one of the most notable lessons from the Jesus Movement is that a passion for the Great Commission cannot be packaged or programmed. This sweeping movement among young people in the late 1960s and early 1970s serves to remind us that the Southern Baptist Convention desperately needs a Great Commission resurgence brought about by a dynamic movement of God's Spirit.[29] This type of movement will not be purchased at the local Christian bookstore, but must be sought humbly by Southern Baptists in our institutions, agencies, state conventions, and local churches. Southern Baptists must remember that our denomination will only be as evangelistically effective as the churches which make up the Convention. Furthermore, local churches will only be as passionate for the Great Commission as their spiritual leaders. Thus, Baptist leaders at every level must focus on loving and serving people more than simply developing new products or programs. Chuck Kelley insists, "From their beginning, Southern Baptists have intended to be an evangelistic people."[30] For this statement to remain valid, leaders of the SBC at all levels must focus on fulfilling the Great Commission rather than advancing personal agendas or promoting pet projects.

Throughout history, Christians have often been accused of hypocrisy by unbelievers. Whether this perception is always justified, there are certainly times when this assessment is accurate. Too often the tongue in our mouth simply does not align with the tongue in our shoe. One of the most tragic displays of hypocrisy can be observed in the lives of those who affirm conservative biblical convictions concerning the realities of heaven and hell and the exclusivity of Christ for salvation, while simultaneously failing to share this truth in both word and deed with the lost world around them.

---

for Jesus Christ (Enumclaw, WA: Winepress, 2001); and Alvin L. Reid, "The Spontaneous Generation: Lessons from the Jesus Movement for Today." *Journal of the American Society for Church Growth* (Spring 2000), 98-105.

[29] See Alvin Reid, "The Great Commission Resurgence." n. p. [cited January 19, 2009] Online: www.alvinreid.com/archives/303.

[30] Charles S. Kelley, Jr., *How Did They Do It? The Story of Southern Baptist Evangelism* (New Orleans: Insight Press, 1993), 6.

While right beliefs should lead to right actions, this has not always been the case. Avant contends, "Southern Baptists need a conservative view of the Bible if they are to grow and be evangelistically effective, but that is far from all they need."[31] Effective evangelism simply does not happen by accident. Danny Akin concludes:

> We can train and we can preach on evangelism. But, we must act. Biblical evangelism must be a constant drumbeat throughout our denomination, in our seminaries and agencies, in our state conventions and associations. If this is not happening at every level, the entity has become irrelevant in fulfilling the Great Commission and should be radically overhauled or shut down and buried like the spiritual corpse it has become.[32]

If the SBC actually exists for "the propagation of the Gospel," then Southern Baptists must stop relishing in the past victories of the conservative resurgence and start combining their efforts for a Great Commission resurgence.[33] It has rightly been stated, "There are no shortcuts to serving, no easy ways to winning, and no snap courses in evangelism. Winning is exciting and far too strenuous for the armchair strategist, the spiritual carpetbagger who always arrives just as the battle is over. Beware, lest we come to the realization that the people of God today may have become a

---

[31] John Paul Avant, Jr., "The Relationship of Changing Views of the Inspiration and Authority of Scripture to Evangelism and Church Growth: A Study of the United Methodist Church and the Southern Baptist Convention in the United States Since World War II" (PhD diss., Southwestern Baptist Theological Seminary, 1990), 283.

[32] Daniel L. Akin, "The Future of Southern Baptists: Mandates for What We Should Be in the Twenty-First Century," *Southern Baptist Journal of Theology* 9 no. 1 (Spring 2005), 77.

[33] *Annual of the SBC*, 1845, 13.

field of evangelism rather than a force of evangelism."[34] May the lessons learned from the Jesus Movement remind all Southern Baptists that our greatest ministry for God's greatest glory is to submit ourselves fully to the Holy Spirit as we joyfully, consistently, passionately share our transformed lives and the Good News of Jesus Christ with others who still desperately need Him. "Not to us, O LORD, not to us, but to Your name be the glory, because of Your love and faithfulness" (Ps 115:1).

---

[34] C. B. Hogue, "The Vision, the Voice, and the Venture," n. d. (Manuscript in the hand of Bobby Lewis), 10. Emphasis added by Hogue.

Section Three

Strategies for the Great Commission

CHAPTER SIX

The Great Commission And Myths About The Unchurched
Thom S. Rainer, Ph.D.

AMERICA could use a Great Commission resurgence. Only 43% of Americans attend church services on a typical weekend.[1] Each new generation is becoming increasingly unchurched.[2] The church dropout rate for young adults 18-22 is 70%.[3] In a given year, only one person is reached for Christ for every 85 church members in America.[4] The lack of focus on the Great Commission is glaring. Unfortunately, the primary concern for some is the status quo for the sake of comfort. The answer seems so apparent: we need to reach these people with the gospel message

---

[1] Frank Newport, "Americans' Church Attendance Inches Up in 2010: Increase Accompanies Rise in Economic Confidence," *Gallup*, June 25, 2010. http://www.gallup.com/poll/141044/Americans-Church-Attendance-Inches-2010.aspx.

[2] For more details see Thom S. Rainer, *Surprising Insights from the Unchurched and Proven Ways to Reach Them* (Grand Rapids: Zondervan, 2008).

[3] For more statistics see Thom S. Rainer and Sam S. Rainer, *Essential Church?; Reclaiming a Generation of Dropouts* (Nashville: B&H, 2008).

[4] See Thom S. Rainer, *Surprising Insights from the Unchurched*.

---

of Jesus Christ. We need to live the Great Commission. Yet I find a lot of confusion about the lost, unchurched, and dechurched populations. Despite the plethora of resources on reaching those who do not attend church, the unchurched in America continues to grow.

When my oldest son, Sam, was four years old, he started running a high fever. At first, my wife and I were not too concerned, as young children often get fevers with viruses and infections. We remained calm and rationalized that his doctor would remedy the situation quickly. But the physician did not have a conclusive diagnosis, and the fever did not break. We took Sam to the emergency room, and numerous attendants tried repeatedly to get the fever to break. Nothing worked. At one point the worried doctor looked at us and said, "Pray that we can find the problem. All we are doing now is treating the symptoms."

To this day I remember asking people to pray for my son's healing. Thankfully, Sam is now grown and a father of his own. The doctors never discovered the cause of Sam's illness. The fever broke without explanation.

Like the worried doctor, too many churches in America today have not come to a diagnosis regarding the unchurched and are trying to treat symptoms. Only a small percentage of churches have recognized the problem of a growing lost and unchurched population in America. These churches have made intentional and successful efforts to reach the unchurched. Many churches, however, have been addressing only the symptoms. A certain worship style, the latest small group, a new church vernacular, or the "right" church name is seen as a panacea to the problem of not reaching the unchurched. Please understand my comments. Many times these "symptoms" need serious work. The church may need to change worship style or rethink its name. Yet the real "treatment" must be at a deeper and more profound level.

The Great Commission calls us to address the problem, not just treat symptoms only. So our research team talked with a group that helped us determine how best to share the healing power of the gospel. This group is the formerly unchurched. Who are the formerly unchurched? They are people who have recently (typically within the past two years) become active in church. For all or a large portion of their lives they were not in church. Some of the formerly unchurched consider themselves Christians even when they did not attend a church. Most, however, were not Christians before they found a church home. We interviewed 353 of these persons.[5] We chose this group because when they tell us why they chose a church, we have an actual case study of someone moving from the ranks of the unchurched to the churched. When the unchurched tell us what *might* attract them to a church, we do not know for certain if they will respond as they indicated. Our study group consisted of people from numerous churches and multiple denominations from all over the nation. Over the course of several conversations and interviews—in person and via telephone—we began to see several themes. This group helped shatter some myths about how the church can reach the unchurched population. In this chapter, let me share with you eight of these myths.

Myth #1: Most unchurched think and act like Anglo, middle-class suburbanites with no church background.

America is becoming more diverse. The United States population is projected to become minority white in 2042, while the American preschool population will become minority white in 2021.[6] As a result, diversity is getting younger. Not only is the younger generation becoming more diverse, diversity is spreading beyond urban cores. More than half

---

[5] Ibid.

[6] William H. Frey, Alan Berube, Audrey Singer, and Jill H. Wilson "Getting Current: Recent Demographic Trends in Metropolitan America," *The Brookings Institution*, March 2009. www.brookings.edu/research/reports/2009/03/metro-demographic-trends.

of metropolitan Hispanics, Asians, and blacks live in the suburbs.[7] This diversity not only applies to race but also socioeconomic status. Once the home to predominantly middle and upper class families, suburban areas now contain the fastest growing poor population— poverty growing five times faster in the suburbs than in primary cities.[8] The American culture has become less segregated. It is now less homogeneous and more heterogeneous.

The unchurched are not part of a monolithic group. Most people acknowledge that the unchurched come from a variety of backgrounds. Yet many church strategies for intentionally reaching the unchurched in a particular community seem to be cookie-cutter approaches originating in areas that may have little in common with the church's community.

For instance, William is a twenty-three year-old African-American with little church background. His grandmother, when asked by William what she wanted for her birthday, said simply, "I want you to go to church with me next Sunday." Reluctantly and seemingly trapped, William agreed.

William was pleasantly surprised. The Memphis-area Baptist church was alive with the hearty singing of black gospel music. The pastor was a great communicator who seemed to know how to speak to the African-American male. He pulled no punches on issues of sin, responsibility, and commitment. No one had to invite William back to church, although several did. He asked his grandmother questions about God, Christ, and the gospel. She patiently explained to him how he could become a Christian. He accepted Christ and then became involved in various church ministries and programs.

---

[7] Ibid.

[8] Elizabeth Kneebone and Emily Garr, "The Suburbanization of Poverty: Trends in Metropolitan America, 2000-2008," *The Brookings Institution*, January 2010. www.brookings.edu/~/media/research/files/papers/2010/1/20%20poverty%20kneebone/0120_poverty_paper.pdf.

"I just didn't know what I was missing," said William. "I can't understand why Christians aren't beating down the doors to share the gospel. Why didn't someone tell me about Jesus before I turned twenty-three?" William is not the stereotypical unchurched person conveyed in books and conferences. He prefers black gospel music. He is challenged by direct and confrontational preaching, and sermons of an hour in length do not bother him. In fact many of the unchurched "rules" were broken by the Memphis church he visited. But he loved the church, and he returned. Unfortunately, many church leaders believe the myth that a methodological model attracts people rather than the philosophical commitment to reach the unchurched in their context. It was not any specific model that reached William. It was the commitment of his grandmother.

Myth #2: The unchurched are turned off by denominational names in the church.

Perhaps one of the biggest surprises in our study was that the name of the church had very little influence on reaching the unchurched. For the most part, neither the presence nor the absence of a denominational name influenced the formerly unchurched's decision to join a church.

When asked, "Did the name of the church influence your decision to join?" we often heard pauses, as if the interviewee was unclear about the question. The pause would often be followed with comments like, "I don't understand" or "What do you mean?" After we explained the question again, the respondent would express surprise at the nature of the inquiry.

Mark is a thirty-nine year-old formerly unchurched person from upstate New York. His response is representative of many of the interviews we conducted. "The name of the church never really entered my mind," Mark told us. "I didn't have a clue what a Wesleyan church was, but that's not what got me interested in the church." Mark's primary influence in coming to church was his sister and her husband. "After all," Mark reflected, "I really don't choose a store because of its name. What does 'Wal-Mart' mean anyway?"

Over 80 percent of the formerly unchurched told us that a church name had little or no influence on their joining a particular church. A further element of surprise came when we asked follow-up questions of the formerly unchurched who said the church name did affect their decision-making process. Nearly two-thirds of respondents indicated that the denominational name had a *positive* influence on their decision. In fact, only 4 out of 100 formerly unchurched indicated that a denominational name had a negative influence on them as they sought a church home.

Readers may ask, "What about the numerous surveys conducted by local churches that indicate certain denominational names are negative in the eyes of the unchurched?" My response is that our research and questions were asked of the formerly unchurched, not the unchurched. The thesis of our research team is that the formerly unchurched provide us insights that we have not previously heard. I would also respond that once a person or event triggers a desire to go to church, the unchurched tend to focus on matters other than the church name. Evelyn serves as an example. At one point in her life "Evangelical Free Church" might have engendered a negative response. But once a certain crisis in her life prompted her to go to church, "I could not have cared less what the name of the church was. I was lonely and hurting and needed to find a community that cared."

Myth #3: The unchurched never attend church.

The word *unchurched* naturally implies that a person has no interest in a church and never attends a church. Our survey of the formerly unchurched, however, indicates that relatively few American *never* attend church. If we defined an unchurched person as one who never attends any kind of church service in a year—including holiday services—the population of the unchurched in America would be small.

Since some church leaders view the unchurched as people completely foreign to the church, they may also assume the unchurched are totally ignorant about biblical or church matters. Our study of the formerly unchurched, however, found that the church was neither strange nor frightening to them when they visited.

"I had attended some Easter services and a few 'regular' services over the past four or five years," Paul of California told us. "I might not have been as familiar with the church as the regular members were, but I wasn't totally ignorant either."

When we asked a portion of the formerly unchurched in our study how often they visited a church a year prior to joining a church, none said zero times. Some of the formerly unchurched attended as many as once a quarter even though they had no church affiliation in the past. Church leaders should realize that the unchurched are not as unfamiliar with the church as we sometimes believe them to be.

Myth #4: The unchurched cannot be reached by direct personal evangelism.

Mark lives in a medium-sized town about sixty miles from St. Louis. He was one of several million unchurched who attend church the previous Easter. "I typically attend a church on Easter," Mark told us. "There was no particular reason for my once-a-year church habit. No major crisis, no guilt trip. It was just something I did."

Mark gladly filled out the guest card as requested in the service. He did not mind hearing from the pastor by letter and receiving information about the church. He also received a call from someone in the church requesting an opportunity to visit him. Mark agreed to receive the two men from church.

"The two guys got right to the point," Mark commented. "They explained to me how I could become a Christian. I received Christ and have been in church ever since."

The seeker-sensitive movement has been a needed wake-up call for dead, inwardly focused churches. The movement has rightly reminded churches to be aware of and be sensitive to the presence of lost persons in worship services. Some churches, however, experience a decline in personal evangelistic efforts when the church focus is on seeker sensitivity. This decline is due to an attitude that sees the seeker-sensitive worship service as the *only* evangelistic effort.

The formerly unchurched in our study left little doubt as to the importance of personal evangelism in reaching the unchurched. Over one-half indicated that someone from the church they joined shared Christ with them. Another 12 percent told us that someone other than a church member evangelized them. Only one-third of the formerly unchurched said that no one made an attempt to share Christ one-on-one with them.

Let me state the obvious—a Great Commission resurgence will not happen without individual efforts at evangelism. The majority of the formerly unchurched who were personally evangelized also told us that someone made an effort to see them within a month of their visit to the church. While the building of relationships with the unchurched is a critical step in reaching them, we heard repeatedly that an evangelistic effort, even by a stranger from the church, had an eternal impact.

Myth #5: We must be careful not to confuse the unchurched with deep and complex biblical truths.

"You know what frustrated me the most when I started visiting churches?" Susan asked us. Susan was a lifelong unchurched person living in the Cleveland area until a life crisis prompted her to seek God. She tried to find him and his truth in the churches she visited. "What really frustrated me was that I had a deep desire to understand the Bible, to hear in-depth preaching and teaching," she continued, "but most of the preaching was so watered-down that it was insulting to my intelligence. I went to one church where the message was on fear. I was eager to hear what the Bible had to say about a subject that described my state of mind."

But Susan was sorely disappointed with what she heard. "It was more of a pop-psychology message. The biblical view was never explained. Bible texts were hardly mentioned," she lamented.

One important lesson we learned from the formerly unchurched is that we should never dilute biblical teachings for the sake of the unchurched. Jennifer, a Minnesota resident, expressed similar sentiments: "You know, I have watched CNBC [a business cable network] for years, since I follow my investments closely," she said. "I remember the first time I watched one of their programs. They used language that contained some strange phrases, like stock splits, P/E ratios, and NASDAQ. Sometimes they explained them, and other times I had to go to the dictionary or the Internet to learn, but I enjoyed the learning experience."

Jennifer continued, "Now that I am a Christian and an active church member, I have been telling my pastor and the church staff that meaty teaching and preaching attracts the unchurched. I think they're listening."

Similar comments to Jennifer's were repeated by many of the formerly unchurched. When we asked if doctrine, or beliefs, of the church they eventually joined was important, the responses were surprising and overwhelming. Ninety-one percent of the formerly unchurched indicated that doctrine was an important factor that attracted them to the church.

Perhaps equally as surprising was the fact that the unchurched were as concerned about doctrine as Christians who had transferred from another church. Almost all of the formerly unchurched responded that doctrine was important, while nine out of ten transfer churched people said likewise. The implications of these findings could be significant in our attempts to reach the unchurched with a Great Commission resurgence. How would our strategies change if we considered the teaching of doctrine to be a major issue in reaching the unchurched?

Myth #6: The Sunday school or small group is ineffective in attracting the unchurched.

I was one of those forecasters several years ago who thought Sunday school was a program that belonged in antiquity, a dinosaur headed for extinction.[9] For some, Sunday school might evoke mental images of dimly lit rooms, walls painted in 1972 yellow, and an eighty-four year-old teacher who uses flannelgraphs. But our research has shown the resurgence of Sunday school in the more effective churches in America. Furthermore, we have learned though this study that the formerly unchurched are positive about and attracted to Sunday school. In fact, the formerly unchurched were more likely to be active in Sunday school than the transfer churched. In a majority of our interviews, it was the formerly unchurched who indicated the greatest allegiance to Sunday school.

We were amazed to find that nearly seven out of ten formerly unchurched were active in Sunday school at the point of our interview. Chris, a formerly unchurched man from Oklahoma, expressed the views of many whom we interviewed: "Look, I'm a new Christian. I've got so much to learn. What better place to learn to fellowship with other Christians than a Sunday school class?" Interestingly, we did notice a slight transition from the nomenclature "Sunday School." Almost 20 percent of the churches in our study did not call their Sunday morning groups "Sunday school," but none of the formerly unchurched expressed any concerns about the name.

---

[9] For the story of my paradigm shift in my attitude about Sunday School, see Thom S. Rainer, *High Expectations: The Remarkable Secrets of Keeping People in Your Church* (Nashville: B&H, 1999).

Myth #7: The most important evangelistic relationships take place in the marketplace.

The marketplace most often refers to the place where we meet people who are not part of our family: workplaces, schools, neighborhoods, and places where we shop and do business. Many good studies and books advocate the training of laity for marketplace evangelism or the development of relationships with the unchurched in the marketplace.

While we do not want to diminish the importance of marketplace relationships for evangelism, our study of the formerly unchurched found that family member relationships were even more important. And of the different family members, wives were the ones most often mentioned as important in influencing the formerly unchurched to Christ and the church. Art, a Florida native, told us a story we heard on multiple occasions: "The reason I'm in church today is because of my wife. When I saw the change in her life, I decided to try it out. Now I'm a Christian and hardly ever miss church."

Art not only told us that family members were the greatest influence in his coming to church, he told us specifically that his wife was the key person God used in the process. We cannot overstate the importance of wives in bringing formerly unchurched husbands to Christ and the church. Thirty-five percent of the formerly unchurched indicated that their wives were the key influence, several times the number of the second-highest influence, children of the formerly unchurched.

We must ask, do most churches today have an intentional strategy to develop these relationships so that the unchurched may come to Christ and the church? Specifically, in those situations where wives are churched and their husbands are not, does the church provide resources, training, and opportunities for these women to reach their husbands for the kingdom? Perhaps the surprising aspect of this portion of the study is that the most receptive unchurched group is living in the homes of those already active in our churches.

Myth #8: The unchurched are concerned only about their needs.

The reasons the unchurched become churched are complex. In the course of our research, we found no one simple explanation. I have observed many strategies for reaching the unchurched that focus on meeting their needs. While there is much to commend about this approach, an exclusive needs-meeting strategy neglects two major issues. First, the unchurched often desire to be challenged. As Bobby of Pennsylvania told us, "I didn't want to be part of a church that puts everything on a silver platter. Even before I became a Christian, I sensed that I needed to be part of something where I could help others."

Our study found churches that expect much receive much, even from many of the unchurched. Perhaps an important lesson we learned from the formerly unchurched is that churches should try to appeal to the unchurched person's altruistic motives. Bobby expressed it as well: "I can tell you before I became a Christian, I knew I wanted to be in a place where I could make a difference. The church needs to hear the message not to water down expectations."

A second major insight gleaned from the formerly unchurched was that the unchurched do not always seek a place of worship for their own needs. Almost one out of three of the formerly unchurched informed us they came or returned to the church for their children. Many of the unchurched seem to know intuitively that "religious training" is good for their children, even though they cannot articulate specific reasons why.

Bobby explained, "I'm a single dad with almost year-round custody of two kids, ages nine and eleven. One of the reasons I wanted to find a church was for them. Though I had never been a member of a church, I just knew that it would be good for them, that it would help me to raise better kids."

While the gospel of Christ clearly calls for believers to help meet the needs of others, the formerly unchurched told us that a church should not communicate an exclusively needs-based message. The unchurched do indeed have motives for seeking churches beyond their personal felt needs.

Asking the Right Questions

More has been written on the unchurched in America in the past twenty-five years than in any similar period of history. Yet with all the research and publications, there remains much confusion on how to reach them. Is it possible we have been asking the wrong people the wrong questions? Are we involved in exercises in futility by researching this large group, most of whom will never attend church? Should we not be talking to those who were unchurched but now attend? It is this group—the formerly unchurched—from whom we have much to learn about a Great Commission resurgence. Perhaps in the process we can learn more about reaching people who do not know Christ. And perhaps we can seek from God new strategies or revive old approaches that may still work.

CHAPTER SEVEN

The Role Of Passionate Students In The Great Commission
Matt Lawson, M.Div.

Occasionally I save Facebook messages from students and then read them again later just for encouragement and a reminder of what God is doing. This message came to my inbox just recently from Breanna, a senior at Sequoyah High School and a new believer in Christ:

> A week ago a guy in my class called me out as a Jesus freak, and I smiled because I was proud to be one. I wasn't sure where he was going to go with it until I sensed his genuine curiosity for Jesus. He asked me every question in the book...some I said "I don't know" to, and others I could answer with reference to scripture. He said he randomly opened the Bible to Matthew and started reading and read all the way to Mark. I was proud of him and listened to see where God would take this...Jay (the guy) asked and asked and asked and I did my best to answer. I told him to keep embracing his

curiosity and that I would be here to help, but that he could find all of the answers in the Bible. I wrote down John 3:16 for him, and he told me that he didn't have a reliable Bible and his was hard to understand, so I came to church and got a free one for him to have…he said that he has been reading, but still has his doubts. I understand where Jay is…because I, and many others, have been in that same place before accepting Christ. Anyways, the magnificence of this story is that just 5 hours before I cried out the most passionate prayer to God in my room and said "use me God, I am tired of being comfortable… challenge me. I want people to know the love you have to offer them…use me, use me, use me!"…and he did. Sincerely, Breanna

Students can love Jesus with all their heart and change the world for Him. Breanna represents hope and optimism for a generation longing to take the Gospel to the ends of the earth. Though she is unique, she is akin to generations of teenagers and young adults who have shared a common thread and passion for the gospel. Recalling revival accounts from his grandfather, Jonathan Edwards once said, "But in each of them, I have heard my grandfather say, the greater part of the young people in the town, seemed mainly concerned for their eternal salvation."[1] History is replete with the truth that students have always played a major role in a Great Commission Resurgence. In fact, many of the greatest revivals in history have come from the hearts and prayers of teenagers who desire to serve God with their entire life.

One of those teenagers was Samuel Mills who lived during the Second Great Awakening when revival fires burst forth into many areas of the country. Not only was this awakening a contributing factor to his

---

[1] Jonathan Edwards, *Jonathan Edwards on Revival* (Edinburgh: Banner of Truth Trust, 1965), 9.

salvation, but Mills himself would later be a major player in continuing the spread and influence of such a revival both to those around him and through mission efforts around the world. He would later be given the title of "the father of American foreign missions."[2]

Samuel Mills' father was a well-known preacher, theologian, writer, and editor. It was said that Mills' father, along with his mother would sit by the fire and tell stories of missionary experiences in Vermont. These stories would spark a hunger within young Samuel for world-wide missionary work. It was this leadership and commitment to Christ by his father, and the devotion through prayer of his mother, that would influence Mills later in his teen years.

Returning from his first year at Morris Academy, Mills explained to his father that he could not think of a better way to spend his time than actively communicating the gospel to the lost world. One particular Saturday afternoon in August 1806, Samuel Mills met with four other students on the campus of Williams College for a time of prayer. While they were meeting, a thunderstorm forced the group to shelter under a nearby haystack where the conversation turned to missionary work in Asia. As the group continued to discuss Asia, Mills saw an opportunity to share his passion and he enthusiastically shouted, "We can do it if we will." Thus, the Haystack Prayer Meetings were born. These students, as well as other occasional members, would continue to meet in the groves and later in a home where they would continue to pray for foreign mission opportunities. The Haystack Prayer Meeting has been cited by many historians as the beginning of the foreign missions movement in America and as the beginning of American missionary outreach abroad. The prayer efforts of Mills and his fellow students would prepare their hearts and the hearts of others to accept a commission to take the gospel to the lost world. While revival spread on many fronts and in many ways,

---

[2] Both Samuel Mills and Adoniram Judson are often called the "Father of American Foreign Missions."

it seems clear that Mills was a major player in fanning the flames of the Second Great Awakening.

The very work of God in the hearts of teenagers praying beneath a few hay bales leads us back to the roots of American missionary work. Here we find a reality that is often overlooked and hardly understood except by those who have the great joy of leading students. Students have the heart and ability to challenge, motivate, and lead a Great Commission Resurgence. Ignoring the potential of students could be detrimental to world evangelization.

Student-led revivals, though they are capable, are not typically world impacting events. As with Mills, a passion is developed within a person, and then it was spread throughout their immediate community before impacting the world. Students you come in contact with on a daily basis are more capable of sparking a revival than we may assume. If you look close enough, you may even notice small revivals happening in your back yard as a result of the passion of a few students. Two students within the ministry I am blessed to lead immediately come to mind.

Johnny is a senior who displays the character of a student on fire for Christ. Johnny was a two-way starter and captain for his high school football team with the hope of a football scholarship. He was a team captain and leader on his team where he used that particular role to impact his teammates for Christ and invite them to our weekly student gathering. It was not until the summer before his senior year that Johnny's passion was taken to the next level. He believed that, even though God had blessed him with the ability and talent to play football, he felt led to quit the team to redirect his focus toward his relationship with God and his campus as a whole. Because Johnny took a stand for God in front of his teammates, his influence and opportunities to spread the gospel among his peers has grown exponentially. Every month, we have the great privilege of baptizing students from his campus who have been saved either directly or indirectly as a result of his influence.

Meanwhile, at the same school, another senior named Hannah has impacted and led a revival among the cheerleaders. The crazy part about Hannah's story is that she's a home-schooled student with a passion for missions and is actively carrying it out on a public school campus. Hannah was given many opportunities to serve the cheerleaders at this school while building friendships with them. Through the relationships that were formed, Hannah was able to invite individual cheerleaders to church with her. Because of Hannah's passion and her willingness to immerse herself in a lost world, a majority of that cheer squad has visited the church and many of them have given their lives to Christ, been baptized, and are now attending and actively involved in our student ministry. This school, which has given opposition to the gospel, has been blown open by the passion of two students who desire to see their peers come to know Christ. These two students have sparked a revival on that campus and its impact is clearly seen.

There are a few observations that are worth discussing when it comes to a student's role within the Great Commission. Each of these observations weighs heavily on my heart and all are a result of being engaged in the lives of students every week. The first observation involves the church body directly:

OBSERVATION #1: Students are over-stressed by the world and under-challenged by the church.

Read this Facebook message from Evan after students were given the opportunity to place a copy of the Word of God in the hands of every student in Cherokee and Cobb County:

> Hey Matt, hope everything's going well for you and the family. Keep my friend Nick Suwalski in your prayers. I've been trying to get him into church all year, but he is very opposed to Christianity. I gave him a lifebook yesterday (sorry it was early, but with him

I wanted him to feel like I was concentrating on him instead of just giving one to everybody) and today he told me he had started to read it and he was somewhat interested. If you knew this guy, even this would seem like a miracle. Keep him in your prayers, and hopefully you'll see him at epicenter in the near future. Love you man. Evan

It is no secret that students today are constantly marketed to and influenced by a world that sees them as nothing more than a means to an end. MTV has a four-fold strategy for developing new programming targeted specifically to pre-teens and teenagers. Their strategy invests significant time, energy, and the necessity of listening to students in order to influence everything from what clothes to wear, what bands to listen to, what language to use, and what new trend is cool.

After listening to Student Pastors across the country for the last nine years in student ministry, I am amazed at how little we process even the simplicity of what we teach or even what we are attempting to accomplish through that teaching. Ken Hamm, founder of Answers in Genesis, suggests in his book *Already Gone* that students are not being lost after high school, but instead are checking out way back in middle school because the questions they have about life are not satisfied by the weak teaching our student ministries are offering.[3] Yet we as the church seem more content to fill time with games and entertainment rather than to lead, teach, instruct, and invest into the lives of those who have the greatest potential to fulfill the Great Commission. Listen to the cries of the students around you to hear the desperation they have to go deeper in their faith. It likely will not seem evident or even present, but students want to be challenged by the gospel.

[3] See Ken Hamm and Todd Hillard, *Already Gone: Why Your Kids will Quit Church and What You can do to Stop It* (Green Forest, AR: New Leaf, 2009).

OBSERVATION #2: Students do not want to play it safe.

It is true. This is an entrepreneurial generation if there ever was one. Did you know that Harvard recently unveiled plans to bankroll MBA student-entrepreneurs? The press release included a statement from first-year MBA student Dan Rumennik, who along with fellow students Jess Bloomgarden and Andrew Rosenthal proposed the idea.

> For entrepreneurially-minded students at HBS, this fund alleviates the financial barrier preventing them from building initial prototypes or test products. This is the greatest challenge for people with an idea but no money," said Rumennik. "It also encourages students to start businesses while in school and to connect with more of their peers who want to do so as well. Finally, it's a great opportunity for students to get experience managing a product as they go about the process of creating a business.[4]

Students, both in the secular world and spiritual, are not afraid to try and fail. They are not afraid to "get their hands dirty." Students are visionaries. They find a dream to latch onto, and they will do whatever it takes to see it through to completion. The problem lies with those who enjoy being "dream squashers." We think we know what is best for students, so we intervene and negate their passion in an attempt to keep them safe. There is often a perception that if we keep the students away from the evils of this world, then it will make them stronger in their faith. Though there may be some legitimacy in this thought, I have to wonder how we expect our students to grow if they are not actively engaging their world by being as Philippians 2:15 says, "lights that shine in a crooked generation."

---

[4] "Harvard Business School Launches Fund for Student Start-Ups: Awards Support Development of Product Prototypes," (Accessed December 20, 2010). Online, www. hbs.edu/news/releases/mvpfund122010.html.

Students are willing to get in the game. They are tired of being left on the bench...or worse...being in the stands. Jonah is one of our students with a desire to impact the world around him. Even in this short and simple message, you can see a fire raging inside of him: "Hey Matt I have set an alarm on my iPod to wake me up in the morning. It plays "Revolution" by the Beatles to remind me to be a revolutionary every day."

The fire exhibited in Jonah's short statement directly compares to the passion of this generation. They are willing to do whatever it takes. They want to see their dream happen. They are willing to be revolutionary. Student Pastors, parents, and adult leaders should be the ones encouraging, guiding, and sharing wisdom with them. This leads us to a third observation:

OBSERVATION #3: Students on the brink of awakening need direction.

I tried to choose my words wisely with this observation. Students do not need regulation or management (which extinguishes their passion). They need the green light to love God with all their heart and the bumper lanes to guide them in the right direction. We need to stop focusing on how or why a student might "fail" and instead, encourage them to be revolutionary. As adult leaders, our desire should be to empower them to make a difference, as well as give guidance and direction as they take part in the Great Commission. Oftentimes as I listen to students, I hear and see the hesitancy in their spiritual life as a result of a lack of encouragement from elder leadership in their lives. When a student knows someone who desires to see him or her make an impact in the Kingdom of God is praying for him or her, encouraging him or her, and giving him or her direction, it can make all the difference in the world... literally. I was convicted of this thought after I read this message from one of our students:

God has recently put it on my heart that the one thing he wants me to do with my life is share the good news of the gospel with the world. God is calling me to missions and it has never been more evident than it is now. However, I don't know how I'll get to that point or where I'm going once I get there. That's why I'm sending this message. I need your help in prayer, advice and any other way you can help me. I know that God wants to use me. I just need prayer that I let Him use me. I can tend to be lazy and I never want to be lazy when it comes to Gods plans for me. Please pray that I stay on fire for God, and I continue to grow and become consistent with everything I do.

Thank you for all you have done for me already. I know I wouldn't be here today if it weren't for the time you have spent trying to show me how important a life lived for God is. Thank you, thank you, thank you! --LP

The value of proper guidance, direction, and the knowledge they are being lifted up in prayer is priceless in the life of a student. Students have a desire to change the world with the gospel of Jesus Christ. Far be it from us, if we stand in their way.

OBSERVATION #4: Students really can love Jesus with all their heart and change the world for Him.

This principle is never more evident than when one sees students serving those around them. Students might not have the money, the connections, or the means that adults may possess, but compared to the hearts of "average Christians," the desire students have to serve outweighs them all. Students have an understanding that menial servant tasks such as yard work or washing a car can directly lead to an opportunity to share the gospel. The following group of students in our ministry illustrates this understanding better than any other I can imagine:

> Within the first week we were on the fish (radio station), within 2 weeks we have gotten 17 boxes for Haiti that will impact who knows how many lives, and we have started our first project (Mrs. Zambrano's house). Imagine what God will do in the first year if, from this point on, we give 100% to God and allow Him to work. It's incredible what He could do. We have given Him about 80% of what we are doing so far. Let's give Him 100% percent and put everything personal aside and allow Him to move. If we truly believe Luke 1:37, the verse we put on all of those cans, then NOTHING is out of our reach. – Rad Ministries

Here is another Facebook message I received from this group of students:

> Pastor Johnny (Hunt) spoke on hill-taking last year. I will never forget it. I haven't taken any hills since that amazing week at camp. I've moved up the hill only to pick a better camping spot. However, if we refuse to be satisfied with our comfy tents, if we run and leave it all behind and we continue until the only way we can go on is if God carries us to the top of the hill, then what will stand in our way? I tell you what, it won't be easy. It's never easy. It has never been easy. But people have done it with much less than we have, and even more incredible is that they did it with nothing but the clothes on their backs and God in their hearts with no friends by their side. We are now without excuse to spread the gospel to the entire earth.

I'm done preaching, I'm done with notes, messages, tweets, and whatever else we do to give these long speeches. I am now for the first time 100% percent devoted to God. He has every aspect that I can think of and I'm praying for Him to reveal anything else I am held captive by. I don't have it figured out at all and I'm nothing special, but God is something special and He does have it figured out. So I'm done with the preaching, its time I truly do something for Christ besides talk. So let's be radicals inside and out. I hope you are all with me. –Rad Ministries

What else needs to be said? There will always be students who have a desire to be revolutionary and change the very world in which they live.

These principles are clearly seen within a very familiar story from Scripture. The Bible shares examples of teenagers doing some pretty revolutionary things from David, Josiah, and Daniel. While those are perfectly acceptable examples, I want to close by looking at the story of Esther. As an unlikely and unknown candidate for such a position of usefulness by God, the story of Esther reads like a well told novel that you just cannot put down. We are all familiar with the story of Esther. King Xerxes of Persia fired the old queen and basically held a beauty pageant to find a beautiful girl who would wear the crown. For such a time as this, God brought Esther into the King's court. However, Xerxes was completely unaware that this seemingly ordinary girl would essentially turn the world upside down.

Esther like most students today is living in virtual anonymity within the Persian Empire. She is thrust into Persia's version of "Next Top Model" and ultimately blows every other female in the Persian Empire out of the water. The text says, "And Esther found favor in the eyes of all who saw her" (Esth 2:15, NASB). This young, unassuming Jewish girl would be the instrument in the hand of God to melt the heart of a king in the favor of the Jews.

Through a series of unlikely events Esther's uncle, Mordecai discovers a plot has been devised by Haman, a servant of the King, to exterminate all the Jews living in the kingdom. The Haman made Xerxes aware of people in the kingdom planning to resist. The King required no convincing and set out to exterminate all the Jewish population in the kingdom. The plan was agreed upon and the decree was rubber stamped with the king's signet ring.

Having learned of Haman's plot, Mordecai gets word to Esther that she must approach the king and ask for his favor and protection. Esther reminds Mordecai that the law allows for immediate death to anyone that approaches the king's court without having been summoned unless the king extends his scepter to him. Mordecai now pleads with his life:

> Do not imagine that you in the king's palace can escape any more than all the Jews. For if you remain silent at this time, relief and deliverance will arise for the Jews from another place and you and your father's house will perish. And who knows whether you have not attained royalty for such a time as this (Esth 4:13-14, NASB)?

After a time of extreme fasting and prayer, Esther approaches the king and wins his favor. Esther invites the King and Haman to a banquet and it is there that Esther exposes her own nationality and warns the king that a plot has been devised to destroy her and her people. The king is disturbed that his queen's life is in danger, though he doesn't yet realize that it is the very plot that Haman had devised. The king demands to know who and where is the person responsible for such a plan. With her life on the line, Esther points her finger in Haman's direction. As the story ends, the king orders Haman to be hanged and his position given to Mordecai.

Let us be honest about our story and ourselves for a moment. When we read the story of Esther, we encounter a momentous event and intervention in the life of the Jewish people. What we have here is nothing less than a people being saved from destruction by the hand of God via the presence of a teenager in the king's court. Because a young, teenage girl was willing to be used by God, an entire nation was spared from genocide. Esther decided that prayer and fasting was the best way for her life to be used by God. The result? He revolutionized an entire empire.

Can you imagine people celebrating a festival 2500 years from now in which students we know played an integral part? If we looked around at the students in our churches, we will see that God is certainly doing a major work in their lives. He is a jealous God who is jealous for His glory. He wants to be known. God declares, "I will be exalted among the nations, I will be exalted in the earth" (Ps 46:10, NASB). While he could use the rocks to cry out and shout his praises, He has chosen to make use of mankind.

It would seem to be a healthy assumption that students today are ready and willing to be involved in God's activity for His purposes. The *Passion Movement* of college students describes themselves as a radical generation of Christ followers rooted in the confession which says "Yes, Lord, walking in the way of your laws, we wait for you; your name and renown are the desire of our hearts" (Isa 26:8, NIV).[5] There can be no doubt that students are already positioning themselves to be in the direct path of God's usefulness. We can learn an important lesson from Esther that God is visibly at work to invite us in His movement. If nothing else, we can see that it is not necessary to force opportunities upon ourselves, but rather to train our students to be prepared when they come our way.

---

[5] For more information about the Passion Movement, see www.268generation.com/3.0/#!about/story.

CHAPTER EIGHT

Developing Missional Churches For The Great Commission
Ed Stetzer, D.Min., Ph.D.

The word "missional" has gone viral. Even Wikipedia has an article about it.[1] The article is not half bad. One thing has become apparent, as "missional" has grown in popularity, that is, people use this term differently. "Missional" is like a Rorschach Inkblot Test for many believers, where people are asked to describe what he or she sees in random inkblots.

We have found that the Rorshach Test tells a lot about what a person is thinking and feeling. The same is true for all of us engaged in the missional conversation. For most people, how we define and use "missional" is shaped by our concerns about what is wrong, or what is right, with the church today.

For some people, the adjective "missional" describes their deep hunger for God to do something new for lost people outside the safe confines of the local church's walls. Others see it as a call to adopt a missionary

---

[1] See www.wikipedia.org/wiki/Missional (accessed July 1, 2012).

posture in their own community and culture. There are others who use the term to describe a shift in church programming from a "come and see" professional presentation to a "go and tell" community based and relational approach. Then, there are those people using the term who are merely parroting it because it is trendy.

The buzz around this term leads some people to look upon it with suspicion, thinking it is simply a new Christian fad. Some of that is going on, for sure. Nevertheless, I would contend that "missional" is a useful term, and the missional "buzz" is not all bad. It is a helpful term that allows us to rethink who we are as agents of the Kingdom. As culture changes, we are often faced with the need to change our own vernacular and conversations. New words—like "missional"—create new questions and deeper dialogue.

We need a shift in the conversation. I am amazed at how many churches (all models, sizes, and locations) are having the same (and often tired) conversations about how many people showed up to attend their services, classes, and events. New churches talk about it. Older, more established churches talk about it. Traditional and contemporary churches talk about it. Sometimes it sounds like the most important thing is how many attended our services and programs. Lots of warm bodies make us feel better about ourselves and what we are doing. Thus, attendance is the primary scorecard for most churches. And, I would add that budget is the close second. We seem content with this as the scorecard. But the term "missional" is slowly shifting the conversation away from discussions on attendance and budgets to commission and relationships. So, new words are not bad things, because new conversations are needed to engage the new circumstances of culture.

As the new conversation begins, we need clarity with our terms. For some, the word "missional" holds out the hope of a new strategy to boost sagging attendance numbers. From my perspective, that is the "buzz" around the term and not its impulse for the church. My point in this chapter is that we need to remove the "buzz" in order to fully explore the meaning of "missional." To do this, we need to understand biblically and theological what God's mission is and how we are called to live it out in our churches and contexts.

Missional is a way of *being* that leads to a way of *acting*. The missional church is made up of Christians who are called through God's gracious redemption to live for Him and His great mission throughout the world and who are sent out to be co-laborers with God to accomplish His mission in the world. This is the mission that God sent His Son on, and it is the mission that He sends His people on. So, missional Christ-followers and missional churches are joining Jesus on mission. They care about the things that Jesus directed us to care about: serving the hurting and loving others (the Great Commandment), and seeking to proclaim the gospel to the lost (the Great Commission).

If missional churches are joining Jesus on His mission, it includes much more than God's heart for the lost people groups among the nations and your lost neighbor, but being missional should never be pursued in way that excludes, lessens the emphasis upon, or fails to see that what is ultimate is God's heart for the lost. In the name of "missional," we must not lose a focus on just how *great* the Great Commission really is. Part of being a missional church is to be passionate about what matters to God. So, missional churches should care deeply for the *ta ethne'* (tribes and tongues) of their community and world. Not only does this mission matter to God. It is the mission that we were created for. God created the world with people who bear His image, and commissions them to fill the whole earth with worshippers of Him. Therefore, it is no surprise that the status quo of the bigger, busier church leaves many (rightfully) dissatisfied. We want to be part of something bigger than ourselves— and rightfully so, for we were created for that. And, I believe a global evangelistic engagement in our communities and into the whole world is a significant part of the answer.

The missional idea begins with God as a missionary God, for He is "The Hound of Heaven" (which is the title of Francis Thompson's now famous poem). From when God searched for Adam (Gen 3:9) to when Jesus knocked on the Laodicean church door (Rev 2:20), our triune God has never waited in anticipation for mankind's attraction to Him. Rather, He seeks people. Eugene Peterson simplifies the concept explained in Romans:

There's nobody living right, not even one, nobody who knows the score, nobody alert for God. They've all taken the wrong turn; they've all wandered down blind alleys. No one's living right; I can't find a single one (Rom 10:10-12, MSG).

Too many churches and Christians ignore the biblical theology of a sent church and God as a missionary. The institutional church is not the dispenser of salvation. It is the message bearer of that salvation. We criticize Catholics who consider the church a vehicle of grace yet we embrace an "invest and invite" mentality that requires people to show up on Sunday morning in order to receive the message of new life. The churches that are exclusively working in a solely attractional model may have a passion to see people experience transformation, but it seems to me that they are missing the inherent flaws in the attractional mindset.

One obvious flaw is that most people who are far from understanding the gospel typically do not attend church. Thus, using a church service to reach them is less effective than living on mission as a Christian for their temporal and eternal good. Statistics consistently confirm that Americans do not and likely will not attend church services. Researcher David T. Olson believes 17.5% of the U.S. population attends a Christian church on a given Sunday.[2] Other scholarly studies come up with a similar number.

The attractional-only church, whether on purpose or unintentionally, conditions everyday Christians to feel no responsibility to have Gospel-

[2] David T. Olson, *The American Church in Crisis* (Grand Rapids: Zondervan, 2008), 28.

focused, spiritual conversations. The "invest and invite" church makes the institutional church (contemporary or traditional) and their trained platform leaders the dispensers of salvation. If people need to go to the pastor to meet God, someone is confused about "who's who" in the gospel story and its proclamation.

The Great Commission and Missional Thinking

Where does the Great Commission belong in this discussion? Well, contrary to what some have written, "missional" and "Great Commission" are not interchangeable terms. "Missional" is not just a new way to say "Great Commission." The missional church is an identification of the people of God on mission because of who God is (and who they are because of their new life in Christ).

Yet, the Great Commission is essential to the missional Christian and church. Remember, the first biblical picture of what we call missional is of God as a missionary, seeking those who have wandered from Him. Second we see God as a sender when He sent His Son into the world to be its savior and king (John 3:16). Then, we find it when Jesus sends the church into the world and the Holy Spirit into its members to empower them: "As You sent Me into the world, I also have sent them into the world" (John 17:18, HCSB).

Jesus was sent from the Father on a mission with an agenda: redemption. He is redeeming people and the world *to* and *for* Himself. And, that means we must be passionate about the advance of the gospel because of Jesus' call and his example. *You can be an evangelistic church and not be missional, but you cannot be a missional church and not be evangelistic.* Let me say it this way. If we are not developing "missional" churches for the Great Commission, we are not developing missional churches—at least in a biblical sense of the word. Yes, handing out coffee, teaching kids to read, and picking up trash in a park can be done for Christ. When we do these types of things, we are seeking to make the world more like Jesus intends for it to be. Seeking to be missional, however, without following the commissions of Jesus is a not joining God on mission. It is merely pursuing a mission that we have created, not one where we follow Jesus on the mission he proclaimed.

Two perspectives must be embraced to develop missional churches for the Great Commission. We need a strong DNA and a corresponding culture that cultivates the conviction that Great Commission lifestyles are critical to accomplishing the mission God. New churches have the opportunity to shape a *Missional DNA* into new congregation. For existing churches, developing new DNA is a retrofit issue. Regardless of the church's age, cultivating DNA is hard work. The concept of being a missionary cannot be taught through reading good books and attempting to modify behavior. The significance and implications of the Great Commission must be fully internalized by core leadership teams in new or existing congregations. It takes time and leadership to cultivate and mature this DNA in the life of the church.

A *Great Commission Ethic* must be championed. The ethic is: We will, as we go, make disciples, baptize, and teach with a focus on people groups in the authority of Jesus Christ. To not do this is to ignore or marginalize the Great Commission, and that opposes biblical Christianity because it opposes the character and work of Christ. He was sent by His Father to establish the kingdom of God on the earth and redeem a people by His death for the kingdom, and He is the Sender of a sent people who are commissioned to speak and live out His message.

The Challenge of Being Missional

What is the greatest challenge for the church or individual who wants to be missional? The first step is to determine what it means to be missional. What is the biblical meaning and theological foundation for this term? The reality is that the term is used in different ways all across the world. Sometimes people use it in ways that we as evangelicals find problematic.

Some people who claim the term do so to promote social justice over (or instead of) personal evangelism. Others who have adopted the term have too narrowly applied it to the call to be a missionary to their local community (intentionally or unintentionally taking the focus off cross-cultural missions). Then there are some who use it to describe a new style of ministry that downplays an emphasis on programs and events.

How should we define the term "missional?" And, where are we going to find what it means to be missional?

Believing the Scriptures to be inerrant, infallible and the sufficient guide of truth that we need for our lives and for our churches, the starting place should be with what the Scriptures say about *God as sender and His purpose for sending* as a place to begin. As Christians, we generally agree that we are "sent." But, affirming this is only a small first step. Being missional means having one's identity shaped by being "sent." We have too long lived with a wall between our public and private lives. Our Christianity too often and too easily gets identified with our private life, our behavior, and our church activities. So, privately and perhaps even corporately as a church, we know that we are sent. But, the truth has not captured how we live. We too often engage our community as consumers and/or as a necessary evil. We rarely engage our community as a missionary. One of the problems in the church is that when we talk about the necessity to engage our community as a missionary, members hear requirement to put something else (another church activity) on an already crowded schedule. In that, the challenge is revealed. It is not about adding something else. It is about being something—a missionary—as you go.

The other issue that we struggle with is God's purpose. What is the role of the church in God's sending of His people, and how does the church relate to the kingdom in this process?

As evangelicals, we need to be aware that "missional" is a problematic term for some older evangelicals because they know their history. For this reason, we should listen to their concerns, and learn from their experience and wisdom. And, they should hear us when we have said that we understand their concerns and agree. They should also hear us in the way we use and define "missional" and why we believe the term is useful. (But, now I am meddling.)

In the 1960s and 70s, leaders began talking about a church built around and for the *missio Dei*, "God's mission." As a result of this broader emphasis, some people began walking away from some of the fundamentals of what it means to be Christian. Some began to devalue the local church, and adopted a fuzzy definition of Kingdom and the redemptive purpose of God. They abandoned things like sharing the gospel of Jesus Christ and the importance of church planting. In the name of the *missio Dei*, they lost the message of gospel proclamation. That was the wrong step to take.

We need a better perspective of the idea. When we talk about being missional, it is with the biblical understanding of what it means to say God is the Sender. Though he is not widely given credit for it, the Southern Baptist missiologists, the late Francis DuBose introduced the word in recent years. DuBose was the head of the World Mission Center at Golden Gate Seminary. His book *God Who Sends: A Fresh Quest for Biblical Mission*[3] reintroduced the word and concept into the evangelical landscape. Chuck Van Engen, professor of Biblical Theology of Mission at Fuller Seminary and former missionary to Mexico has, in recent years, been important in giving context to the term "missional." Yet, it was *The Missional Church*,[4] edited by Darrell Guder, that would introduce the concept to most readers. Later, leaders like Tim Keller, Reggie McNeal, and Alan Hirsch have had great influence in the missional movement.

---

[3] See Francis M. DuBose, *God Who Sends: A Fresh Quest for Biblical Mission* (Nashville: Baptist Sunday School Board, 1983).

[4] See Darrell L. Guder, ed., *The Missional Church: A Vision for the Sending of the Church in North America* (Grand Rapids: Eerdmans, 1998).

The Missional Idea in Scripture

If we are going to understand our role in the kingdom of God, we need to understand God's sending purposes and our right response to that commissioning. If we are going to get what it means to live missionally, we have to understand that God sends us according to His redemptive plan for the world, and we have to respond to that call. The word *missio* is a Latin word meaning "sent," and the equivalent word in Greek is *apostolos*, meaning "sent ones." The whole idea behind the adjective "missional" is that we are sent.

A nine-year-old boy was sent to the store by his mother to buy a head of lettuce. This was the first time he had ever been on such a mission. His older brother and sister had always been sent before. He had money in his pocket. He knew right where he was going. He went into the supermarket, got it, paid for it, and returned home feeling proud of himself. The only problem was that he brought home a cabbage. Why? It was green, round and had leaves. Was this mission a success? No. He was willing, he had gone, and he had returned triumphant. But no, he had not achieved the intent of the one doing the sending—not to mention that the boy hated coleslaw.

The story of the little boy gives insight concerning the tension created through the *missio Dei* movment. Completing the assignment given by the sender is the critical factor. In a post-resurrection appearance to the disciples, Jesus said to them, "'Peace to you! As the Father has sent Me, I also send you.' After saying this, He breathed on them and said, 'Receive the Holy Spirit. If you forgive the sins of any, they are forgiven them; if you retain the sins of any, they are retained'" (John 20:21-23, HCSB). Jesus sends His disciples to proclaim delivery through the forgiveness of sins. That is clearly an essential part of the mission and shapes how we view being missional. No social, political, or ethical scorecards should replace the specific mission of Christ. When sins are forgiven and new life is experienced social, political, and ethical arenas in our culture will change. Churches and individuals are right when they live for the good of their world in these areas. God is glorified when there is more peace and justice in His world. But these arenas are not the ultimate focus of God's mission and why He sends us. Christ died to save sinners. We proclaim, explain, and deliver that Good News.

Mission is *not* just going—do not miss this. Mission is *not* only about getting on the foreign mission field and doing something. Mission is understanding the work of God, and joining Him in it. It seems even in the Great Commission Jesus makes this point. He says, "All authority has been given to Me in heaven and on earth. As you go…" Apparently, the going part, at some level, is assumed. The assumption is you will go—the verb form "go" implies a command to go. Some people express a unique and special call to go to another city, state, or country. But, Jesus is not dealing with that in Matthew 28. He is simply saying you live, you go to and fro everyday, and "as you go" be on mission.

The question is: what do you do when you go? To answer the question, we need to look to the God who sent us because it is His mission, not ours. If we do not understand His purpose, we can do good things and still fail. So when we talk about mission and being missional, we need to remember that generating mission *activity* is not the mission. The mission is tied into the nature of who God is and the nature of the gospel itself. We take our cue from God's activity, and our lives are to be ordered and shaped by what God's mission for His world is. Playing missional without being gospel-centered and Great Commission engaged only means you have a personal agenda. The term missional has changed the conversation in the church, and that conversation is largely good. But we must keep a perspective of gospel-centrality in the process.

God is a sender by nature, and has been sending for a long time. It is not just a phenomenon of the New Testament. In Genesis 12:1-4, Abraham was sent by God to be blessed and to be a blessing. Abraham's obedience resulted in his joining God on mission. Another example is seen in the life of Isaiah. He encountered the holiness of God (Isa 6) and became aware of his own sinfulness. God asked, "Whom shall go for us, whom shall we send?" Tied up in the nature of God himself—in the nature of God the Father, the Son and the Holy Spirit—He is a sender.

Because God by nature is a sender, it implies two simple ideas. First, there is One who sends; and second, there are people to whom we are sent. But, it is not that God just sends us anywhere; God sends us somewhere. You are called and sent on mission; the only question is where and among whom. It could be to the Pokot in East Africa or to a cultural mosaic of urban Los Angeles. We are called because we have a Sender, but we also have a people to whom we are sent. This is the reason we plant or lead so many diverse churches, because ultimately God is a sender by nature.

When you understand that God is a sender, you are simply responding to the character of God and His purpose for His world when you live sent. And because you live sent, it means you will live and lead differently. We join Him in that mission so that everyone—from every tongue, tribe, nation, every people group, every population segment, every cultural environment—hears the good news of Jesus Christ and is reached by a church appropriate to its cultural setting.

God Sends the Son and the Spirit

Truth number one is that God is a sender by nature. The second truth that shapes how we conceive of what it means is the God, who sends, sent his Son, Jesus the Christ, the second Person of the Trinity, into the world to reconcile the world to Himself. We must not miss this. Being missional must never be reduced to doing good things and calling it the kingdom of God. It must always be conceived of as Christocentric. Paul teaches us in Ephesians that it was God's plan from before creation to unite all things under the reign and rule of His Son. So, the one who created all things has been placed as head over all things (Eph 1:9-10). Everything being redeemed is being redeemed by Him. Everything that will be judged will be judged by Him.

John 1 teaches important truths on the person and work of Jesus for developing our Christology. John writes, "In the beginning was the Word and the Word was with God, and the Word was God. He was with God in the beginning. All things were created through Him, and apart from Him not one thing was created that has been created. Life was in Him and that life was the light men. That light shines in the darkness, yet the darkness did not overcome it" (John 1:1-5, HCSB). From these words, we learn that Jesus was with God the Father at creation, and He is identified with the nature of God. We learn that everything was created by Him. He gives life and light to all humanity, and nothing overcomes His power or goodness. Then, John the Baptist entered the story as a man *sent* from God, who came as a witness about the power and goodness of Jesus and His mission (v. 7). Jesus' mission is described in John 1:11-14: "He came to His own, and His own people did not receive Him. But to all who did receive Him, He gave them the right to be children of God, to those who believed in His name, who were born, not of blood, or of will of flesh, or of will of man, but of God. The Word became flesh and took up residence among us (HCSB)." John records the words of Jesus telling us that this mission is an expression of God's love (John 3:16), and the ultimate aim of this mission is for us to live with our God and Creator of all eternity.

John's Gospel is clear about the way this mission is accomplished. Forty times Jesus says or implies, in essence, "I am sent." It teaches us that the Father has sent the Son for the greatest of purposes. John's Gospel begins with the incarnation when the Word became flesh, and it ends when Jesus' words remind us to live as sent people. The sending God also sent the Spirit to fulfill His mission. "But the Counselor, the Holy Spirit—the Father will send Him in My name—will teach you all things and remind you of everything that I have told you" (John 14:26, HCSB). Over and over again, we see this. God is by nature a sender. God sent the Son. God sent the Spirit. We don't want to get so focused on this that we spend all of our time saying, "God is a sender, God is a sender, God is a sender," so that it becomes a theoretical exercise. I think that is part of the problem in modern missiology today; it has become largely a theoretical exercise. So, in effort to motivate (or, cajole), we search for verses to show that God is a sender. We appeal to Isaiah 6 and Matthew 28.

However, in repeating the truth that "God is a sender," we have failed to say, "Here I am. Send me" (Isa 6:8, HCSB). It is a disconnect between believing that God calls and sends, and being willing to be sent. Perhaps we have stopped contemplating that it is the personal Creator of the universe who has a glorious pursuit for His creation this is calling and sending us. Perhaps we simply have missed that we were created to advance the name of God throughout the whole earth, and God redeemed us to fulfill that purpose through us. Perhaps we have forgotten that Jesus told His disciples to wait until the Spirit comes before they start the mission, and the Spirit came and the disciples went. We have the same Spirit in us today, and we have the same mission. Perhaps we have overlooked that when Jesus commissioned His disciples there were some there who were full of faith and some who doubted (Matt 28:17). Because we believe that God only sends those with risk-taking faith, we conclude that God cannot send us. Perhaps we have not heard that when He sends us, He sends us with His peace (John 20:21) and the assurance that He has overcome the world (Matt 28:18, John 16:33).

Ultimately, churches and individuals make the choice to hear the sending voice of God and obey it. Obedience begins with embracing that God has a glorious purpose for His mission and He initiates the mission by sending His Son and His people. The truth is either we are sent or we have missed our orders.

God Sends the Church

The sending God sends the church. We, the church, are His sign *in* the world and *to* the world. Paul wrote of the church's calling to be a divine instrument for the divine mission. It is, he stated, through the church "God's multi-faceted wisdom may now be made known...to the rulers and authorities in the heavens (Eph 3:10, HCSB)." But, I find that too many people believe they can love Jesus and hate His wife. They claim to have a great love for the Lord, but they hold a great disdain for the church. We must recognize that this instrument, this vessel, this imperfect bride is God's choice to spread His "multi-faceted wisdom," so that His glory might be shown in the world. Yes, sometimes she is a mess, but she is still God's choice. We are God's choice.

In Acts 13 the church responded to the sending nature of God himself, specifically the Spirit of God: "As they were ministering to the Lord and fasting, the Holy Spirit said, 'Set apart for Me Barnabas and Saul for the work that I have called them to'" (v. 2, HCSB). So the church in Antioch sent them out. They had fasted, they had prayed, they had laid their hands on them, and then they sent them out. The church was and is an agent of God's sending. As a part of the church, we must fully embrace God's strategy for His mission as the church sends us on mission.

Mission Gets Compartmentalized

In different ways, missions have been compartmentalized. What became of this is a view of missions as a specific activity or ministry of the church and only specially called people participated in it. Historically, in the early part of the twentieth century, there was a desire to elevate missions as a discipline in Christian settings. So people began to distinguish between evangelism and missions. Evangelism was defined as telling the good news and propagating the gospel in Christendom—particularly Europe and North America. Missions became a cross-cultural focus that involved an academic discipline that had to be done differently. They knew that crossing cultural boundaries—such as reaching the Iban in Malaysia—would need different skills to proclaim the gospel. So we created a discipline from that perceived difference, and that discipline was called "missions."

Also, the term "missions" was, at times, used to describe the inferior status of non-Christendom churches, rather than describing the work of advancing the gospel, certain ministry outpost were called "missions," instead of a church. In the early twentieth century, believers living in countries outside Christendom were not part of any "church." Thus, in the nineteenth century, Christians in China were not part of a Chinese church; they were part of an Anglican church in London as a "mission." They were not full communicants. Believers in the Two Thirds World were in an Anglican mission or a Baptist mission or a Presbyterian mission. Effectively the "missions" status relieved these churches from the responsibility of doing missions themselves, and ultimately, created the idea that only established churches from certain parts of the world could do missions.

But, over time, leaders began to recognize that all churches were called to participate in God's sending work. They realized that churches in every region have a task and a responsibility to send people to the uttermost parts of the world to proclaim the good news of Jesus Christ. No matter the place of origin, the world is the responsibility of every church. So the language has begun to change. New works were no longer called "missions" but churches, because Christians began to realize that the church is wherever God had planted it. Furthermore, wherever the church was, it was on mission. In other words, the mission was from everywhere and to everywhere. The church is sent and is a sender, in every time and in every place.

In due course, people noticed that the West needed to be re-evangelized. As people wondered how the churches would "win back" the West, grand conversations about missiology emerged. In part, that face gave rise to the term "missional." Being missions-minded was not and is not sufficient; we have to be missional. It is an important distinction.

In the denomination in which I serve, we have many missions-minded churches, giving large amounts of money to missions. Cooperative giving to missions is a central idea of what it means to be a part of my denomination. But the challenge is that many times, in spite of being mission-minded with great global thinking, we miss the impulse of being the sent people of God to our local culture. I fear that in the shadows of our own steeples people far from Christ have never heard the good news communicated to them in a way that they can understand. We need to recognize that the church sends people but the church herself is also sent. The challenge is that many of us have not yet figured out how to be sent into our own community. Being missional means we have to live sent here, to our place and among our people.

I frequently speak at conferences and training events. I remind them that in spite of their exposure to the greatest church minds of the day (the *other* speakers), they should resist the tendency to live as if they are "sent" to their (the speakers') communities. Often, pastors and leaders hear about what's going on with Wayne Cordeiro in Hawaii or Andy Stanley in Atlanta, and say, "I want to be just like that." What happens is that you begin to think that the key to what they have done is the way in which they have done ministry. It is easy to forget that when we are sent to a place, and that, in many ways, *the how of missional ministry is determined by the who, when, and where of culture.*

Go Where God Sends

So here is the challenge. You are not sent to the people where Greg Surratt ministers in South Carolina. I have preached there and it is an amazing church. But you are not sent to those people in that neighborhood. Do not be guilty of community lust or demographic envy-thinking, "If I could just have a people like Tim Keller is trying to reach." Most are going to lead churches in areas that just do not seem that great, but they should be great to you. Most will plant or lead churches in areas where famous church leaders do not go, but God sent you there. We should cry out like John Knox did of Scotland when he prayed, "Give me Scotland or I die." Whether it is the blue-collar, middle-class bowlers or downtown indie rockers, will you reach them with the good news of Jesus Christ? It is essential for us to go on mission where God has sent us because we are called to a people not a methodology. To be effective we must be passionately in love with the unique people to whom we are called.

Again, Ephesians 3:6-11 is helpful in reminding us that God would make known the mystery of His eternal purpose *through the church*. Also, Paul wrote, "How can they call on Him in whom they have not believed? And how can they believe without hearing about Him? And how can they hear without a preacher? And how can they preach unless they are sent (Rom 10:14-15 HCSB)?" So if you are going to be a missional believer or pastor, if you are going to have a missional church, it has to be tied up in the sent-ness of individual believers and the church collectively.

One of the wonderful things that came out of the great missiological discussion of the 1950s and the 1960s was the idea that doing missions was not all about the church. God is working outside of the church. "How?" and "Why?" are the real questions. Acts 16 helps inform us. Paul had a vision of a certain Macedonian man requesting help. Yet there was no church in Macedonia. Paul responded to the calling. He went to a place by the river where woman normally assembled to pray and found a business woman, named Lydia. There was still no church. But God was already at work in Macedonia. The story continues to include the planting of a church and the stories of life change. Paul did not introduce God in Philippi. Paul joined God on His mission in Philippi.

We learn an important point here. *The church is not the center of God's plan—Jesus is—but it is central to God's plan.* The church *is* central to God's mission to proclaim the story of Jesus to every man, woman, and child. What churches do is central to what God is doing in the world because God is working through His church. We find that in the church the invisible kingdom made visible, but not completed.

Evangelicals have gone to great lengths to distance themselves from some of the theological errors that took place in recent history of "mission" thinking. Specifically, when many mainline Protestants deemphasized the proclamation of the gospel, one missiologist said they abandoned two billion people—the lost two billion. When they lost the gospel, evangelicals said they did so because they cared for everything except the gospel. So evangelicals decided to care exclusively for the gospel, but sometimes they forgot the agency through whom God is working—the church. Jesus said that He came to proclaim good news to the poor, but this is the same Jesus who said He came to seek and save those who are lost. God who so loved the world does not limit Himself to working through the church, but He uses the church for His mission and for His agenda. The agenda is bigger than just our local church but is inclusive of it. Thus, it is critical that as members of local churches, we understand what God is seeking to accomplish in declaring the gospel and caring for the hurting.

The Goal of the Mission

The mission is not the goal of the mission. It involves joining Jesus on His mission, working for the Kingdom, and proclaiming the gospel. Many important things are involved—and the Bible speaks to their importance.

In 1 Corinthians 15, Paul provides a succinct explanation of the gospel, "Now brothers, I want to clarify for you the gospel I proclaimed to you; you received it and have taken your stand on it. You are also saved by it if you hold to the message I proclaimed to you—unless you believed to no purpose. For I have passed on to you as the most important what I also received" (1 Cor 15:1-3, HCSB). Paul led by making sure they understood the gospel first. He indicated it was of first importance. He continued: "that Christ died for our sins according to the Scriptures, that He was buried, that He was raised on the third day according to the Scriptures"

(v. 3b). So here Paul laid out the fullness of what the gospel is, what is of first importance, and why it matters.

Jesus said, "The Messiah would suffer and rise from the dead the third day (Luke 24:46, HCSB)." This is fundamental to the gospel. Both in Luke 24 and 1 Corinthians 15 the gospel is about a bloody cross and an empty tomb. So if we are going to be tied into the mission of God and think in missional ways, then the mission of God has to include the proclamation of the gospel—a bloody cross and an empty tomb. But Jesus does not stop there. After referring to His death and resurrection, Jesus says, "repentance for forgiveness of sins would be proclaimed in His name to all nations beginning at Jerusalem. You are witnesses of these things" (Luke 24:47-48, HCSB). Jesus explains that the very nature of the gospel connects to the propagation of the gospel. Paul echoes Jesus words that the gospel is about a bloody cross and an empty tomb. But why does Jesus indicates that spreading the gospel is fundamental to the nature of the gospel? Because *mission* is not the goal of the mission. The *gospel* is the goal of the mission. This is so because the gospel is the only way to connect people to the Christ, which is the ultimate goal of the mission. So, what is that gospel?

The gospel is the good news that God, who is more holy than we can imagine, looked upon with compassion, people, who are more sinful than we would possibly admit, and sent Jesus into history to establish His Kingdom and reconcile people and the world to himself. Jesus, whose love is more extravagant than we can measure, came to sacrificially die for us so that, by His death and resurrection, we might gain through His death and resurrection and by his grace what the Bible defines as new and eternal life.

God's mission is more than the Great Commission but it must include the Great Commission because God's mission is not complete without proclamation of the gospel and making of disciples. Missional churches should focus on kingdom endeavors like mercy ministries, they should be a sign of the kingdom in how they live as ambassadors, and they should show grace-filled hearts to their neighbors, but not at the expense, though neglect or ambivalence, of the Great Commission. The churches that have embraced the goal of God's mission have decided to live out the values of the kingdom sometimes even against their personal preferences so that the gospel become understandable to the culture in which they reside.

Cultural Relevance and Living Sent

The gospel is always a stumbling block. But, the fact that so many people reject the gospel before they get to the gospel is a painful reality. In our well-meaning bid to "make the Bible and God relevant," we often marginalize ourselves from the very culture we seek to reach. The Bible and God are relevant in this culture and in every other culture. He and His gospel are relevant. Always! We are the roadblocks to relevancy, not the Bible. We live in a way that makes God seem irrelevant, but He is not to blame.

A missional church with a Great Commision passion will care about relevance—making the message clear. Cultural awareness, relevance, and engagement are an important element of missional theology and being on mission yet these are not the only elements. Our churches are to be biblically faithful, culturally relevant, and counter-cultural communities. Being biblically faithful is possible without being culturally relevant or counter-cultural communities. Being biblically faithful and counter-cultural is also possible. But to be true to all three elements is challenging. Part of our task of being missional is to be all three. Being missional means we live, act, and think like a people living on mission.

I was in Romania a few years ago with one of my former students, Chris. He had never been out of the country until then. Driving around Bucharest, we passed the American embassy and discovered that it was on high alert. You could see all these Marines with their guns ready and the American flag flying proudly. But Chris had never been out of the country before. He did not understand how American Marines could have weapons ready and American flags could fly on Romanian soil. The answer is related to what Scripture says about how we are to live sent.

In 2 Corinthians 5, Paul refers to himself, and, I think, to all believers as an ambassador. When you are leading a missional church, you are establishing an embassy (to use a diplomatic term). You are involved in making the invisible kingdom of God break through to become visible through the development of a church in that time and that place. You are representing God in an alien land. Paul speaks about what it means to be sent as representing and participating in the mission of reconciliation:

> From now on, then, we do not know anyone in a purely human way. Even if we have known Christ in a purely human way, yet now we no longer know Him like that. Therefore if anyone is in Christ, there is a new creation; old things have passed away, and look, new things have come. Now everything is from God, who *reconciled* us to Himself through Christ and gave us the ministry of *reconciliation*: that is, in Christ, God was *reconciling* the world to Himself, not counting their trespasses against them, and He has committed the message of *reconciliation* to us. Therefore, we are ambassadors for Christ; certain that God is appealing through us, we plead on Christ's behalf, 'Be *reconciled* to God.' He made the One who did not know sin to be sin for us, so that we might become the righteousness of God in Him" (2 Cor 5:16-21, HCSB).

Paul's imagery is that we represent a sovereign king from another kingdom. When you plant or develop your church—whether in Mississippi or Manhattan or Madrid—you are establishing an embassy whose purpose is to propagate the good news of the King from another kingdom. This is what it means to live sent. This does not simply mean we go for the good of the city, though it does include good for the city. This does not simply mean loving the poor, though it does include love for the poor. We go for what missiologists call a "transforming mission." Sometimes we say that sharing Christ through planting churches and serving the community are two sides to the same coin. But this is a bad metaphor because it implies that those two sides have to be flipped one to the other. The mission is not two things; it is one thing. A "transforming mission" changes us and people far from God because we live sent.

I have planted several churches and led in revitalizing several others. The reason I love church planting is the simple focus of planting and sharing the gospel. The good news of Jesus Christ being communicated and transforming the lives of people in the community around me is what evangelistic ministry is about. Admittedly the pressure changes as a new church grows. You will feel the pressure to do so many other things, many of them considered to be good ministries. But holding to a missional theology will remind you that the nature of the mission leads to the transmission of the Gospel. It should be true of all churches as they pursue a missional position that they hold the mission of God as primary. The mission is not the mission; the proclamation of the good news of Jesus Christ is central to the mission.

Paul said, "We are ambassadors for Christ; certain that God is appealing through us, we plead on Christ's behalf, 'Be reconciled to God'" (2 Cor 5:20, HCSB). When you lead a church, recognize that the church must be three things: biblically faithful, culturally relevant, and a counter-culture community. Put the gospel, the authority of Scripture, and the centrality of the gospel of Jesus Christ in the center of all you do.

Some ministries teach you to ignore culture. Do not listen to them. Their view hurts the mission of the church. They teach you to preach against culture. Yet, preaching against culture is like preaching against someone's house—it is just the place where they live. There are good things in it and bad things in it too. But our task it not to preach against a house. Our task is to engage those who live in the house (near and far from us) with the good news of Jesus Christ. We need to engage people in culture with a biblically faithful message.

To engage culture with a biblically faithful message, we also need to culturally relevant methods. Again, fundamental to the nature of the gospel is the proclamation of the gospel. But even further, fundamental to the proclamation of the gospel is being sent *to people*—and that means we must understand those people. Cultural relevance is understanding and communicating with the people God has sent you to reach. People are afraid of that term because it seems to be a compromise. It need not be.

Cool and trendy does not necessarily mean culturally relevant because the definition changes from community to community across America. It changes even more dramatically across cultures. I would encourage you to be a church that seeks out those who are far from an understanding of the gospel and make the gospel comprehensible to them. Everyone who interacts with your church ought to understand what is going on while he or she is there. That is what being culturally relevant means. It is an issue of communication, making sure church forms, style, and method support and aid gospel proclamation. One important focus of being culturally relevant is to create an environment where people are comfortable, at ease and their defenses are disarmed, so they can receive the message of the gospel.

You cannot always be sensitive. The gospel is *not* sensitive to the conscience or practices of the lost. The cross is scandalous and causes people to stumble across it. It is supposed to offend the sinner, pierce their conscience, and convict their soul. But the church should never create an environment, systems, or rules that cause people to stumble before they even get to the cross. Instead, as ambassadors, we should speak winsomely and act graciously toward those in need of our King's message.

Your church must be biblically faithful, culturally relevant, and finally a counter-culture community. Tim Keller talks about being "counterintuitive." He explains we are to do those things in the name of Jesus Christ that might surprise, transform, and be salt and light in a community. The purpose is that the name and fame of Christ might be more widely known.

So, What Does it Look Like?

I think part of the challenge is to keep "missional" from dying as a buzzword but flourishing as an idea that presses believers forward into God's work. "Missional" is not a new word for cutting edge and contemporary. And, it should not be used as the adjective for every ministry so we can pretend we have missional music, missional quilting, and missional lighting. Instead, we need to ensure that missional is a driving force for how we live out God's work. I have already warned about the dangers of the theoretical without the practical. God's sending us is a big idea. Simply stated, it means participating in the mission of God, being theologically formed, theologically shaped, and theologically sent. That means perhaps a different kind of church.

So I encourage you, when you look at your community, to fall deeply in love with it. Remember when Jesus walked down that mountain outside of Jerusalem? He looked over Jerusalem and wept for it. The people were like sheep without a shepherd. When you lead a church, say, "Dear God, I want to lead a biblically faithful church, rooted in the soil of the culture where I am; a church that becomes a counter-culture community representing you as an ambassador, as a king from another kingdom—an invisible kingdom that begins to be made known here through the gospel to the glory of Jesus Christ."

CHAPTER NINE

Ensuring Passion For The Great Commission Results In Evangelistic Action: Forming And Evaluating One's Philosophy Of Evangelism
Matt Queen, Ph.D.

Author's Note

WHILE completing my MDiv at Southeastern Baptist Theological Seminary, I first met Dr. Alvin L. Reid. After enrolling in several classes he taught, I entered the PhD program in evangelism in order to learn under Dr. Reid's tutelage. For a number of years, I served as his teaching fellow. During that time Dr. Reid strongly encouraged me to write and to teach, aspects of my ministry that I continue to this very day. I am indebted to Dr. Reid for his investment in me and my ministry. Throughout his ministry Dr. Reid has attempted to ensure that believers' passion for the Great Commission results in evangelistic action; therefore, I have written the following article to honor this particular mark of his ministry.

Introduction

A lady once criticized the evangelism methods used by Dwight L. Moody, famed nineteenth century American pastor, to win people to saving faith in the Lord Jesus Christ. In response Moody replied, "I agree with you. I don't like the way I do it either. Tell me, how do you do it?" Moody's critic answered, "I don't do it." Moody quipped, "In that case, I like my way of doing it better than your way of not doing it."

Like Moody, I would rather be a criticized personal evangelist than a non-evangelistic critic. Sometimes another's critique of our evangelism is biblically warranted. At other times critical comments about our evangelism discourage us without cause. Perhaps the evangelistic enterprise would be served best if before 1) we critique and/or question the evangelistic practices of someone else, and/or 2) our evangelistic practices are critiqued and/or questioned by someone else, we sternly look ourselves in the mirror and say, "I question your evangelism!"

What questions might a believer ask himself in order to assess his evangelistic practices? In *Tell It Often—Tell It Well* Mark McCloskey offers three essential questions every believer should ask himself in order to assess his evangelism and its methods biblically. In addition to McCloskey's three questions (which are enumerated first in the list below), I suggest five additional questions. A believer's response to each of these questions assists him in discerning 1) whether or not someone else's critique of his evangelism proves warranted, and 2) what aspects of his evangelism fall short of the biblical ideal and need adjusting.

Concerning your practice(s) of evangelism:

1. Does the New Testament teach it?[1]

Evangelism finds its origin in the New Testament. A believer who assesses his evangelistic practices should begin by ensuring his evangelism conforms to the evangelistic doctrines, instructions, and principles found in the New Testament. McCloskey offers a few follow-up questions that frame the context of this particular question for personal evangelistic assessment. These questions include the following: "Is my approach to evangelism grounded in theological convictions regarding salvation, the gospel, and evangelism? Is it grounded in the certainties of God's plan to redeem a lost creation, the lostness of man, and responsibilities of our ambassadorship?"[2]

Concerning theological convictions regarding salvation, the gospel, and evangelism, Alvin Reid correctly states: "A conviction about a great salvation leads to a passion for evangelism."[3] However, even someone passionate for evangelism either can hold to erroneous theological convictions or alter his theological convictions over time. A believer's theological convictions concerning salvation inevitably contribute to the gospel content he presents to unbelievers. Therefore, a personal evangelist's theological convictions and the message he proclaims must be tested continually by New Testament doctrine, instructions, and principles. Because it serves as the authoritative and foundational source for evangelism, the New Testament must inform the reasons for and way(s) in which a believer evangelizes.

---

[1] Mark McCloskey, *Tell it Often-Tell it Well: Making the Most of Witnessing Opportunities* (San Bernardino: Here's Life, 1986. Reprint, Nashville: Thomas Nelson, 1995), 185.

[2] Ibid.

[3] Alvin Reid, *Evangelism Handbook: Biblical, Spiritual, Intentional, Missional* (Nashville: B&H, 2009), 141.

2. Did the first-century church demonstrate it?[4]

The first-century church initially received the Great Commission of our Lord, who passed it down to all ages of His church. For this reason a believer interested in assessing his evangelism should consider the philosophy, practice, and pattern of the apostolic church. To assist someone in this dimension of his evangelistic assessment, McCloskey suggests the following supplemental considerations: "Has my philosophy and practice of evangelism been modeled by the first-century church? Have the theological realities that drove the first-century church to proclaim the gospel with boldness and sensitivity caused me to develop similar patterns for communicating my faith?"[5]Biblical evangelism results from one's evangelistic consistency with the philosophy, practice, and pattern of the early church.

The first-century church employed an evangelistic philosophy that endeavored to evangelize as many as possible, as quickly as possible, and as clearly as possible. Though they employed other evangelistic methods, Luke recorded numerous times in which the apostles (*e.g.*, Acts 2:12-41; Acts 3:11-26; Acts 4:5-12; Acts 5:19-21), deacons (*e.g.*, Acts 6:8-7:60; Acts 8:4-6, 12, 40), and disciples (*e.g.*, Acts 2:5-11) of the early church evangelized as many people as possible, by preaching the gospel publically.

Additionally, members of the first church also evangelized as quickly as possible. The New Testament indicates at least two reasons for the rapid rate of their evangelism. First, in order that the gospel of Jesus Christ not "*spread* any further among the people," the elders, rulers, and scribes charged Peter and John not to speak or teach in the name of Jesus (Acts 4:17-20, emphasis added). However, Peter and John claimed that they could not help but to speak of what they had seen and heard. Second,

---

[4] McCloskey, *Tell it Often-Tell it Well*, 185-186.

[5] Ibid.

upon being brought back before the Jewish council a second time for evangelizing in the temple, the high priest questioned why Peter and John continued to *"fill* Jerusalem" with their teaching (Acts 5:27-29, emphasis added). Peter and John responded that they must obey God and not men.

In addition to its evangelistic philosophy and practice, the apostolic church also provides a pattern for evangelistic proclamation. A personal evangelist faces temptations to adopt worldly, even sinful, standards in order to gain a hearing and become relevant.[6] Nevertheless, he must be convinced that an evangelistic lifestyle incorporates a pattern, or lifestyle, of biblical holiness. While not every evangelistic approach practiced today can be found in Scripture (for example, internet evangelism), an evangelistic practice consistent with Scripture conforms to its standards of holiness, as the first-century church practiced it.

3. Does it work?[7]

While a believer should evangelize with all excellence and purge ineffective practices, McCloskey has something else in mind here. He frames the intended meaning of this assessment question by offering another: "Does my philosophy and practice of evangelism make me effective in getting the gospel out to as many as possible, as soon as possible and as clearly as possible?"[8] In other words, does what you believe about evangelism encourage or hinder your practice of it?

---

[6] Though not commenting on this particular temptation, Edward Rommen articulates the danger of yielding to such a temptation when he writes: "We are under great pressure to adapt the [g]ospel to its cultural surroundings. While there is a legitimate concern for contextualization, what most often happens in these cases is an outright capitulation of the [g]ospel to the principles of that culture." *Get Real: On Evangelism in the Late Modern World* (Pasadena: William Carey Library, 2010), 371.

[7] McCloskey, *Tell it Often-Tell it Well*, 186.

[8] Ibid.

Permit two words of warning concerning one's beliefs and his commitment to a working (or active practice of) evangelism. First, someone merely believing in the necessity and importance of evangelism does not guarantee that he will evangelize. Second, no matter how "biblical" someone perceives his beliefs to be, any belief that deters him from evangelizing inevitably will lead him to deter others from evangelizing.

Numerous helpful campaigns, apparel, and apps exist to assist a personal evangelist in evangelizing consistently. Though space limitations prevent including all of them in this essay, permit me to suggest one helpful way that encourages consistent evangelism in a believer. Paige Patterson suggests a believer incorporate the following "soul-winner's prayer" in his daily prayers: "Dear God, give me the opportunity to share the gospel today. When it happens, help me to recognize it. When I recognize it, give me the courage to proceed [to evangelize]."[9] Although the prayer itself cannot guarantee an evangelism that works, who could doubt that a believer genuinely and daily asking God for 1) an opportunity to evangelize, 2) the recognition of that opportunity, and 3) the courage to act on that opportunity would not work at his evangelism?

4. Does it ground itself in the authoritative command of Jesus found in the Great Commission?

McCloskey suggests we ought not to ask ourselves, "Why are men not coming to us?" Rather we must ask ourselves, "Why are we not going to men?"[10] Though many symptoms prevent us from going to men with the gospel, they all result from disobedience to Jesus' authoritative command in the Great Commission.

---

[9] Paige Patterson, "Jesus is Lord, But is He Really?," www.swbts.edu/mediaresources/audioplayer.cfm?audioToPlay=chapel/Chapel090612_fd1.mp3&fdi=_fd1. (accessed on January 27, 2013).

[10] McCloskey, *Tell it Often-Tell it Well*, 191.

In his day William Carey confronted such disobedience when he published *An Enquiry into the Obligations of Christians to Use Means for the Conversion of the Heathens*. He described the Great Commission disobedience of believers in his day when he wrote:

> [B]ut the work has not been taken up, or prosecuted of late years (except by a few individuals) with the zeal and perseverance with which the primitive Christians went about it. It seems as if many thought the commission was sufficiently put in execution by what the apostles and others have done; that we have enough to do to attend to the salvation of our own countrymen; and that, if God intends the salvation of the heathen, he will some way or the other bring them to the gospel, or the gospel to them. It is thus that multitudes sit at ease, and give themselves no concern about the far greater part of their fellow-sinners, who to this day, are lost in ignorance and idolatry. There seems also to be an opinion existing in the minds of some, that because the apostles were extraordinary officers and have no proper successors, and because many things which were right for them to do would be utterly unwarrantable for us, therefore it may not be immediately binding on us to execute the commission, though it was so upon them.[11]

Nevertheless, he contended that all believers have a duty to obey the Great Commission of our Lord. Otherwise, he argued, why do we continue to baptize in obedience to His command? Why do we honor the obedience of others who have evangelized throughout history? Why, then, do we believe we have available to us the divine promise of His Presence?[12]

---

[11] William Carey, *An Enquiry into the Obligations of Christians to Use Means for the Conversion of the Heathens* (Leicester: n.p., 1792), 8.

[12] Consult Ibid., 8–9.

Evangelism is not the result of mere coincidence. Evangelism rarely occurs when someone relegates it to a pastime activity. Evangelism ensues when a believer in Jesus Christ submits himself to the authoritative command of Jesus and disciplines himself to make disciples.

5. Does it demonstrate urgency considering the reality of heaven and hell?

Concerning the reality of heaven and hell, evangelism can be described in terms of two, opposite extremes—either lethargic or urgent. Though most Evangelicals identify themselves as believing exclusivists, those who exercise a less-than-urgent kind of evangelism appear as practicing universalists. If heaven and hell really exist and someone's eternal destiny in one or the other depends on whether or not he repents of his sins and believes in Jesus Christ's death, burial, and resurrection for salvation, how then will he believe and be saved if he does not receive the gospel by means of evangelism (*cf.*, Rom 10:14-17)?

Some well-meaning commentators have critiqued urgent evangelism driven by the reality of heaven and hell. Their critiques do not dispute the reality of hell; rather, they indicate that urgent evangelism motivated by final states minimize the importance of discipleship. Although the practices of a few modern-day personal evangelists may validate these concerns on occasion, urgent evangelism in light of the reality of heaven and hell (as one observes was practiced in the New Testament, and as faithful, Great Commission believers practice today), neither precludes discipleship nor necessitates the exclusion of it.

An unbeliever will not be saved on the basis that *we* have heard and now believe. Rather, *he* must hear the gospel of Christ in order to believe! Therefore, ensure you exhibit an urgency to evangelize as many as possible, as soon as possible, and as clearly as possible.

6. Does it consider the role of the Holy Spirit?

According to the Bible, a personal evangelist and the Holy Spirit cooperatively partner with one another in the evangelistic enterprise. Evangelism that fails to depend upon the Spirit of God has a tendency to become manipulative. On the other hand, the Holy Spirit does not evangelize on His own apart from the evangelistic witness of a believer. Rather, He assists a believer in his proclamation of the gospel to an unbeliever.

Alvin Reid suggests the following five ways that the Holy Spirit specifically aids a believer in his witness: 1. He empowers [him] to witness (Acts 1:8); 2. He gives [him] wisdom (Luke 12:12); 3. He gives [him] boldness (Acts 4:31); 4. He helps us in [his] praying (Rom 8:16); and 5. He gives [him] the burning desire to see people saved (Acts 4:29-31).[13] Reid also calls to a believer's attention to the evangelistic role of the Holy Spirit in an unbeliever. He identifies that the Spirit precedes the evangelistic conversation (Acts 10:1-15), convicts the unbeliever of sin, righteousness, and judgment (John 16:7-11), and regenerates a repentant sinner that believes in Christ for salvation (John 3:5-6).[14] Taking into account the multifaceted role of the Holy Spirit in evangelism, a personal evangelist must rely on the Holy Spirit in preceding (*e.g.*, Acts 10:19-22; Acts 8:27-35), empowering (*e.g.*, Acts 1:8; Acts 6:10), and emboldening his witness (*e.g.*, Acts 4:8-13; Acts 4:29-31), as well as convicting an unbeliever of his sin and need for Christ (*e.g.*, John 16:8-11) and sealing him for salvation after he hears the gospel and believes in Christ (*e.g.*, Eph 1:13-14).

These days, some experts tout one particular way to package the gospel in order to evangelize successfully. Other specialists prescribe the primacy of a long-term relationship over a comprehensive gospel proclamation in order to evangelize missionally. Still other authorities advocate the

---

[13] Reid, *Evangelism Handbook*, 158.

[14] Ibid., 159-161.

dumbing down of holiness standards in order to evangelize persuasively. Altogether, these kinds of strategies create a new form of pragmatism—method-dependent evangelism that deemphasize and/or neglect the role and power of the Holy Spirit in a personal evangelist who proclaims the entire gospel to unbelievers. A believer who evangelizes without utilizing a helpful technique may experience frustration. However, a believer who evangelizes without depending on the Holy Spirit will find failure.

7. Does it incorporate the Scriptures?

The previous assessment questions appeal to evangelism that incorporates a biblical model derived from the New Testament, the practice of the first-century church, and the Great Commission. This question, on the other hand, helps a believer assess the extent to which he includes the Scriptures in his gospel presentation.

The New Testament presents two obvious reasons for incorporating the Scriptures in one's gospel presentation. First, hearing the Word of Christ is prerequisite for biblical faith (Rom 10:17). Second, evangelistic proclamations in the New Testament overwhelmingly incorporate the Scriptures (*e.g.*, Luke 24:14-32; Acts 2:14-41; Acts 3:11-26; Acts 4:1-12; Acts 7; Acts 8:4, 35; Acts 13:13-49; Acts 16:25-32; Acts 17:10-13; Acts 18:5, 28; Acts 20:27; Acts 26:22-23; Acts 28:23-27).

A personal evangelist often summarizes the gospel in his own words or in the words of someone else (if he utilizes a witness training model). Whether he uses his own words or the words of another, a personal evangelist should ensure that his evangelistic proclamation incorporates and structures itself around the Word of God. When he evangelizes, a personal evangelist must incorporate Scripture in his presentation of the gospel in such a way that proves consistent with both the text's immediate context and intended meaning.

8. Does it call for a decision?

A personal evangelist does not evangelize merely to convey information about Jesus. Rather, a personal evangelist evangelizes in order to call people to faith in Jesus. Edward Rommen states, "Given the personal nature of the [g]ospel, evangelism is essentially the issuing of an invitation to participate in the restoration offered by Christ."[15] He continues, "Talking about conversation instead of conversion misses the point, since the end result of evangelism is an acceptance of the invitation and a radical transformation of the recipient's life."[16]

An evangelistic presentation must include a call for decision for at least two reasons. First, evangelistic presentations recorded in the New Testament include a call for unbelievers to believe in Jesus Christ for salvation and to repent of their sins (e.g., Matt 3:2; Matt 4:17; Mark 1:14-15; Acts 2:38; Acts 3:19; Acts 14:15; Acts 26:20). Second, unbelievers do not know how to respond to the gospel apart from receiving instruction through an evangelistic invitation (e.g., Luke 3:10-14; Acts 2:37; Acts 16:30). A personal evangelist's aim should emulate the desire of August Hermann Francke when he writes, "As far as I am concerned, I must preach that should someone hear me only once before he dies, he will have heard not just a part, but the entire way of salvation and in the proper way for it to take root in his heart."[17]

On the basis of these reasons, ask yourself, "Does my evangelistic proclamation incorporate an invitation to receive Christ as recorded in the New Testament?" Also ask yourself, "After I present the gospel to an unbeliever, does he know how he can receive the gospel?" In the New

---

[15] Rommen, *Get Real*, 183.

[16] Ibid.

[17] Paulus Scharpff, *History of Evangelism: Three Hundred Years of Evangelism in Germany, Great Britain, and the Unites States of America*. Helga Bender Henry, trans. (Grand Rapids: Eerdmans, 1966), 46.

Testament, those who hear the gospel make a decision, whether positive or negative, in regards to what they have heard (*e.g.*, Acts 17:32-33). The inherent nature of the gospel elicits a response on the part of those who hear it. Do you present the gospel in such a way that your hearers realize they have a decision to make? Or, do they leave the conversation indifferent and unaware of their responsibility to receive the forgiveness of sins, reconciliation with the Father, eternal life, and the indwelling of the Holy Spirit by believing in Christ for salvation and repenting of their sins?

Conclusion

What a believer thinks about evangelism influences his evangelistic practices, or the lack thereof. However, what the Scriptures say about evangelism must inform and correct a believer's evangelistic practices. Though not an exhaustive list, the previous eight questions can assist a believer in evaluating his philosophy of evangelism so that he is able to ensure his passion for the Great Commission results in biblically-informed, evangelistic activity.

CHAPTER TEN

Myths Surrounding The "Gift Of Evangelism"[1]

Larry Steven McDonald, D.Min., Ph.D.

Author's Note

WHILE completing my PhD at Southeastern Baptist Theological Seminary, Dr. Alvin Reid served as the mentoring professor overseeing my studies. I also served as his Teaching Fellow, frequently lecturing in his courses. For several years I taught evangelism courses adjunctively with Dr. Reid at Southeastern College and Seminary. I am indebted to him for his investment in my life and ministry. Throughout his ministry Dr. Reid has emphasized that every believer has the joy, privilege, and responsibility of sharing Christ with unbelievers. The following article is presented to honor this particular mark of his life and work for Christ's kingdom.

---

[1] An earlier version of this chapter was presented at the Evangelical Theological Society meeting in Orlando, FL, November 1998 and appeared as "Rethinking the Gift of the Evangelist: Reflection on C. Peter Wagner's Teaching," *Journal of the American Society for Church Growth*, 10 (Fall 1999): 15-28.

Introduction

"Discovering Your Spiritual Gift" has become a common topic of discussion in evangelical churches. Small group classes as well as sermon series regarding the topic stimulate great curiosity. Initially this interest in gifts focused almost entirely upon the gift of tongues and the gifts of healing. Since then a more balanced and holistic emphasis has taken place, with a few exceptions. The development of spiritual gifts inventories or questionnaires has been a product of this focus.[2] C. Peter Wagner, a major leader in church growth, has been on the cutting edge of developing the spiritual gift emphasis. Thom Rainer testifies to the important role Wagner has played by stating, "Of all the contributions he [Wagner] has made, one of the major ones has been his discussion of the relationship between church growth and spiritual gifts discovery."[3]

Wagner believes that one gift in particular is the most instrumental for church growth. He states, "It is obvious that the one gift above all others necessary for church growth is the gift of evangelist."[4]

Because Wagner is a leading figure on spiritual gifts, his view of the gift of evangelist must be considered and evaluated. This chapter, therefore, will examine the same.[5] New Testament passages related to this gift will

---

[2] For example, see C. Peter Wagner, *Finding Your Spiritual Gifts: Wagner-Modified Houts* (Ventura, CA: Regal, 1995) and Larry Garner and Tony Martin, *Gifts of Grace: Discovering and Using Your Spiritual Gifts* (Jackson, MS: MS Baptist Convention Board, 1995).

[3] Thom S. Rainer, *Eating the Elephant: Bite-Sized Steps to Achieve Long-Term Growth in Your Church* (Nashville: Broadman and Holman, 1994), 189.

[4] C. Peter Wagner, *Your Church Can Grow: Seven Vital Signs Of A Healthy Church*, rev. ed. (Ventura, CA: Regal, 1984), 83.

[5] Wagner's most extensive teaching on the gift of evangelist is found in *Your Spiritual Gifts Can Help Your Church Grow*, updated and expanded ed. (Ventura, CA: Regal, 2012), 162-181; and *Your Church Can Grow*, 83-93. The following section will be a summary from these two books.

also be presented. Finally, Wagner's teaching will be compared with New Testament passages. My position is that while Wagner has indeed made worthwhile and important contributions, he over-extends the use of the biblical gift of evangelist and under-extends the responsibility of every believer to be involved directly in evangelism.

Wagner's Teaching on the Gift of Evangelist

Wagner believes the gift of evangelist found in Ephesians 4:11 specifically refers to the office of evangelist. In his view, it is not too "far-fetched" to presume that the one who holds the office of evangelist also possesses the gift of evangelist. Existing for the edification of the body (Eph 4:12), this gift of evangelist promotes church growth in quality as well as quantity.

Wagner teaches that not every Christian is an evangelist nor should try to be. He believes this explains why "total mobilization" efforts have not worked and have instead brought about frustration, failure, and negative results. Wagner is quick to point out, however, that every Christian is to be a witness. Citing a distinction between spiritual gifts and Christian roles, Wagner maintains that Christians lacking the gift of evangelist are prevented from sidestepping the responsibility to share Christ. Although every Christian may not possess the gift of evangelist, every Christian does bear the role of being a witness.

Wagner illustrates this point in two ways. He first points to physical bodily functions with primary and secondary organs. For example the uterus, being the primary organ in reproduction could not reproduce without healthy secondary organs of the digestive, respiratory, nervous, and circulatory systems. Likewise, evangelism, being the primary spiritual reproductive organ needs healthy secondary organs (other spiritual gifts) for church proliferation. Church growth and church health are therefore interrelated.

Second, Wagoner illustrates that many gifts have corresponding roles. Faith, for example, is listed as a spiritual gift (1 Cor 12:9; 13:2). As such it is assumed that not all Christians possess the gift of faith. Still, all Christians are called to a role of living a life characterized by faith (Heb 11:6). Comparably, not all Christians are endowed with the gift of evangelist, but all Christians carry the role of being witnesses.

Wagner defines the gift of evangelist as "the special ability that God gives to certain members of the Body of Christ to share the gospel with unbelievers in such a way that men and women become Jesus' disciples and responsible members of the Body of Christ."[6] He believes one discovers this gift through experimentation, examination of feelings, evaluation of effectiveness, and confirmation from the body. This gift of evangelist is intended for a man or woman, lay person or professional, ordained or un-ordained, full-time or part-time, and for personal or public ministry. It can be exercised in settings denominational or interdenominational, as well as mono-cultural or cross-cultural. Its use may be to build up existing churches or initiate new ones.

According to Wagner only 5-10% of a local church body has the gift of evangelist. He feels security in this percentage based upon his studies in case after case.[7] Additionally Wagner cites a basis for his premise. Following His ascension, Jesus left a group of 120 believers, only 12 of whom were apostles (10%) with the task of propagating the gospel. The remaining 108 bore the role of being faithful witnesses. Wagner believes if 10% of a local church body exercises the gift of evangelist, a 200% per decade growth rate would be a realistic expectation.

---

[6] Wagner, *Your Spiritual Gifts*, 164.

[7] Wagner states he has thoroughly tested this hypothesis but he does not offer documentation. It appears to me he has done more of an informal sampling from pastors. The illustrations Wagner gives of this percentage are limited to two cases: Coral Ridge Presbyterian with D. James Kennedy and Trinity Congregational with David Libby. See *Your Church Can Grow*, 86-87; 89-90 and *Your Spiritual Gifts*, 168-169.

Practically speaking, Wagner believes about one-half of one percent of those possessing the gift of evangelist actively use it.[8] He further states that when evangelism is lacking, typically the 90% who do not have the gift of evangelist are blamed. Wagner denounces this counterproductive practice and proposes instead a mobilization of the 9.5% who have the gift of evangelist but are not using it.

Wagner progresses to an area that even he acknowledges as controversial: Can evangelism be overemphasized? Because his answer goes against the grain of evangelical thought Wagner quickly claims that his entire life has been committed to fulfilling the Great Commission. He also states that every Christian needs to know that God wants people to be saved, needs to be a witness, and needs to be prepared to share his faith as opportunity presents it. Wagner then states,

> Having said this, it is time we admitted that there are many good, faithful, consecrated, mature Christian people who are in love with Jesus Christ but who are not, do not care to be, and for all intents and purposes will not be significantly involved in evangelization in any direct way. Indirectly, yes. They will contribute to the growth of the Body of Christ like the lungs and the small intestines and the kidneys and the thyroid gland contribute to human reproduction. And they will carry out their role as witness when circumstances so dictate. But they won't go around looking for opportunities to share their faith.
>
> It is a misunderstanding of biblical teaching, in my opinion, to try to convince every Christian that he or she has to be sharing the faith constantly as a part of their duty to the Master. We do not tell them that they

---

[8] Wagner, See *Your Church Can Grow*, 88.

145

have to teach all the time or pastor others all the time
or be an apostle or a prophet or an administrator or
a   leader or a missionary if they haven't been given
the spiritual equipment to do the job well. To make
people   feel guilty if they ever get gas and don't
share Christ with   the filling station attendant or if
they don't leave tracts   for the mailman or if they
don't witness to the waitress   in the restaurant may
actually harm the Body of Christ more than help it.[9]

Wagner illustrates through his own life experience. When traveling
by air, Wagner takes with him 8 to 12 pounds of reading material in
his brief case, thereby exercising his gift of knowledge. He prays and
searches for an isolated seat where he is not likely to be disturbed and
considers it a good flight if he is left alone. In the event that someone does
sit beside him, Wagner asks the Lord to keep that person quiet unless
their heart is prepared to hear the gospel message. More times than
not, he abstains from conversation with the adjoining passenger, being
too preoccupied with his spiritual scholarly gift. Wagner continues this
thought by saying, "The Lord is not going to hold me responsible for
what I did as an evangelist, but he is going to hold me responsible for
what I do with my gift of knowledge. On the other hand, those with the
gift of evangelist should make every effort to converse with the people
next to them on the plane and expect them to accept Christ before the
next landing."[10] He concludes by saying, "My role as a Christian is to be
a witness for my Lord at any time, and I am delighted when God gives
me the opportunity. But I have found that whenever I force it, I tend to
blow it. So I let God do it for me."[11]

---

[9] Wagner, *Your Spiritual Gifts*, 170.

[10] Ibid., 175.

[11] Ibid., 178.

New Testament Passages Related to the Gift of Evangelist

The word "evangelism" comes from the Greek work *euaggelion* which is used seventy-two times in the New Testament, fifty-four of which are in Paul's writings.[12] Meaning "good news," it is often translated with the word "gospel,"[13] but it is never associated with "gift" or "gifts." Although it is very common to hear people speak of "the gift of evangelism" the Bible never speaks of it.[14] Ed Stetzer, President of LifeWay Research, shares concern about this misunderstanding as he states, "I hear many people saying they don't have the 'gift of evangelism' and thus believing it is not their responsibility to do evangelism (since they don't have the 'gift'). And, since evangelism can be a challenge at times, that seems to be a 'gift' that people don't want."[15]

The word "evangelist" is used only three times in the New Testament (Acts 21:8; Eph 4:11; and 2 Tim 4:5) and comes from the Greek word *euaggelistes* and means "one who announces good news." Each one of these passages will be examined along with the Great Commission in the book of Matthew.

Phillip, the Evangelist

Phillip is first mentioned in Acts 6 as one of the seven chosen to meet the practical needs of the widows. These seven were described as "men of good repute, full of the Spirit and of wisdom" (Acts 6:3).[16] He is next

---

[12] See David Watson, *I Believe In Evangelism* (Grand Rapids: Eerdmans, 1976), 32.

[13] Lewis A. Drummond, *The Word Of The Cross: A Contemporary Theology Of Evangelism* (Nashville: Broadman, 1992), 204-205.

[14] See Malcolm McDow, "Evangelism and Spiritual Gifts," Evangelism Today (November 2, 1996): np.

[15] Ed Stetzer, "No Such Thing as 'the Gift of Evangelism,'" www.edstetzer. com/2010/07/the-gift-of-evangelism.html. (accessed 1/8/2013).

[16] All Scripture texts are taken from the English Standard Version, unless otherwise noted.

mentioned in Acts 8 following the stoning of Stephen, another of the seven. With Saul's persecution scattering the Christians out of Jerusalem, Phillip traveled to Samaria and "proclaimed to them the Christ" (Act 8:5). Accompanied by miraculous events (Acts 8:6-7, 13), Phillip's preaching spawned great crowds who were very attentive to his message (Acts 8:6). Even Simon, who formerly practiced magic, was converted and baptized by Phillip.

As news of the revival reached the apostles in Jerusalem, Peter and John were sent to investigate this "Samaritan Awakening." Praying for this movement of God, Peter and John witnessed the Samaritan people receiving the Holy Spirit. Within the context of these exciting miracles Phillip is led away by an angel to a desert road in order to tell "the good news about Jesus" (Acts 8:35) to an Ethiopian court official. This passage concludes with the Ethiopian believing and Phillip baptizing him. It is commonly believed this encounter brought about the introduction of Christianity to Northeast Africa.[17] Immediately following the Ethiopian's baptism Phillip disappears and continues to preach "the gospel to all the towns until he came to Caesarea" (Acts 8:40). Preaching to cities all along the Mediterranean seaboard, Phillip becomes a forerunner to Paul's missionary journeys. Phillip's ministry in Acts 8 has been summarized as "that of 'evangelizing' or 'announcing the gospel' (vv. 4, 12, 35, 40) with the intent that the hearers believe in Jesus (vv. 5, 12, 35, 36)."[18] About twenty years went by before Phillip was mentioned again in Acts.[19] Paul and Luke were on Paul's last journey to Jerusalem when they visited Phillip's home in Caesarea for several days. Luke describes Phillip as "the evangelist, who was one of the seven" (Acts 21:8).

[17] See R.E. Perry, "Phillip," in the *Zondervan Encyclopedia of the Bible*, rev. ed. (Grand Rapids: Zondervan, 2009), 859.

[18] George W. Knight III, *The Pastoral Epistles: A Commentary on the Greek Text* in the New International Greek New Testament Commentary (Grand Rapids: Eerdmans, 1992), 457.

[19] F.F. Bruce, *The Book of Acts* in The New International Commentary on the New Testament (Grand Rapids: Eerdmans, 1954), 424.

Timothy, the Pastor Evangelist

Described as a disciple who had a good reputation, the first mention of Timothy is found in Acts 16 when Paul and Barnabas traveled through Lystra. It is commonly believed Paul had met Timothy on an earlier visit in the area during his first missionary journey (Acts 14). Timothy's mother and grandmother, Eunice and Lois, were devout Jewish women (Act 16:1; 2 Tim 1:5), and they faithfully raised Timothy in the Old Testament Scriptures (2 Tim 3:14). Timothy's father was Greek (Acts 16:1) and is assumed to have been an unbeliever. Timothy traveled extensively with Paul in addition to fulfilling Paul's ministry assignments for him. Paul felt so deeply about Timothy that he called him his "true child in the faith" (1 Tim 1:2) and described him as having a "kindred spirit" (Phil 2:20, NASB). Having been left by Paul in Ephesus (1 Tim 1:3) to deal with false doctrine, it is commonly believed Timothy became the Pastor of the Ephesian church.

Two letters were written to Timothy by Paul in order to encourage him in his pastoral ministry. In the midst of a charge for Timothy to be faithful in proclaiming the word, Paul tells him to "do the work of an evangelist, fulfill your ministry" (2 Tim 4:5). Usually thought of as a "fairly young man who was somewhat retiring, perhaps even a bit shy,"[20] it is possible that Timothy did not possess a natural orientation to evangelism. At any rate, such introverted qualities would not easily result in a personality that readily engages others. Thus Paul would be writing to give Timothy an extra push to be involved in evangelism.[21] The picture of Timothy is of a young man coming from mixed racial and religious backgrounds, young and introverted. Paul had to encourage him to "fan into flame the gift of God" (2 Tim 1:6). Already juggling his personal problems

---

[20] B. Van Elderen, "Timothy," in the Zondervan Encyclopedia of the Bible, rev. ed. (Grand Rapids: Zondervan, 2009), 856.

[21] Leith Anderson, "Personal Challenges for 21st-Century Pastors," Bibliotheca Sacra 151 (July-September 1994): 260.

along with his pastoral duties of dealing with doctrinal issues within the church, Timothy is instructed by Paul to do the work of an evangelist. I fear that many such pastors today would respond to Paul by saying, "I do not have that gift!"

The Gift of Evangelist

In Ephesians 4:7-8 and 11, Paul speaks of "the gift of evangelist" by stating, "But grace was given to each one of us according to the measure of Christ's gift…and He gave gifts to men…and He gave the apostles, the prophets, the evangelists, the shepherds and teachers." This is the only passage in the New Testament that speaks of the gift of evangelist.

Scholars describe this list of gifts by using diverse words such as "offices,"[22] "functions,"[23] "spiritual gifts,"[24] "missionaries"[25] or "leadership gifts."[26] Various views are taken on this passage because the list of gifts appears to be different from the ones in Romans 12, 1 Corinthians 12 and 14, and 1 Peter 4:10-11. Ken Hemphill, Founder and Director of North Greenville University's Center for Church Planting and Revitalization, states this by saying, "The listing of gifts in Ephesians is unique because it included only persons who might be thought of as 'leaders'."[27] He indicates this passage "adds an important clarification on how gifted

---

[22] Millard J. Erickson, *Christian Theology*, 2d ed. (Grand Rapids: Baker, 1998), 891.

[23] Hauck Friedrich, *"Euaggelistes,"* in the *Theological Dictionary of the New Testament*, vol. II (Grand Rapids: Eerdmans, 1964), 737.

[24] Wagner, *Your Spiritual Gift*, 173. Wagner initially describes this gift as an office but practically treats it as all other gifts.

[25] Drummond, *The Word of the Cross*, 302.

[26] A. Skerington Wood, *Ephesians – Philemon*, vol. 11 in The Expositor's Bible Commentary (Grand Rapids: Zondervan, 1978), 58.

[27] Kenneth S. Hemphill, *Spiritual Gifts: Empowering the New Testament Church* (Nashville: Broadman, 1988), 195. Hemphill also reiterates this point in his recent work, *You are Gifted: Your Spiritual Gifts and the Kingdom of God* (Nashville: B & H, 2009), 142-162.

---

leaders are to equip the gifted members."[28] MacArthur concurs as he states, "to the church overall He [Christ] gives specially gifted men as leaders."[29]

What then becomes the determining factor in deciding how to view this list and specifically, the gift of evangelist? It seems to me that Paul communicated the determining factor by stating the purpose of these gifts. The gifts' purpose is to "equip the saints for the work of the ministry, for building up of the body of Christ, until we all attain to the unity of the faith and of the knowledge of the Son of God, to a mature manhood, to the measure of the stature of the fullness of Christ" (Eph 4:12-13). This listing of gifts is intended for leaders who will equip the rest of the body. The gift of evangelist then is intended for leaders who will focus upon training Christians in how to lead people to Christ. Hemphill states, "Here, for the first time, there is a clear statement concerning the relationship between those gifted for leadership and other gifted members of the community. The leaders must promote the ministry of the saints and equip them so that all may work together for the edification of the body."[30] Michael Green concurs as he states, "in Ephesians 4:11 the emphasis is all on teaching. The gifts of the ascended Christ to his church are apostles, prophets, evangelists, pastors and teachers, all of whom are called to equip the Christians for service."[31]

What then should be the focus of the evangelist? First, the evangelist is to himself be a proclaimer of the good news of Jesus Christ. This might take place through an itinerant ministry, ministry within a local church,

---

[28] Kenneth S. Hemphill, *You are Gifted: Your Spiritual Gifts and the Kingdom of God* (Nashville: B&H, 2009), 158-159.

[29] John F. MacArthur, Jr., *Ephesians in* The MacArthur New Testament Commentary (Chicago: Moody, 1986), 140.

[30] Hemphill, *Spiritual Gifts*, 195.

[31] Michael Green, *I Believe in the Holy Spirit* (Grand Rapids: Eerdmans, 1975), 193-194.

on the mission field, or in church planting in unchurched areas.[32] He is to set an example by his lifestyle in order to motivate the church toward evangelism.

Second, the evangelist is to train Christians in how to share their faith. Earl Radmacher, former president of Western Seminary, pointedly addresses this by stating,

> One might ask then, `What is the specific role of the evangelist, if it is not his job to come at appointed times and conduct intensive soul-winning efforts?' It would seem, from the text that we have considered, that the evangelist has a part in equipping the saints. Then his particular part must be equipping them in the work of presenting the Lord Jesus Christ to the lost person; thus, in place of the typical two-week evangelistic service that we have in many of our churches, I would suggest that it might be well for us to consider the possibility of spending two weeks in the intensive training of our membership in the work of evangelism. Make no mistake about it, the pastor and the evangelist are not exempt from personal soul-winning activity. In fact, they must lead the way, but the messengers of evangelism include the entire body of Jesus Christ.[33]

Radmacher's point is well made even though he sets up an "either/ or" situation. I participated in a Billy Graham Crusade in 1975 which included months of evangelistic lay training prior to the actual week of the meeting. The training I received became the foundational layer of my

---

[32] John R.W. Stott, *The Message of Ephesians* in The Bible Speaks Today (Downers Grove: InterVarsity, 1979), 163.

[33] Earl D. Radmacher, "Contemporary Evangelism Potpourri, Part II" *Bibliotheca Sacra* 123 (April 1966): 166.

Christian walk. An evangelist and his team can and should be leading the way in both the act of evangelism as well as training in evangelism.

The Great Commission

If the gift of evangelist is a leadership gift, what is the average Christian's part in evangelism? The Great Commission given by Jesus is recorded in Scripture five times (Matt 28:19-20; Mark 16:15; Luke 24:47; John 20:21; Acts 1:8). Jesus did not direct His marching orders for the church primarily toward those with the gift of evangelist. Instead, these final commands were given to every believer in Christ. Green elaborates by saying, "One of the most striking features in evangelism in the early days was the people who engaged in it. Communicating the faith was not regarded as the preserve of the very zealous or of the officially designated evangelist. Evangelism was the prerogative and the duty of every church member."[34] Evangelists are to lead and train, but every Christian is to participate in fulfilling the great commission. As Stetzer indicates, "all believers are given the ministry of reconciliation (2 Cor 5:18)."[35]

At times evangelism streams from the natural overflow of a Christian's life. But it must be realized that evangelism does not take place only within the context of emotional motivation. Evangelism comes from a heart of obedience to Christ's command. Because of the vitalness of evangelism, some have argued that it is one of the spiritual disciplines of the Christian walk. This presupposes that without the inclusion of evangelism in everyday life, the growth of the Christian is stunted. Donald Whitney says, "evangelism is also a Discipline in that we must discipline ourselves to get into the context of evangelism, that is, we must not just wait for witnessing opportunities to happen." He continues by saying, "Isn't the main reason we don't witness because we don't

---

[34] Michael Green, *Evangelism in the Early Church* (Grand Rapids: Eerdmans, 1970), 274.

[35] Stetzer, "No Such Thing."

discipline ourselves to do it? Yes, there are those wonderful, unplanned opportunities…that God brings unexpectedly. But I maintain there is a reason for most Christians to make evangelism a Spiritual Discipline."[36] Whitney is not alone in sounding this emphasis. Wayne McDill states, "There is a direct correlation between personal Christian discipline and the spiritual boldness which is necessary to evangelistic zeal and effective leadership."[37] All Christians are mandated to share Christ with the lost and to seek them out.

An Evaluation of Wagner's Teaching on the Gift of Evangelist

As one examines Wagner's teaching on the gift of evangelist, several very positive aspects are apparent. There is no doubt Wagner is personally committed to the Great Commission. Through his teaching and writing he has helped many churches in the expansion of the kingdom. Indeed, for many years he has been instrumental in the Charles E. Fuller Institute of Evangelism and Church Growth as well a Professor of Church Growth at the School of World Missions at Fuller Theological Seminary. Also, he has personally impacted many pastors by pioneering the Doctor of Ministry degree in Church Growth at Fuller Seminary. Currently he serves as the President of Global Harvest Ministries and Chancellor of Wagner Leadership Institute in Colorado Springs. These achievements are admirable and have made a positive impact on the kingdom of God.

Despite these contributions, there are several shortcomings in his teaching on the gift of evangelist. First, Wagner has a tendency to observe events in churches and then read those back into Scripture, therefore making them the norm. For example, Coral Ridge Presbyterian Church had 2,500 members, 250 of whom were involved in Evangelism Explosion.

---

[36] Donald S. Whitney, *Spiritual Discipline for the Christian Life* (Colorado Springs: NavPress, 1991), 100-101.

[37] Wayne McDill, *Evangelism in a Tangled World* (Nashville: Broadman, 1976), 170.

This church had a decadal growth record of 200%. Wagner therefore concludes that any church should have 10% of its members operating with the gift of evangelist, also producing this 200% decadal growth. He believes this can be documented in Scripture for when Jesus ascended there were 120 people waiting in Jerusalem. The 12 apostles were specially trained in proclaiming the gospel; therefore 10% had the gift of evangelist. Wagner's allowing experience to interpret Scripture is a slippery slope that easily gives way to errant deductions. Scripture never distinctly supports Wagner's assumption. But Scripture clearly emphasizes the importance of leaders who are gifted as evangelists being responsible to train and lead all of Christ's followers in evangelism.

Second, Wagner states he has done extensive case studies on his statistics regarding the percentage of people who have the gift of evangelist (10%) as well as their impact upon the local church (200% decadal growth). But Wagner never offers documentation of these studies much less details how he compiled his data and analyzed it. He tends to make bold and sweeping statements and expects the reader to take him at his word.

Third, Wagner over-extends the importance of the gift of evangelist. He places too much importance upon a person needing the gift of evangelist in order for them to be effective in evangelism. In effect he basically emphasizes that a person who does not possess this gift cannot be effective. However, Scripture emphasizes the importance of leaders who are gifted as evangelists being responsible to train and lead all of Christ's followers in evangelism. As to the effectiveness of the Christian's evangelizing efforts, Scripture emphasizes that it is the work of the Holy Spirit in the non-believer's heart to "convict the world concerning sin and righteousness and judgment" (John 16:8).

Fourth, Wagner has under-extended the responsibility of the Christian to be involved in direct evangelism. He paints the picture that evangelism is to be dreaded and avoided by most Christians. Regardless of his well-worded attempts to differentiate between the gift of evangelist and the role of a Christian witness, his logic falls apart in light of the Great Commission given to all Christians.

Wagner's view of the gift of evangelist and his view of the role of a Christian witness are riddled with many pitfalls. Considering these shortcomings his perspective on this subject should not be followed.

Conclusion

No one has sacrificed or inconvenienced themselves more than did our Lord Jesus Christ when He left the perfection of Heaven to assume the frailty of human life where He was mocked, beaten, and killed. Jesus came to seek and save the lost. Prior to leaving this earth, He commissioned his followers to continue in His footsteps. He provided leaders with the special gift of evangelist, who through their example and training are to guide His Church along the right path of evangelism. Among the great joys of the Christian life should be the participation of every Christian in seeing the Great Commission fulfilled. Stanley Gale states, "Everyone who has come to know and follow Jesus Christ is given the responsibility to 'make disciples of all nations.'"[38] As Christ's followers we are each also called to go out of our way, to step outside of our own comforts, to seek out the lost as we "go into all the world and proclaim the gospel" (Mark 16:15), and to be His witnesses "to the end of the earth" (Acts 1:8).

---

[38] Stanley D. Gale, *Warfare Witness: Contending with Spiritual Opposition in Everyday Evangelism* (Ross-shire, Scotland: Christian Focus, 2005), 27.

CHAPTER ELEVEN

Understanding Great Commission Ministry
David A. Wheeler, Ph.D.

"Christianity doesn't get more basic... It is seeing value in, and loving and caring for, and reaching out to, and spending time with "the least of these."
— Chuck Swindoll[1]

WE are all familiar with the old phrase, "the proof is in the pudding." What you may not know is that the original saying was a few words longer and actually makes much more sense when you think about it. According to the website *Phrase Finder*, the original saying is "the proof of the pudding is in the eating."[2] This can be explained as follows:

> The meaning becomes clear when you know that 'proof' here is a verb meaning 'test'. The more common meaning

---

[1] Chuck Swindoll, *Compassion: Showing Care in a Careless World* (Waco, TX: Word, 1984), 60.

[2] "The Proof of the Pudding" www.phrases.org.uk/meanings/proof-of-the-pudding. html (Accessed July 1, 2012).

of 'proof' in our day and age is the noun meaning 'the evidence that demonstrates a truth' - as in a mathematical or legal proof. The verb form meaning 'to test' is less often used these days, although it does survive in several commonly used phrases: 'the exception that proves the rule', 'proof-read', 'proving-ground', etc. When bakers 'prove' yeast they are letting it stand in warm water for a time, to determine that it is active.[3]

This same principle reigns true when approaching the Great Commission and how it relates to ministry. All too often, Christians seem to focus on the command to "make disciples" without considering if the spiritual "yeast" has been activated for ministry. It sounds bad, but in many cases the sad result is a church that is neither "great" nor on "mission" with God!

The Unfortunate Dilemma

In an October 2003 article written by James Draper, former President of LifeWay Christian Resources, he records what he calls a "sobering accusation" against Western Christianity. He quotes David Watson, an Anglican priest, who writes two sentences that Draper says have haunted him for over 21 years:

It is widely held that the battle of the century will be between Marxism, Islam, and Third-world Christianity. Western Christianity is considered too weak and ineffective to contribute anything significant to the universal struggle.[4]

Draper continues:

That's a sobering accusation I've been unable to discredit. I fear that the church in America has wandered down

---

[3] Ibid.

[4] James T. Draper, "Sobering Accusation" in *Facts and Trends*, October 7, 2003.

one path when we should have taken the other. The path opposite our current direction is the path of a disciple...I believe Jesus is in search of disciples but is having difficulty finding any in the evangelical church in America. We've turned churches into comfortable country clubs for members when, in fact, the church is designed for those who are not members. People shop for churches like they shop for automobiles or for groceries. People want something that fills their needs. We have missed the boat because we think Christianity is about us. It is not. It's about God and His kingdom come on earth as it is in heaven. He has chosen Christians to play a significant role rekindling in showing the world what His kingdom looks like...Western Christianity has retreated from the battle for the souls of men to hollow pursuits of self-comfort.[5]

If Watson and Draper are right, the future of the American church is in serious disarray. The obvious question is, "What needs to happen in order for the church to become effective again?" Or, more specifically in reference to this context, "Where did the American church get off course in reference to ministry and the Great Commission?"

Understanding the Heart of Great Commission Ministry

In order to answer the questions above related to the American church getting sidetracked and losing its effectiveness, we must first understand how ministry ultimately fits into the mandate of the Great Commission. There are, after all, certain parameters that need to be established in order to fully comprehend how ministry dovetails into the biblical imperative to "make disciples." Consider the following observations:

---

[5] Ibid.

1. Great Commission Ministry is Incarnational Rather than Institutional.

All of my students at Liberty University and Liberty Baptist Theological Seminary are required to do several ministry projects each semester. Aside from the complaining by a few "super spiritual" students who do not feel they should be required to share their faith or be involved in ministry projects for a grade, I am usually encouraged by the positive responses from the students. They love volunteering at feeding centers and working with needy children through Liberty's Campus Serve ministry in downtown Lynchburg, VA. Just this past semester, we had over one-hundred students travel over an hour to assist a church in Roanoke, VA, with their Fall Festival! At the very least, I am proud that our students desire to serve!

However, not to diminish the impact of such opportunities, but mere participation in these events does not necessarily mean that our students understand the incarnational connection between ministry and the Great Commission. In the book *Evangelism Is,* when explaining the biblical nature related to developing a lifestyle that glorifies God, Dave Earley uses the incarnational picture of Christ as the example to be followed. He explains:

> In John 1:14, we read: "And the Word [Jesus, *logos*, message] became flesh and dwelt among us, and we beheld His glory, the glory as of the only begotten of the Father, full of grace and truth." The Greek term for "flesh" (*sarx*) is used when referring to "flesh, muscles, tissue and the like." The implication is that Jesus, who was born physically, was a human being through and through. The word *incarnation* is taken from the Greek *in carne* or, literally, "in the flesh." "Dwelt," used in John 1:14, is an Aramaic term that could be translated "pitching one's tent." Linking the two ideas together,

we see that Jesus did not merely shout the good news at us from heaven. No, He literally became one of us and "pitched the tent" of His life among us so He could get the message of God to us in a manner that was "full of grace and truth."[6]

Therein lies the difference in being involved in ministry and actually "pitching one's tent" among people who are hurting. All too often, the church has grown accustomed to sponsoring large ministry events that are momentarily designed to mobilize congregations into situations where their help is needed. There is nothing inherently wrong with this approach. I applaud any attempt at becoming the hands and feet of Christ, even if it is only for an afternoon!

However, when these events are over, it is worth noting whether those who participate take the same urgency for ministry back to their neighborhoods and work places? If not, while it is admirable, the end result misses the point of how ministry and the Great Commission are incarnationally joined together. In short, the Great Commission should drive believers to adopt a daily lifestyle of ministry, not merely an afternoon of limited service!

There is the attitude that authentic ministry can only be achieved by meeting at the church building and "going out" somewhere to serve. Unfortunately, that is a purely institutional approach that in in my opinion creates an atmosphere of addition rather than biblical multiplication.

In the end, Great Commission ministry requires surrendered disciples who are willing to cloth themselves in the nature of Christ, thus becoming His hands and feet 24/7 to a hurting world beginning in their Jerusalem and spreading to the nations! Thus, "real" ministry is not something one does to fulfill his duty to God. On the contrary, ministry that is driven

---

[6] Dave Earley and David Wheeler, *Evangelism Is...: How to Share Jesus with Passion and Confidence* (Nashville: B&H, 2010), 184.

by the Great Commission is an incarnational expression of who you are as a child of God!

2. Great Commission Ministry is Missional Rather than Attractional.

In the book, *Planting Missional Churches*, Ed Stetzer explains the concept of what it means to live a missional existence. He states:

> Missional means actually doing mission right where you are. Missional means adopting the posture of a missionary, learning and adapting to the culture around you while remaining biblically sound. Think of it this way: missional means being a missionary without ever leaving your zip code.[7]

He goes on further to explain that a missional church is called to go "on-mission" with Christ. This simply means "being intentional and deliberate about reaching others."[8] This does not mean, however, that being missional is about merely "putting more time into reaching out to the neighborhood."[9] Rather, "being missional begins with a profound conviction that we are invited to join in the mission of God and that the church does not exist for itself, but rather for the world around us who God so desperately loves."[10]

To be truly missional, one has to be sold out to the concept of biblical multiplication. This means that every believer should be expected to

---

[7] Ed Stetzer, *Planting Missional Churches: Planting a Church that is Biblically Sound and Reaching People in Culture* (Nashville: B&H, 2006), 19.

[8] Ibid.

[9] John Bailey, "The Missional Church" in *Pursuing the Mission of God in Church Planting* (Atlanta: NAMB, 2006), 39.

[10] Ibid.

---

reproduce themselves as passionate evangelists in their neighborhoods, homes, and workplaces.

Contrary to this biblical philosophy is the "attractional" approach that only requires believers to invite friends to church services to hear the gospel being presented by a pastor or church leader. Unfortunately, this has become the accepted interpretation of fulfilling the Great Commission in most congregations. Let me be clear, this approach is not biblical as a disciple-making model and will ultimately compromise God's desire for natural reproduction! Above everything, Great Commission ministry is missional!

3. Great Commission Ministry is Intentional Rather than Random.

I often hear pastors and church leaders talk about ministry in terms of "doing random acts of kindness." Aside from not being very strategic, I find this concept to be contrary to the spirit of the Great Commission, not to mention the vision of Christ.

When it comes to living out the Great Commission through ministry, we should always be intentional in our approach. Experience reveals that serving others will usually create a positive atmosphere in which to build relationships. But it must not end there!

Keep in mind that ministry alone will not redeem mankind. This can only occur as an act of the Holy Spirit when the person is confronted with the truths of the Gospel. Therefore, while Great Commission ministers should be willing to serve regardless of the sacrifice in time or money, they should be equally committed to the proclamation of the gospel! As I often remind young ministers when trying to emphasize this point, "that which we intentionally ignore...we intentionally will NOT do!"

4. Great Commission Ministry is an Act of Surrender Rather than a Pursuit of Self-Fulfillment.

There is no doubt that we live in a world that is dominated by the narcissistic concept, "what's in it for me?" Unfortunately, I have found this to be especially true in the church where politics and personal agendas tend to overrule obedience to living out the Great Commission through selfless ministry. Jesus attacks this kind of attitude in when He proclaims:

> If anyone desires to come after Me, let him deny himself, and take up his cross, and follow Me. For whoever desires to save his life will lose it, but whoever loses his life for My sake will find it. For what profit is it to a man if he gains the whole world, and loses his own soul? Or what will a man give in exchange for his soul (Matt 16:24-26, NASB)?

The key to this passage of Scripture is found in the words, "whoever desires to save his life will lose it, but whoever loses his life for My sake will find it." Therefore, Great Commission ministry is an act of total surrender. A man must be willing to "lose" his life in the pursuit of serving Christ or he is not being true to the spirit of ministry or the biblical call of the Great Commission!

The Proof is in the Ministry

Just like the pudding analogy mentioned earlier, the real proof of one's biblical understanding of the Great Commission is manifested through a life of dedicated ministry. In the end, the evidence of how "Great" the biblical "Commission" is in our lives is found in the many ways that we obediently respond to God as He thrusts us into His mission field.

With this in mind, the following principles provide a rubric of sorts in order to be involved in Great Commission ministry:[11]

---

[11] Under a different heading and contextual application, these principles are also utilized in *Nelson's Church Leader's Manual for Congregational Care*, Edited by Kent Spann and David Wheeler (Nashville: Nelson, 2010), 74-77.

Learn to Identify Needs

The first step in developing a lifestyle of ministry is very simple. Learn how to identify the needs of the people. Police officers are trained to spot certain things immediately. If there is a problem or something suspicious going on, a good officer will be able to recognize it and handle it in a professional and effective way. Much in the same way, we as Christians need to train ourselves to spot needs in other people's lives so we can then minister to those needs. Of course, this mindset stems from one thing: a selfless heart. It is so easy in today's culture to become consumed by all the things we need. After all, we have jobs that demand our attention, families that demand even more attention, and bills that must be paid. All these things can be overwhelming and will blind us to the needs of other people. However, for the Christian this should not be the case.

Matthew 6:32-33 states plainly that while the unsaved spend their lives chasing after their own needs, Christians ought to first seek after the kingdom of God and His righteousness. In other words, as Christ followers, we need to first be concerned with advancing God's kingdom and not our own. That means taking the focus from ourselves and aiming it towards those around us who are in desperate need of an encounter with Christ. Jesus modeled this attitude perfectly in John 4. In this chapter Jesus and his disciples travel through Samaria, (this went against Jewish religious tradition). Verse 4 states that "it was necessary" that Jesus went through Samaria. This was undoubtedly confusing for His disciples, because as good Jews they would never travel through Samaria. We do not find out why Jesus went that way until we get to verse 7, where we observe His encounter with the woman at the well.

Being omnipotent and led by the Holy Spirit, Jesus was aware of the woman's need. Rather than purposefully traveling around Samaria, like most Jews, Jesus traveled through it for the purpose of ministering to the woman, and eventually the whole town of Sychar. The application that we can glean from this, is that Jesus' main concern was not simply meeting his own earthly needs. Rather it was meeting the needs of others, like the woman at the well.

Go Where Needs Are

The next step to developing a Great Commission lifestyle of ministry is to go where the needs are. Returning to the example of Jesus in John 4; we can see that Jesus not only identified the needs of the people, but He went to them regardless of how it looked to others. As His followers, we need to have the same attitude and drive when it comes to living out the Great Commission. We need to identify needs and be willing to go to where those needs are, even if it means going into unpleasant or unfamiliar settings. So many times we avoid the slums and downtown alleys, and focus our witnessing efforts with less abrasive places and people. This was not the approach of Christ.

The woman at the well was not the type of person with whom any of the Jews would have felt comfortable addressing. Not only was she a "half-breed" according to the Jews, but she was also an adulterous woman. In the typical Jewish mind, this made her less than human. Historically, Samaritans were the offspring of Jews that had intermarried with people of other faiths and mixed pagan traditions and teachings with those of Judaism. With that in mind, it is not hard to understand why the Samaritans were viewed so lowly by the Jews. Not only were they not full-blooded Jews, but they had compromised their theology and teachings and abandoned the faith of their fathers.

This makes the events of John 4 even more spectacular. At that moment, the disciples must have felt a thousand miles outside of their comfort zone. However, this did not hinder Jesus. As Christians, we need to be willing to step out of our comfort zones and interact with cultures that might not be the same as ours. We need to go where the needs are most apparent.

Initiate a Plan

The third step in developing a Great Commission lifestyle that is characterized by compassion is to initiate a plan of ministry. When Jesus related the woman at the well, He had a strategy. He listened to her politely, and spoke to her in a non-aggressive tone. He confronted her with the truth without embarrassment or manipulation. Then, when she was ready, He offered the ultimate solution to her problem…an opportunity to be redeemed!

Therefore, once we identify the needs of people in our spheres of influence, we must initiate a plan to help meet that need. This step often centers on doing intentional acts of kindness for these people, simply because they are loved by God and made in His image. After all, is not that what Christ's sacrifice was all about? Did He not come to us while we were yet sinners, and die even for the ones who were hurling insults at Him while He hung on the cross? Indeed, the incarnation of Jesus should be seen as the ultimate expression of empathetic ministry.

Think about it, Jesus identified the world's need for forgiveness and a restored relationship with the Father. As a result, He was willing to come where the need was, namely to earth; and so He wrapped Himself in human flesh and came as one of us. He also initiated a plan to meet the desperate need of humanity; which was to die on the cross in our place in order to make restoration to the Father possible for all people. Last, He did not leave us to our own devices to figure out how to live the Christian life. Rather, He sent "another," the Holy Spirit who is our comforter and sustainer. This leads us to the last step to developing a Great Commission lifestyle of ministry.

Be Willing to Stay

Once we initiate a plan to meet the needs of the people, we need to be willing to stay. In John 4, after Jesus had ministered to the people from

Sychar, He stayed with them for two more days. Why is that? It seems logical that He stayed with them longer because He cared for them and wanted to develop intentional relationships for the sake of communicating the gospel. As a result, in John 4:42, the Samaritans eventually proclaimed with great joy, "Now we believe, not because of what you (the woman) said, for we ourselves have heard *Him* and we know that this is indeed the Christ, the Savior of the world."

This is exactly what we need to do as we develop lives that are characterized by Great Commission expressions of ministry. We must be willing to forge relationships with people in our spheres of influence. These people need to know that they are not just numbers, and that we are not simply marking off "evangelism" or "ministry" on our personal lists of weekly things to accomplish as religious duties. Once this happens, and we begin to immerse our lives in serving God and impacting others, the Great Commission becomes much more than a mere suggestion, it is our passport to a life of authentic ministry!

CHAPTER TWELVE

Striking The Match: Strategic Evangelistic Short-Term Missions
George G. Robinson, D.Miss.

From Being a Missionary to Living Missionally

In the summer of 1996 I had the opportunity to travel on a short-term mission trip (STM) from Atlanta, where I was a public school teacher, to the country of Panama. Upon my arrival I was paired up with a translator named Jorge and a kind lay-leader named Itzel. Our task was simple: go house to house through Itzel's village and share the biblical message of the gospel with as many people as possible and gather those who believe to form the nucleus of a new evangelical church.

I had come to faith in Christ my senior year at the University of Georgia and was discipled by some men who understood the importance of personal evangelism. So what our little band set out to do in Western Panama that week was not completely out of the ordinary for me—though the results would certainly shape my life from that point forward. You see, by the end of the week several dozen of Itzel's neighbors had come to repentance and faith in Christ alone and our week ended with a small gathering of this harvest under a tin roof in the middle of her village. Everything in my life changed in light of what God did that week through the proclamation of His gospel. I could not look at my career goals, relationships, or finances the same. So upon my return I began making plans to attend seminary with my new bride, Catherine, where we could be equipped to invest the rest of our lives in evangelistic missions.

One year later we arrived on the campus of Southeastern Baptist Theological Seminary (SEBTS) and my first class was "Practicum in Personal Evangelism" with a vibrant young professor named Alvin Reid. I saw in Dr. Reid a man who simply oozed a consistent passion for the gospel and an urgency for the task of personal evangelism. It was from him that I learned what it meant to live "missionally"— although that particular word had not come into widespread use yet in those days. So I had come to seminary to prepare for a future ministry assignment, but God in his grace allowed me the privilege of studying and ministering alongside a man that taught me to live every day as a missionary. And now over a decade later I have the privilege of calling Alvin my mentor and colleague as I get to teach both missions and evangelism in the very place where God had led me to study. To this day I tell my students that being a missionary has less to do with one's geography than it does one's identity. All Christ-followers are called to live as missionaries—or missionally if you will. That is an enduring lesson that I first learned from the man to whom this book is dedicated and it is one I will never forget.

Striking the Match

After studying and learning to live missionally at SEBTS, I had the great privilege of serving in South Asia as an International Mission Board missionary with the Southern Baptist Convention. Part of my job there was to host several short-term mission teams and incorporate them into my church planting strategy. Through those experiences I became convinced that these short-term evangelistic teams could be used as catalysts in a longer-term field-based strategy. Several years later I joined the staff of e3 Partners Ministries, where I led hundreds of lay-persons to engage in evangelistic cross-cultural missions. It was a great joy to equip those "ordinary" people to live with missional intentionality overseas and then watch as they brought that same evangelistic fervor back to their communities, workplaces and schools in the United States.

During this phase of my ministry I worked with other leaders at e3 Partners to refine the use of short-term evangelistic teams that would partner with indigenous Christians to assist them in starting new multiplying house churches. Our goal was to see these interdependent partnerships catalyze church planting movements in the thirty-plus countries where we worked. Church planting movements are similar to wildfires in that both have a small beginning but given the right conditions, they rage and spread to affect everything around them. Spiritually speaking, the goal of any missionary, regardless of length of term, should be to start a "wildfire" that literally changes the spiritual and cultural landscape of the target people. Most of the time, however, wildfires do not just happen. There must be a source or a catalytic event. Sometimes wildfires are started through a lightning strike without the help of man at all. Church planting is definitely the work of God for He alone brings life to the spiritually dead by setting hearts ablaze for His glory. But God, in His sovereign grace, chooses to use His Church and His children as fire starters. We are like matches used to ignite fires throughout the world. The fires God uses us to ignite are not destructive however. Instead, when the gospel goes forth and reproducing churches are established, these movements are to be likened to burning off the undergrowth which brings new life to the land. With that thought in mind, the remainder of this chapter is based upon the metaphor I developed—*Striking the Match*—that provides a theoretical framework for organizing truly strategic evangelistic short-term missions.[1]

The Purpose of a Match

Ages ago, parents came up with a warning that addresses the inexplicable fascination that their children have with fire: "Don't play with matches!" Why? Because a person that has interest in matches without much knowledge about fires can really cause a lot of problems. Import that age-old warning we all received into the metaphor that serves as the framework for this chapter: the admonition of not playing with matches needs to be heard by many who are leading short-term work trips and calling them short-term missions.[2] Too many people are striking matches and tossing them to the ground without any idea of how to truly start a fire. Unfortunately, many have forgotten that the purpose of a match is to start a fire. Instead, they are like children that find a book of matches and strike one after another just to watch the match go up in smoke. Short-term mission teams are like a match—they are catalytic in nature and should be treated as such.

How to Start a Fire

Backpackers know that the most important part of starting a fire is what you do before you strike the match. Those who brave the remote places of the earth today recognize just how crucial fire is to survival. I remember a backpacking trip I took over a decade ago in the Great Smoky Mountains National Park. It was mid-winter, and snow was falling before we left the

---

[1] A more in-depth treatment of this topic is available in my book entitled *Striking the Match: How God is Using Ordinary People to Change the World through Strategic Short-term Missions* (Franklin, TN: e3 Resources, 2008).

[2] The word "mission" is tied to the biblical term *"apostolos"* which entails being sent out with a message. Therefore I believe that proclamation of the gospel is central to missions. If proclamation is not present, what remains is a service-oriented work trip.

trailhead. Within an hour the once clearly marked trail was blanketed with fresh white powder and every opening between two trees looked like a trail. My friends and I quickly became disoriented, and soon we were lost. By late afternoon we had wandered for miles trying to find something that looked familiar. We were cold and hungry. Our water bottles were frozen inside our packs. All of our food had to be cooked. We desperately needed fire.

When we finally found our way out of the woods, to our amazement we had made a full-circle and were back at the trailhead. So we quickly set up our tent and went to work building a fire. One friend cleared the fire pad. Another gathered small tinder. I gathered some larger sticks. We took the time to meticulously build a small tee pee out of the smaller tinder and then added the larger sticks around that initial structure. Finally we struck the match and prayed that it would create a flame much larger than what was initially flickering. As we held the match to the small tinder the flame began to grow, and in a matter of time we had a blazing campfire that would bring us warmth and allow us to enjoy warm food and drink. For us, life was in the fire…kind of. We really were not in any danger because our car was just beyond the campsite. But real backpackers do not sleep in cars. Then again, real backpackers do not camp at the trailhead either. We may not have conquered the trail, but at least we had managed to start a fire.

The Match

The most common way to start a fire is with a match. A match, much like an STM team, has a limited amount of time with which to accomplish its intended purpose before it burns out. Most matches will burn for about 5-10 seconds, and if it fails to ignite a fire on some other object that can serve as fuel, it is no longer useful. Matches are non-renewable resources, as are short-term mission ventures. If you take a match and throw it onto the ground it might occasionally start a significant fire, but that is not the best way to ignite a wildfire. The best way to start a fire is to make the conditions right for burning by preparing a small, strategically organized gathering of kindling.

The Kindling

For the sake of the metaphor we will say that the kindling of missions is made up of indigenous national leaders in whatever location one works. There is a precise way of organizing that kindling to maximize the potential for starting a raging fire. In order for STM to be strategic, there must be adequate focus on preparing the kindling in advance. One must prioritize partnerships with indigenous national leadership by going to the target area ahead of a short-term team to learn how we can best serve their church planting goals. If you are focusing on an unreached people group (UPG) then you will want to partner with field-based missionary personnel or any near-culture Christians that may be in the region. Often during those initial meetings national leaders that have no vision for church reproduction will emerge. That is why it is crucial to convene a preparatory equipping meeting involving all leaders who will be hosting the STM team. Interdependent partnerships are formed when there is a mutually agreed upon and mutually beneficial goal. The purpose of this meeting should be to insure that all are in agreement to prioritize starting a wildfire through establishing reproducing indigenous churches as the primary goal for the partnership. This collaborative meeting should then seek to determine the appropriate roles of each participant including how a short-term evangelistic mission team could help advance the establishment of reproducing indigenous churches. By conducting such an equipping meeting, trip leaders are in effect arranging the kindling and making the conditions right for a fire. Tom Steffen notes, "For ongoing church planting to continue within and outside of a people group, the national leaders must own the vision, be equipped to implement it, and be given the opportunity to accomplish it successfully...[church planters must] create a world vision, see it take root, train nationals to accomplish it, and delegate full responsibility to them to carry it out."[3]

Orientation of the Evangelistic STM Team

In order to guard and facilitate a church planting movement (CPM) vision, it is equally crucial to orient the North American STM team prior to their arrival on the field giving them similar training to what the national leaders received during the preparatory equipping conference. This training should focus on the simple, biblical principles of intentional evangelism that lead to church reproduction. Oftentimes STM orientation is so narrowly focused that team members fail to see how they fit into the long-term strategy. This mistake could be costly in several ways. If the team does not see the bigger picture of church planting then they could become overly pragmatic in their evangelism and foster an easy-believism that results in a "Christian" veneer in the host culture. A myopic approach to STM also leads to disillusionment when evangelistic efforts meet resistance or fail to see immediate results. But when the team understands their role in the greater context of a long-term church planting strategy they are more apt to contribute in substantive and sustainable ways. Thus, biblical priorities such as the role of prayer, discipleship, and leadership development should be addressed in the context of the greater goal of igniting or fueling a CPM.[4] This element of equipping the STM team is akin to making sure you have good matches in your matchbook. There is nothing more frustrating than trying to start a fire with either wet matches, or worse, no matches at all.

---

[3] Tom Steffen, *Passing the Baton: Church Planting that Empowers* (La Habra, CA: Center for Organizational & Ministry Development, 1993), 170.

[4] David Garrison, *Church Planting Movements: How God is Redeeming a Lost World* (Wigtake Resources, 2003), 262-266.

Ignition

When both sides in this potential interdependent partnership have been prepared through equipping for the shared goal of planting reproducing churches, the time has come to "strike the match" by introducing the short-term mission team to the prepared kindling of indigenous national leadership. The STM team goes into the journey with the understanding that their role is a temporal, but a catalytic one. They also understand that their goal is to partner with the nationals in such a way as to empower them, so that by the time the journey comes to an end, indigenous leaders are ablaze with vision, training, and encouragement. Throughout the process both the STM team and the host nationals are praying that the Holy Spirit blows on the emerging flame and fans it through many people coming to Christ, many disciples being made, and many new churches planted. In my previous ministry at e3 Partners where I worked with others in the development of this strategic approach to STM, we found more often than not that God answers this prayer and we have seen hundreds, sometimes thousands come to Christ through these interdependent partnerships that we call church planting campaigns. The vast majority of those new converts were the fruit of personal evangelism (rather than crusade-type events), all of which are immediately placed under the care of a trained national leader who is committed to establishing a new church in the target area by making disciples and gathering in the harvest to form a local body.

Fanning the Flame

Following the catalytic event of striking the match during the evangelistic STM, churches should continue to partner with the indigenous leadership through helping them to further develop national strategies to engage under-reached/underserved areas. STM partnerships usually result in localized fires. National strategies are meant to spread that blaze throughout the region by adding fuel to the existing fire through indigenous church planting. Leadership must continually equip more and more people with a vision to spread the wildfire. I have had the privilege to be a part of several national strategies that resulted in fires spreading across cultural barriers and even into other surrounding countries as leaders began to send teams out from their newly established churches to repeat the process. It is truly a blessing when these strategies continue to unfold and develop without the assistance of North American teams. What God starts with a match that is quickly consumed, He turns into a wildfire that spreads a passion for His glory through church planting movements.

Missional Match-Making

One of the glaring critiques of most of what is called STM is that it is hedonistic in that many participate for what they can get out of the experience. While participating in missions solely for what you personally gain is unbiblical and often harmful to the indigenous work, there are indeed personal benefits that come as an overflow of involvement in God's global plan of redemption. I have often heard people quip that one should not travel overseas to do something they are not willing to do at home. While I agree with that statement in theory, I would add that if participation in a cross-cultural evangelistic STM experience results in people returning to their own context living with greater missional intentionality, then maybe we should be working to get more people involved in *Striking the Match*.

Time and again I have seen people's evangelistic zeal come alive while living out the mission of Jesus on a short-term assignment. Overcoming cultural barriers in an attempt to communicate the gospel faithfully does something to a person. Among other things it usually results in his/her reflecting on why he/she has not been living with missional intentionality back home. I have seen this happen to many people over the last decade. A businessman whose job was in international sales came back and began to lead his church to engage cross-culturally at home. He is now a lay mission leader in one of the largest Southern Baptist churches and has begun to engage his clients with the gospel in parts of the world that are considered unreached. A senior in high school proclaimed the gospel and helped start a church in a slum area outside of Lima, Peru and returned to his high school to catalyze a movement of his classmates coming to faith in Christ. He went on to organize teams to engage residents of low-income housing and is now assisting with a church plant in his home town. A young banker traveled with me to South India and spent a few weeks engaging Hindus and Muslims with the gospel helping to start a house church in a village where there had previously been no evangelical presence. He returned home and spent the next year engaging his co-workers and clients with the gospel and is now one of my students at SEBTS leading efforts in local evangelism while preparing to be a church planter. And it was a short-term evangelistic mission back in 1996 that started me on the journey of living with missional intentionality wherever I am.

Conclusion

It is probably obvious at this point that I disagree with many who try to argue for a hard and fast distinction between the roles of clergy and laity in the work toward completion of the Great Commission. A quick internet search regarding STM will yield countless rants about how damaging this lay-movement is becoming. We should all take the advice of Gamaliel when he spoke to the Sanhedrin regarding the group of commoners that they thought were damaging the Kingdom in the 1st century. He prophesied saying that if the paradigm shift being ushered in by the Apostles was of human origin, it would fail. But if the movement was truly of God, it could not be overcome by all of the professional activism that could be mustered up by the Sanhedrin. Why? Because they would in essence be fighting against God, not man.

This chapter has provided a framework for how ordinary people can take part in what I believe is a movement that has been birthed by God. My mentor, Alvin Reid, is fond of speaking about movements. And people listen to him primarily because he is not speaking from an ivory tower, but from the city streets. He himself is leading a movement of ordinary people living with missional intentionality to engage the lost with the timeless message of the gospel, and I have been and continue to be a beneficiary of his leadership in that respect. He taught me that all Christ-followers can and should take part in God's mission to set the nations ablaze through living as though every day is a mission. Reader, God desires for you to take part in His global plan of redemption no matter what level of training you have or what position you hold. However, He wants you to be strategic in doing so. If you desire to be a fire starter, then it would help to work within the framework of the process introduced in this chapter. Take time to make the conditions right by gathering kindling through equipping both nationals and the STM team. Strike the match with an intentionally evangelistic partnership that has church planting as its end goal. Add fuel to the fire through coaching and encouraging indigenous leadership in the development of an ever-expanding church multiplication strategy. And pray with perseverance for the Holy Spirit to blow and spread the flame so that a Christ-honoring movement begins where many come to faith in Christ and grow to maturity in the context of a multiplying indigenous church—both near and far.

Section Four

The Challenge

CHAPTER THIRTEEN

An SBC Vision For Fulfilling The Great Commission
Danny Akin, Ph.D. and Bruce Riley Ashford, Ph.D.

Authors' Note

ALVIN Reid has been a friend, as well as colleague at Southeastern Baptist Theological Seminary for many years. He is known and loved by many people. For students, he is a favorite classroom instructor and eager mentor willing to spend time with students outside of the classroom. For faculty members, he is a jovial colleague eager to spend time discussing the latest book he has read. For fellow church members, he is a dedicated teacher and servant. For all of us, he is a source of contagious enthusiasm for the gospel. In light of this, we are happy to be invited to participate in this collection of essays in his honor.

We had opportunity to write the present essay encouraging the Southern Baptist Convention (SBC) to give her best effort toward fulfilling the Great Commission. We could think of no better essay to honor our friend and colleague, Alvin Reid. Toward that end, the following pages will delineate six crucial factors for the success of the SBC's cooperative mission as we move forward together in reaching the nations with the gospel. Our mission must be one that is (1) revealed in the Christian Scriptures, (2) based upon God's mission, (3) focused on the nations, (4) focused on this nation, (5) driven by biblical theology, and (6) centered on the gospel.

A Mission Revealed in the Christian Scriptures

The character of God is the basis for a Great Commission Resurgence. In the Bible's opening act of creation, we learn that he is a God of life and love. In the aftermath of the Fall, we find that he is still a God of life and love, setting in motion His plan to redeem His image-bearers and restore his creation. It is this same God who gave the Great Commission, who empowered the early church of Acts in her mission, and who will empower us in ours. Our knowledge of these teachings, indeed our confidence in them, stems from the narrative set forth in the Christian Scriptures. If we cannot trust the Scriptures, we have nowhere to turn for a trustworthy word about God and his character, or the church and her mission.

The churches of the SBC confess that the Scriptures are *ipsissma verba Dei*, the very words of God. Time and again, the Scriptures claim to be the word of God. We know that the Scriptures are inspired, or literally "God-breathed" (2 Tim 3:16). The words of Scripture are more sure even than Peter's eyewitness experience of our Lord's life and ministry (2 Pet 2:16-21). Indeed the Scriptures instruct us not to allow our human traditions to make the word of God "of no effect" (Mark 7:13).

This doctrine of inspiration is foundational. Because the Scriptures are inspired, we confess that the biblical autographs are perfect (Prov 30:5-6), meaning that they are without error. Christian Scripture is infallible—it will not lead us astray (Ps 19:7). It is inspired in the whole and not merely in the parts (Rom 15:4), as given in the autographs (2 Pet 1:21). God has given us the Scriptures through the pens of human authors (2 Sam 23:2) who used human language (Matt 4:4). In other words, the Bible is the Word of God written in the words of men. Moreover, it is sufficient to instruct us concerning life and salvation (2 Tim 3:15), sufficiently clear for us to comprehend (Ps 119:105), and sufficiently powerful to convict sinners and deliver the good news of God's salvation (Heb 4:12). Finally, the Scriptures are Christocentric: the purpose of Scripture is to present Christ (Luke 24:44-49). Christ himself stands at the center of the Scriptures—he is the linchpin of the canon and the towering actor in the drama of history.

This is our confession. Although it may be treated as intellectual leprosy in the academy, and although modern and postmodern socio-cultural currents are diametrically opposed to it, we stand firmly upon this doctrine. Other issues pale before this one. The doctrine of Scripture is a "watershed" of theological conviction, and its significance reaches across the whole of the Christian mission.[1] When we lose conviction concerning God's Word, we will surely feel the effects in other doctrines and in the life and practice of the church. If we lose our way in relation to the Scriptures, we will lose our way in Christology and soteriology. If we do not have a sure word from God, we will soon lose our mission.[2]

---

[1] This is the point Danny Akin makes when he writes, "we must never forget that the 'war for the Bible' is not over and it will never end until Jesus returns. Launched by Satan in the Garden of Eden, 'has God said' will continue to be under assault, and we must be ever on guard and ready to answer those who question its veracity and accuracy." Daniel Akin, "Axioms for a Great Commission Resurgence" (Wake Forest, NC: Southeastern Baptist Theological Seminary, 2009), 10.

[2] For further reflection, we commend Paige Patterson, "Beyond the Impasse: Fidelity to the God Who Speaks," in Robinson B. James and David S. Dockery, eds., *Beyond the Impasse? Scripture, Interpretation, and Theology in Baptist Life* (Nashville: Baptist Sunday School Board, 1992), 149-168, and David S. Dockery, *Southern Baptist Consensus and Renewal: A Biblical, Historical, and Theological Proposal* (Nashville: B&H, 2008), 16-57. The Patterson chapter is

A Mission Based upon God's Mission

Scripture and mission go hand in hand. Baptists have missional convictions because they are a people of the Book.3 Our network of churches possesses a missional DNA. History informs us that the majority of the early Baptist networks arose from a need for interchurch cooperation in missional endeavors and that the SBC is no exception since cooperation in missions has been her raison d'etre from the very beginning.

In the remainder of this essay, the reader will notice three golden threads. The first thread is the mission of God, revealed in the biblical narrative of creation, fall, redemption, and new creation. The biblical narrative reveals that the uncreated Triune God created this world from nothing. God created and fills a good world with his image bearers from whom he will make a kingdom of priests. This world reflects God's glory and points continually to him. God's first image-bearers, however, sinned against him, setting themselves up as autonomous, and in so doing, they alienated themselves from God, each other, and the rest of the created order. As a result, they and we are dead in our

---

helpful in exposing how an errant view of Scripture issues forth in an errant mission. The Dockery chapter is an extended argument that, for Baptists, Scripture, global missions, and cooperation go hand in hand. None can be separated from the others.

3 We use the word "missional" in a particular manner, to denote a certain posture or impulse among Christians and churches. A person who lives missionally, as we use this term, is one who sees all of life as an arena for God's glory, who sees himself as "sent," whether he lives in Mumbai, Moscow, Memphis, or Milan. The word "missionary" carries connotations of professional overseas service, but to call a person "missional," in our usage, implies that he takes a missionary posture no matter what his geographic context. We recognize that many who use this term do not share our theological convictions. This is the central concern of Keith Eitel's article, "Shifting to the First Person: On Being Missional," Occasional Bulletin of the EMQ, 22:1, 1-4. Eitel warns that many who use words such as "missional" reject absolute truth in general, and absolute biblical revelation in particular. We share his concern, and hope that this chapter will help to provide sufficient context for our use of this word.

trespasses, and the good world God created is marred by the ugliness of sin, the consequences of which are far more pervasive than we might typically imagine.

In the aftermath of man's rebellion, God immediately promised to send a Savior, one born of a woman, one who would redeem the nations and restore God's good world. Indeed, from the third chapter of Genesis onwards, the Scriptures bear witness to the triumphant march of God who accomplishes the redemption He promised through the Savior He sends. The Savior came, was crucified to cancel the debt that we could not pay, rose from the dead, and is seated at the right hand of God the Father. Further, He will return again, bringing with him a new heavens and earth, where the redeemed of the nations will worship him forever and ever.

The second thread is *the church's mission,* which is set firmly in the context of God's mission. The church finds itself between the third and fourth plot movements in redemptive history, between the time when he sent his Son to purchase redemption and the time when he will have gathered the redeemed of the nations and created the heavens and earth anew. We bear witness to the Sent One, to glorify him in both word and deed. Just as he will return one day to receive the worship of the redeemed and to restore his good creation, so the church's mission includes both redemptive and creational aspects.[4] In its redemptive aspect, the church bears witness to the gospel in word and deed so that she may be an agent of grace to a lost and perishing world. In its creational aspect, the church works out the implications of the gospel in every dimension of society and culture. In so doing, it provides a sign of the kingdom that has been inaugurated and will come in all its fullness in the *parousia*.

---

[4] It is fitting that the book of Revelation encapsulates both the redemptive and creational aspects. Revelation 5 speaks to the redemption of men and women from every tribe, tongue, people, and nation, while Revelation 21-22 speaks to the restoration of God's good creation, as he provides a new heavens and earth.

The third thread is *the church's cross-cultural and cross-linguistic mission*. Throughout the Scriptures, God makes clear that he will glorify himself among the nations. In Solomon's prayer, for example, we learn that God will make known to the nations his great name, his strong hand, and his outstretched arm. In Psalm 67, we learn of a God who will make his salvation known among all the nations and to whom all the peoples of the earth will give their praise. In Matthew's gospel we find our Lord commanding us to take the gospel to the nations, while in Luke's we find him promising that his name will be preached to all nations. Finally, in Revelation, we are given a glimpse of those redeemed worshippers from among every tribe, tongue, people, and nation (Matt 28:16-20; Luke 24:46-49; Rev 5, 7). These passages and numerous others make clear God's mission to redeem worshipers from every people and nation in his good creation.

God has woven these golden threads deeply into the tapestry of the biblical narrative. To remove any of the three threads is to distort the overall picture: God's mission—to win the nations and to restore his creation—frames the church's mission. The church's mission, in both its redemptive and cultural aspects, frames the cross-cultural and cross-linguistic aspects of her mission.[5] Mission, therefore, begins with God and culminates in God. He organizes, energizes, and directs it. The danger is that we lose sight of this, thereby divorcing missiology from theology, and thence making the church's mission in our own image, which is nothing less than idolatry.

---

[5] By this, we do not mean that our international missionaries will pay the same attention to the cultural mandate that they will to their evangelistic mandate. It is our opinion that Southern Baptist missionaries should focus their energies on church planting, and in particular on church planting among unreached people groups. However, the churches that we plant should seek to glorify God in every conceivable manner among their people group. These churches' efforts, therefore, would optimally include efforts to work out the implications of the gospel in every dimension of their respective cultures.

A Mission Focused on the Nations

The SBC has always had international missions at the center of its concern. This is no secret. The Triennial Convention met for the express purpose of organizing international missions activities in general and the work of Luther Rice and the Judsons in particular.[6] The SBC, after having been established in 1845, soon formed the Foreign Mission Board, through which churches have supported thousands of missionaries. Today, the number of SBC missionaries hovers just above 5,000, while the budget of the International Mission Board (IMB) is approximately $300 million.[7] Because of a serious shortfall in recent funding, the IMB has reduced its number of personnel. If we are not careful, our "focus on" the nations might become a "passing glance toward" them.

An Awkward Tension

Reflection upon the biblical narrative makes it clear that our efforts often fall short. Revelation 5 serves to illustrate the point. This chapter portrays perhaps the most breathtaking and glorious vision in all of Scripture. In it, God gives a vision to John, the disciple whom Jesus loved, who was being held captive in his old age on the island of Patmos. In the midst of the vision, John sees the four living creatures and the twenty-four elders prostrate before the Lord, singing a new song, saying: *"You are worthy to take the scroll, and to open its seals; for You were slain, and have redeemed us to God by your blood out of every tribe and tongue and people and nation, and have made us kings and priests to our God; and we shall reign on the earth"* (5:9-10, NKJV). And again, together with all of heaven, they were singing with a loud voice: *"Worthy is the Lamb who was slain to receive power and riches and wisdom, and strength and honor and glory and blessing"* (5:12, NKJV).

---

[6] Dockery, *Southern Baptist Consensus and Renewal*, 38.

[7] In 1997, the SBC's study, "Covenant for a New Century," recommended that Foreign Mission Board (FMB) change its name to the International Mission Board (IMB).

In this passage, which reveals to us the consummation of God's redemptive purposes, we note two truths in particular. First, we note that there is something so profoundly true, and so deeply good, and so strikingly beautiful about our God that he finds for himself worshipers among every type of person on the face of the earth. He brings his salvation not just to every continent, and not merely to every nation-state, but also to every "tribe and tongue and people and nation"—to every people across the span of history and to the farthest reaches of the globe. In doing so, he makes clear that he is superior to all other "gods" and that he is intent upon winning the nations to himself. This is no footnote to redemptive history. It stands front and center. God killed his Son in order to redeem the nations. In the words of our Lord, "This gospel of the kingdom will be preached in the whole world as a testimony to all nations, and then the end will come" (Matt 24:14, NKJV).

Second, we learn that this salvation comes through Christ alone. John tells us that the creatures and elders sing to the Lamb: "You were slain, and have redeemed us to God *by your blood*." Salvation is wrought by the shed blood of the Lamb of God. For this reason, Luke describes him as the chief cornerstone of the church and writes: "Nor is there salvation in any other, for there is *no other name* under heaven given among men by which we must be saved" (Acts 4:12, NJKV). In this vein, Paul writes "through *[Jesus Christ]* we have received grace and apostleship for obedience to the faith among *all nations* for His name" (Rom 1:5, NKJV). And it is for this reason that we sing: "There is a fountain filled with blood, drawn from Emmanuel's veins, and sinners plunged beneath that flood lose all their guilty stains."[8]

But we must not allow these two points to stand alone. We must place beside them two glaring realities. The first reality is that there are several billion people who have little or no access to the gospel. They could search

---

[8] William Cowper, "There is a Fountain," in *The Baptist Hymnal* (Nashville: Convention Press, 1991), 142.

for days and months and years and never find a Bible or a Christian or a church. The second reality is that there has been perhaps no network of churches at any time in history which is as well placed as ours to take the gospel to the nations. There are those who have never heard the gospel, to whom we could easily take the gospel, and yet we do not. The question we all must ask is, "Why?"

Here is the bottom line: If we believe that salvation comes through Christ alone, and if we know that two billion people have little or no access to the gospel, then we are faced with a dilemma. Either we build Great Commission churches and accomplish the task that God has given us, or we force the Lord to plow around us to accomplish his will. Indeed, the Lord will accomplish his will. The question before us is, "Will we be found in his will or watching from the sidelines in disobedience?" We are hopeful it will be the former.

Five Clear Challenges

As we fulfill our mission to the nations, we face many decisions, including the five following challenges. *With a limited number of missionaries, to which parts of the globe do we send missionaries?* It is our conviction that the majority of international missionaries should be sent to unreached and unengaged people groups, those who have little or no access to the gospel. As we mentioned above, there are vast stretches of the globe (Asia and Africa in particular) where there is no church capable of reaching its own people. Our churches must take the gospel to these people groups. As Jerry Rankin has argued, this does not mean that we discontinue our partnerships in the parts of Latin America or Sub-Saharan Africa where there are indigenous churches capable of reaching their own people, but it does mean that the majority of our resources should probably be directed toward the unreached and unengaged.[9]

---

[9] Jerry Rankin, *To the Ends of the Earth: Churches Fulfilling the Great Commission* (Richmond: International Mission Board, 2005), 6. Rankin points out that in 2001 Southern Baptists finally reached a total of 5,000 missionaries under appointment,

When we send our workers to the unreached and unengaged, what are we sending them to do? Should they primarily preach the gospel? Feed the hungry? Heal the sick? It is our belief that, ultimately, we are sending missionaries to make disciples by means of *planting churches* (and training indigenous church planters) that will preach the gospel, feed the hungry, and minister to the sick. It is these churches, and not primarily the missionaries, who will preach the gospel and work out its implications in all aspects of their society and culture: in their families, workplaces, and communities. God works primarily through his church; therefore, he would have us to extend his kingdom by means of his church."[10] We seek to plant churches whose immediate goal is to plant other churches until there is a cascading chain of churches planting churches. Indeed, we hope to see churches planted within walking distance of every house in the world.

When we plant these churches, how will we ensure that we do so in a way that is biblical and appropriate to their respective contexts? How can we guarantee that we are not planting American churches on Iraqi, Nigerian, or Vietnamese soil? In brief, the answer lies at the intersection of three imperatives. First, we must preach the gospel and plant churches *faithfully*, in a way that conforms to the Scriptures. In a phrase, we seek to plant healthy, biblically-defined churches. Second, we must preach the gospel *meaningfully*, using words and categories and teaching styles that enable the hearer to understand the gospel in the same way that the preacher

---

but that this is not nearly enough. For example, at the time Rankin's book was written, the IMB had appointed one missionary unit for every 4.6 million lost people in South Asia.

[10] In Matthew 28:18-20, we are commanded to make disciples of all nations. If we are to "make disciples" of the nations, we must do so through the planting of churches, because discipleship can only be fully accomplished through the local church. For further biblical-theological treatment of the mandate and implementation of church planting, see John L. Nevius, *The Planting and Development of Missionary Churches* (Hancock, NH: Monadnock, 2003); Roland Allen, *Missionary Methods: St. Paul's or Ours* (Grand Rapids: Eerdmans, 1962); and David Hesselgrave, *Planting Churches Cross-Culturally: North America and Beyond* (Grand Rapids: Baker, 2000).

intends it. Third, we must preach the gospel and plant the church *dialogically*, in conversation with the host culture as national believers prayerfully seek to allow the gospel to critique the very language and categories of their own culture. If we will hold these three imperatives in tension, we have good reason to hope that the churches arising from native soil will be biblically faithful and appropriate to their contexts.

In what ways may our American churches fulfill their calling to the nations? First and foremost, we must find ways to build the Great Commission into the DNA of our churches. Mission is not a "ministry" of the church; it is at the heart of who she is. This means that in our preaching and teaching ministries we need to trace the message of mission throughout the Scriptures and publicly invite our members to commit a summer or two years or even a lifetime working among the nations. In our community ministries, we need to reach out to the immigrants, foreign exchange students, and others, who live in our cities. In our mission ministries, we might work with the IMB to adopt an unreached people group as the church's own, and then seek the guidance of the IMB's seasoned workers on how to proceed in ministering to that people group.[11]

---

[11] This provides a natural opportunity for partnership between a local church, IMB missionaries, and national partners (unless there are not yet any national believers and churches). When an American church embarks upon mission trips without such a partnership, there are three potential pitfalls. First, the church will have limited insight on how to make their work fit within a broader long-term strategy. Second, the church often will find itself crafting the trips primarily according to what is best for the local church team rather than what is best for the people group to whom they are ministering. Third, the church will be tempted to focus too much on certain *perceived* needs of the nationals and, in so doing, create an unhealthy dependency upon the American church. For a church's short term mission trips to be truly strategic, they must be part of a long-term field-based strategy in collaboration with missionaries and (if a national church exists) with seasoned national partners. George Robinson has addressed all three of these issues in *Striking the Match: How God is Using Ordinary People to Change the World through Short-Term Missions* (Franklin, TN: E3 Resources, 2008). Also, see Robert J. Priest, ed., *Effective Engagement in Short-Term Missions: Doing it Right!* (Pasadena, CA: William Carey, 2008).

In what way might our seminaries and colleges assist our churches in fulfilling our calling to the nations? They may do so by not divorcing theology from missiology and by not quarantining missiology to a lonely corner of the campus. Theology may be the "queen of the disciplines," but it will be a distorted theology indeed if it is not forged in the fire of mission. We must be careful to teach the books of the Bible and the classical theological loci with reference to the biblical narrative and God's missional character.[12] In so doing, we will find ourselves teaching about God with reference to his missional heart. We will teach about the church in relation to her missional calling. We will teach about the end times in light of the ingathering of the nations. Some institutions will need to be careful not to allow their missions department and missions professors to be viewed as second class citizens. Others, however, must take care to ensure that their evangelistic zeal is buttressed by sturdy theology. In riveting theology to mission, we will produce students who can build and sustain Great Commission churches.

A Mission Focused on This Nation

Our Convention Must Confront the Brutal Facts

In Matthew 28:18-20, Jesus commands us to make disciples of *all* nations. This includes our own nation—the United States of America—and yet the truth is that we are failing to meet the challenge. While the population of our nation increases, the population of our churches has not kept pace. While the United States becomes increasingly diverse, the Southern Baptist Convention remains a mostly middle-class, mostly white, network of mostly-declining churches.[13] This is a painful truth, and to ignore this fact is the worst form of denial.

---

[12] Russell D. Moore makes this point in "A Theology of the Great Commission," in *The Challenge of the Great Commission: Essays on God's Mandate for the Local Church*, eds. Chuck Lawless and Thom S. Rainer (Hanover, MA: Pinnacle, 2005), 49-64.

[13] For statistics on the SBC's decline, see the statistics released by LifeWay Resources in June 2009: www.lifeway.com/lwc/article_main_page/0%2C1703%2CA%2525 3D169332%252526M%25253D201340%2C00.html.

It is not as if the churches of the SBC have not tried to reach their own towns and cities. Many of them have worked hard to reach their cities and many of them have more or less succeeded. But the truth of the matter is that we are losing the battle. Our nation is becoming increasingly post-Christian and we are not stemming the tide. Perhaps one of the reasons that we are losing the battle is that we are "aiming at" a culture that no longer exists. The SBC built its programs and its personality, if you will, in the 1950s. But we find ourselves in a socio-cultural context that varies significantly from that of 60 years ago. Many of our churches no longer have the luxury of communicating the gospel within a city that has basically one culture. Instead, they find themselves communicating across numerous cultural and sub-cultural divides.[14]

In years past, many of us found ourselves ministering in regions heavily influenced by Christianity, but now often we do not. Many, if not most, of our neighbors had sufficient knowledge of the biblical narrative to understand "sermonese," but now they do not. In a previous era there were common categories for moral discourse, but now these categories are less and less common. There was a day when we were able to build our churches by inviting people to church events but now we find it hard to do so. So, how do we conceive of the task of communicating the gospel effectively to the various cultures and sub-cultures of our own country? How can we create and implement a missiology that will enable us to win the lost, make disciples, and plant churches in an increasingly larger array of American socio-cultural contexts? In a nutshell, how can we build missional churches and a missional convention?

---

[14] One particularly helpful treatment of ideological diversity in the United States is Gertrude Himmelfarb, *One Nation, Two Cultures* (New York: Vintage, 2001). Himmelfarb argues that the United States is a divided nation. On the one hand, there is a religious culture that has common categories for discourse and common convictions on ethical issues. On the other hand, there is an elite culture that is very permissive on moral issues and does not share the religious culture's moral language and categories.

Our Mission Must be Cross-Cultural

The United States is increasingly multicultural, multiethnic, and multilinguistic, as immigrants from around the world now live in our own cities and suburbs. Many of the tribes, tongues, and peoples of Revelation 5 are right here on our doorstep. Further, there is a dizzying variety of sub-cultures within the broader American culture, each with their own distinctive beliefs and ways of life. Many of them do not have even a basic understanding of Christian worldview or vocabulary. *Southern Baptists missionaries and pastors in North America must take their own cultural contexts as seriously as Southern Baptist missionaries take their international contexts.*

We must seek to understand the cultures and sub-cultures around us so that we can preach the gospel *faithfully* and *meaningfully* within the framework of our neighbors' cultural and social contexts, and plant churches that are at home in the culture. We must preach the gospel *faithfully*, allowing it to be defined and delimited by the Scriptures. We must also preach the gospel *meaningfully*, so that the hearer understands the gospel in the same way that the preacher intends it. The concept of the gospel might be foreign to them, but we may communicate it in language and constructs that are not. By doing so, we are able to preach the gospel *clearly* within the framework of the audience's cultural, sub-cultural, and situational contexts.

The way we preach the gospel affects the way the audience receives it. Many church planters, pastors, teachers, and authors have pointed out that if evangelical churches are to be missional, they must make changes in their preaching. Southern Baptists are no exception. When Southern Baptist churches were ministering in the Bible Belt in the mid-to-late twentieth century, they ministered to a population who had some (or much) knowledge of the biblical narrative, and there was a common language for moral discourse. But in the 21st century, we find ourselves in a context where many people have little or no knowledge of the Scriptures or Christian language. How do we communicate the gospel effectively in this situation? Tim Keller is one church planter who has written extensively on this challenge.[15] He argues that:

- The missional church avoids 'tribal' language, stylized prayer language, unnecessary evangelical pious 'jargon', and archaic language that seeks to set a 'spiritual tone.'

- The missional church avoids 'we-them' language, disdainful jokes that mock people of different politics and beliefs, and dismissive, disrespectful comments about those who differ with us.

- The missional church avoids sentimental, pompous, 'inspirational' talk. Instead, we engage the culture with the gentle, self-deprecating, but joyful irony the gospel creates. Humility + joy = gospel irony and realism.

- The missional church avoids ever talking as if non-believing people are not present. If you speak and discourse as if your whole neighborhood is present (not just scattered Christians), eventually more and more of your neighborhood will find their way in or be invited.

- Unless all of the above is the outflow of a truly humble-bold gospel-changed heart, it is all just 'marketing' and 'spin.'[16]

---

[15] Tim Keller is the founding pastor of Redeemer Presbyterian Church in New York City, New York. Keller founded the church in the late 1980s, and since then has seen the church grow to more than 5,000 in attendance (in addition to 5,000 sermon downloads per week), most of whom were unchurched before finding Redeemer. More significantly, perhaps, is the fact that Redeemer's church planting center has facilitated over 100 church plants. In January 2007, *Outreach Magazine* named Redeemer the top "Multiplying Church" in America. www.outreachmagazine.com/docs/25innov_JA07.pdf.

[16] Tim Keller, "The Missional Church," (June 2001) www.redeemer2.com/resources/papers/missional.pdf. Also, this material is explained in Tim Keller and J. Allen Thompson, *Church Planter Manual* (New York: Redeemer Church Planting Center, 2002), 224-225.

To Keller's admonition, we would add this clarification. We are not proposing to give up biblical-theological language, the very grammar and vocabulary of our faith. Instead, we are proposing to speak to those who are gathered in such a way that they can understand the gospel. And we do so precisely so that we can draw them into the biblical world, where they will find a better set of categories for understanding God and his world as well as a deeper and more profound vocabulary for speaking of those things.

Our Mission Must be Multi-Faceted

In addition to proclaiming the gospel from inside of the four walls of a church building and in addition to community outreach programs and door-to-door visitations, we must continually remind ourselves and our congregations that everything we do matters to God. Drawing upon Martin Luther's concept of *vocatio*, we must teach that every believer has the privilege and responsibility of bringing glory to God in each of his callings: family, church, workplace, and community. The workplace, in particular, is an oft-neglected calling in which we are given an almost unparalleled opportunity to bring God glory and to love one's neighbor.[17]

Further, God has given us the ability and responsibility to work out our faith in the various spheres of culture, including especially the arts (e.g. literature, music, movies, visual art), the sciences (e.g. biology, physics, chemistry, sociology, anthropology, psychology) and the public square (e.g. law, politics, economics, journalism, moral philosophy). For the gospel-minded Chrsitian, there is no room for indifference or hostility towards these aspects of human culture. We are not given the option of abdicating our responsibility to glorify God across every square inch of

[17] The best brief introduction to Luther's treatment of calling is Gene Veith, *God at Work: Your Christian Vocation in All of Life* (Wheaton: Crossway, 2002).

his good creation.[18] Instead, we are called to engage the culture arising from the society in which we live and minister, critiquing and developing it according to God's Word. In so doing, we sow the seed of the gospel throughout every dimension of our cultural context, providing a sign of God's Kingdom.

Our Mission Must be All-Encompassing

Not only is our task cross-cultural and multi-dimensional, but it also stretches across the geographic and demographic spectrum. We must reach both the small towns *and* the great cities of the United States. While evangelicals and Baptists have been fairly successful in the South, we have been less successful in the great cities of the northeast and the west. We recognize the strategic nature of urban involvement and seek to heighten Southern Baptist involvement in the largest, least churched, and most influential American cities. Urban centers such as New York, Washington, D. C., Boston, and Los Angeles are the nerve centers of North American socio-cultural activity, having massive influence on our continent and across the globe, and yet they are among the least churched cities in America.

We must reach both the down-and-out *and* the cultural elite. Southern Baptist churches have been fairly effective at reaching the upper and lower middle classes in the Bible Belt, but often we have not reached the

---

[18] Among the most helpful books treating Christianity and culture are D. A. Carson, *Christ & Culture Revisited* (Grand Rapids: Eerdmans, 2008), Michael S. Horton, *Where in the World is the Church?* (Phillipsburg, NJ: P&R, 2002) and T. M. Moore, *Culture Matters* (Grand Rapids: Brazos, 2007). Carson's text is a meta-level theological treatise on the Christian's place in culture, while Horton's text is a popular level, practical treatment of the church's role in its cultural context. Moore's monograph is a concise, intermediate level manifesto for Christian cultural engagement. David Dockery's treatment of Christian Higher Education exemplifies the outworking of our faith across the various dimensions of culture. David Dockery, *Renewing Minds: Serving Church and Society through Christian Higher Education* (Nashville: B&H, 2008).

cultural elite or the poor and disenfranchised. In reaching those who are "down and out," we must be prepared to build churches that intentionally minister in the inner cities, are willing to embrace those with HIV, and are happy to include those who may never be able financially to contribute in a significant way to the church. When we minister to these men and women, we recognize that they are God's image-bearers and deserve our love and attention every bit as much as anyone else.[19] In reaching those who are the cultural elite, we must intentionally reach out to artists, scientists, philosophers, moral and political movers, and many others. In so doing, we are "swimming upstream," ministering to those who in turn may have significant ability to influence our society and culture for the sake of the gospel.

We must build churches that do serious-minded student ministry, both for youth and college students. It will be a good day indeed when an increasing number of our churches' student ministries are known more for sound doctrine and genuine cultural savvy than they are for cutesy Bible studies and superficial cultural gimmickry.[20] Moreover, we pray that the day comes when more of us seek, consciously and consistently, to win our nation's college campuses to Christ. In the classrooms of our American universities sit the students who are the future of our nation and in many cases the future of our churches, as well as international students who are the future of their nations and of their nation's churches. We must make student ministry a priority in our churches, even during those times when it seems not to bear spiritual fruit and even during those times when it does not make sense financially.

---

[19] In the Gospels, we learn that the most "religious" people, the Pharisees, were able to attract only people just like them. They circled the world in order to find one convert, but Jesus attracted all kinds of people: tax collectors, prostitutes, lepers, etc. Jesus, not the Pharisees, must be our model.

[20] This is not to degrade the solid student ministries in many of our churches. There is a revival of interest in our churches for theologically sound and culturally savvy student ministry.

Our Mission Must Center on Church Renewal, Church Planting, and Cooperation

Our mission will not succeed without healthy churches. This requires, first and foremost, an emphasis on church renewal. We must always be renewing and reforming. This is the only way to ensure that our churches are sound in their doctrine, consistent in their evangelism, intentional in crossing cultural and linguistic boundaries, and contextual in their cultural forms. It is only from the wombs of healthy churches that we might see a church planting movement that is capable of reaching our own country. It is only healthy churches who will faithfully and meaningfully proclaim the gospel of our Lord and build churches across cultures and sub-cultures, languages and races, vocations and dimensions of culture, cities and suburbs, rich and poor, young and old.[21]

Second, our mission requires aggressive and intentional cooperation in church planting. The churches we plant must be sound in their doctrinal orientation, contextual in their cultural forms, and aggressive in their evangelistic and mission orientation. In order to make this work, we need renewed commitment from our churches, local associations, and state conventions. For local associations, this is an opportunity to demonstrate that their existence matters. In days gone by, local associations provided local churches with mission resources and advice that are now being provided by other institutions, networks, and people. For some state conventions, this provides an opportunity to return to their roots and stem

---

[21] Many resources are available to help pastors and their congregation work toward church health, of which we mention the following three. First, IX Marks ministries offers a website, a journal, and books on the topic of church health: www.blog.9marks.org/. Second, Thom Rainer has authored more than a few helpful books dealing with church health and growth. Thom S. Rainer, *The Book of Church Growth* (Nashville: B&H, 1993); Thom S. Rainer and Eric Geiger, *Simple Church* (Nashville: B&H, 2006); Thom S. Rainer and Daniel L. Akin, *Vibrant Church* (Nashville: LifeWay, 2008). Third, Ed Stetzer and Mike Dodson's recently published *Comeback Churches*, a study of 300 revitalized churches. Stetzer and Dodson, *Comeback Churches* (Nashville: B&H, 2007).

the tide of churches that are bypassing these conventions, refusing to give money to what they consider to be inefficient bureaucracies.[22]

Third, our mission will not fare well if it is not cooperative. This includes local church cooperation with other churches, local associations, state conventions, seminaries, and agencies. The daunting nature of our task demands that if any of the above associations is unwilling to fulfill their missional calling, then healthy churches will seek other ways to cooperate in order to fulfill the calling God has given them. It is the hope and prayer of the churches of our convention that the associations, conventions, seminaries, and agencies that we now have will prove to be sufficiently willing and able to take on this God-given calling.[23]

A Mission Driven by Biblical Theology

For three decades now, the churches of the Southern Baptist Convention have united over their belief in the inspiration, inerrancy, and sufficiency of Holy Scripture.[24] Unlike those (such as Schleiermacher or Freud) who see Scripture as a human construction void of supernatural revelation, and unlike those (such as Barth or Lindbeck) who see Scripture merely as a *witness* to divine revelation, we confess that the Christian Scriptures are the very words of God. This we have made very clear. What we have not made clear, however, is whether we are committed to allowing our high

---

[22] Daniel Akin, "Axioms for a Great Commission Resurgence," 16-18. Manuscript of sermon preached April 16, 2009, Binkley Chapel, Southeastern Baptist Theological Seminary. Manuscript available at www.apps.sebts.edu/president/wp-content/uploads/2009/04/acts-1-4-8-axioms-for-a-great-commission-resurgence-tt2.pdf.

[23] If the associations and state conventions prove unwilling or unable to invest their resources in church planting and renewal, many of our best churches will bypass those associations and conventions and form informal partnerships of their own. We do not wish to see this happen.

[24] Of course, not all Southern Baptist churches would affirm the inerrancy of the Scriptures. However, the majority of Southern Baptist churches do, and this is reflected in confessional statements such as the *Baptist Faith & Message (2000)*.

view of Scripture, and the concomitant doctrines of historic Christianity, to determine and shape our methods in ministry and mission.

Because the Christian Scriptures are indeed the very words of God, we want to mold our strategies and methods according to those words.[25] And while this might seem to be a yawningly obvious observation, we must pay careful attention in light of the fact that often we *do not* allow the Scriptures to drive our methods of evangelism, discipleship, church growth, and church planting. We find ourselves speaking loudly about inerrancy, while undermining that same conviction by our practices.

One of the significant challenges in upcoming years, therefore, is ensuring that we build a theologically-driven missiology in which Scripture and sound doctrine provide the starting point, the parameters, and the trajectory for our method and practice. "It has become apparent," David Dockery writes, "that a firm theological foundation is important for faithful Gospel proclamation. Pastors, theologians, evangelists, and lay people must work harder at closing the gap between theology and the work of evangelism so that our theology is done for the church and our proclamation is grounded in biblically based theology."[26] We must consciously, carefully, and consistently seek to understand the biblical narrative and its implications for church practice, and in particular for our missiological method. Building a theologically-driven missiology is hard work because (1) as our global, national, and cultural contexts change from era to era our missiology must be re-worked and re-written afresh; and (2) proof-texting does not suffice to handle such complexities faithfully. Many of the particular challenges that we face are not addressed explicitly by Scripture. Rather, we must call forth

---

[25] Thom Rainer makes this point in *The Book of Church Growth* in which he devotes one-third of the book to an exposition of the classical loci of systematic theology, explaining how those doctrines should drive our church growth strategies. Thom S. Rainer, *The Book of Church Growth: History, Theology, and Principles* (Nashville: B&H, 1993).

[26] David Dockery, *Southern Baptist Consensus and Renewal*, 94.

the deep-level principles in the Bible and allow them to speak with propriety and prescience to the issue at hand.

This is not to say that we may not learn from extra-biblical sources. Arthur Holmes is right: All truth is God's truth. We benefit from reading widely in history, current affairs, philosophy, anthropology, sociology, psychology, marketing, and other disciplines. It is God who has given mankind the capacities to develop such disciplines and who allows us the great privilege and responsibility of using those for his glory. While it is in Scripture alone that God has provided us knowledge of special doctrines (*e.g.*, the Trinity, the Incarnation, and salvation by grace through faith alone), it is through our human faculties that God has provided us knowledge of other aspects of his good creation. God is the giver *both* of Scripture *and* of the created order, and the two are not in conflict with one another. When properly interpreted, they agree.[27] Therefore we do not ignore what we learn from extra-biblical sources, but we also must not allow anything other than biblical doctrine to have the driver's seat in forming our method and practice.

Take, for example, the biblical *doctrine of God*, which is absolutely central to the life of the church but in some ways is overlooked in the mission of the church. The Scriptures describe how God does all that he does for the sake of his name, for his renown, for his glory. He created man for his glory (Isa 43:7) and chose Israel for his glory (Isa 49:3). He sent our Lord Jesus Christ so that the Gentiles would give him glory (Rom 15:8-9) and then vindicated his glory by making propitiation through his Son (Rom

---

[27] This is not to say that theologians and (natural or social) scientists never disagree. Often they do, but the disagreement is not found in any inherent conflict between Scripture and the natural world, but rather in theologians' and scientists' interpretations of the two. Either group might err and either group is therefore subject to correction. Because of our idolatry and the effects of the Fall, God's special revelation provides "the lenses" through which we study the created order. See David K. Clark, *To Know and Love God: Method for Theology* (Wheaton: Crossway, 2003), 259-294.

3:23-26). He sent the Spirit to glorify the Son (John 16:14) and tells us to do all things for his glory (1 Cor 10:31). He will send his Son again to receive glory (2 Thess 1:9-10) and will fill the earth with the knowledge of his glory (Hab 2:14; Isa 6:1-3). Indeed, all of this is so, "that at the name of Jesus every knee should bow, of those in heaven, and of those on earth, and of those under the earth, and that every tongue should confess that Jesus Christ is Lord, to the glory of God the Father" (Phil 2:10, NJKV).

God in all of his blazing glory stands at the center of the universe. He is the fountainhead of all truth, all goodness, and all beauty. And it is the increase of his glory that is God's ultimate goal and man's ultimate purpose.[28] *An implication of this doctrine is that if our ultimate goal is to glorify God, we are set free from unbridled pragmatism.* Ultimately, we seek to please God rather than to manipulate or coerce professions of faith, church growth, or church multiplication. We are directed away from the temptation to engage in evangelism and discipleship that subverts the gospel or the health of the church, and are free to proclaim the gospel God's way and leave the results to God.

We believe theological and missiological method must be tethered to the *doctrine of Christ*. It is said that a Hindu once asked Dr. E. Stanley Jones, 'What has Christianity to offer that our religion has not?' He replied, 'Jesus Christ.' Indeed, Jesus Christ is central to Christian belief and practice, and he is the driving force in our missiology. He stands at the center of the universe, at the center of the Scriptures, and at the center of our missiology. It is part and parcel of the church's mission to proclaim the Scriptures, which proclaim none other than Christ himself. Both

---

[28] Jonathan Edwards, in his *The End for Which God Created the World*, gives the most well-known and extended reflection upon this doctrine. Technically, *The End* is the first part of a two-part book by Edwards entitled *Two Dissertations*. See *Two Dissertations, Ethical Writings*, ed. Paul Ramsey, *The Works of Jonathan Edwards*, vol. 8 (New Haven: Yale University, 1989). It should be noted, however, that although Edwards was a Calvinist, this doctrine is not one that should be trumpeted primarily or exclusively by those who are Calvinists.

the Old and New Testaments are Christocentric—Christ himself is the axis of the testaments, the linchpin of the canon. The purpose of the Scriptures is to present Christ (Luke 24:27). *One implication of this doctrine is that our preaching should be Christocentric.* We should preach both the Old and New Testaments and should preach them both with Christ at the center. It is very possible to preach expository messages, verse by verse through the Bible, that are not, in any meaningful sense of the word, *Christian*. Instead of being distinctively Christian, our messages are often moralistic and legalistic, differing very little from the moral exhortations of a Jewish rabbi or Muslim mullah except that we attach an "appendix" about Christian salvation at the end of the message.[29]

The *doctrine of the Holy Spirit* also is not incidental to the church's mission. In addition to the Spirit's agency in teaching, convicting, illuminating, empowering, and restraining, the Spirit also gives gifts to each person (1 Cor 12:11) and enables believers to bear fruit (Gal 5:22-23). These gifts and fruit are most fully put on display in the harmony that is found among a community of believers. *An implication of this truth is that church planting is often best done in teams*, as the multiple members of a team use their spiritual gifts together, and bear fruit together one with another. The result is that those who are watching will see more clearly what Christ intends for his church. *Another implication is that a new convert can immediately be considered a "new worker," a part of the team*, as he is surely already gifted by the Spirit and capable of bearing fruit. Immediately he can give testimony to Christ and edify fellow believers.

---

[29] This is Graeme Goldsworthy's point in *Preaching the Whole Bible as Christian Scripture* (Grand Rapids: Eerdmans, 2000). Goldsworthy observes that many pastors and lay people find it difficult to preach meaningfully, and Christianly, from the Old Testament. He applies biblical theology to the task of preaching Christ-centered sermons. Other helpful texts for preaching the OT canon are Bryan Chappell, *Christ-Centered Preaching* (Grand Rapids: Baker, 2005) and Craig G. Bartholomew and Michael W. Goheen, *The Drama of Scripture* (Grand Rapids: Baker, 2004).

In the biblical *doctrine of man*, we learn that God created man in his image and likeness, so that man would worship and obey him. The creation narrative teaches us that Adam was in a rightly ordered relationship with God, with Eve, and with the rest of creation. At the Fall, however, Adam and Eve rebelled against their creator, setting themselves up as autonomous. In so doing, they became idolaters. We, Adam and Eve's progeny, have rebelled against our creator, setting ourselves up as autonomous—we are serial idolaters, enemies of God, seeking goodness and happiness on our own, apart from him. Our relationship with others is broken—rather than loving our fellow man, we find our relationships marked by gossip, slander, abuse, rape, war, murder, and other symptoms of the Fall. Our relationship with the created order is broken—rather than unbroken harmony and interdependence, we experience pain, misery, and natural disaster. Our relationship with ourselves is broken—we are alienated even from ourselves as we use our capacities inappropriately (spiritual, moral, rational, relational, creative, etc.) to perpetuate our idolatry rather than to worship the living God. The effects of the Fall are profound and comprehensive, penetrating man at all levels of his being.

Upon recognition of the horror of the Fall and its effects upon man, *we must plant churches that seek to glorify God and minister to man at all levels of his being*. These churches will realize the deep and pervasive effects of the Fall on the human heart, and preach a deep and powerful gospel message that is the human heart's only hope. They will use all of the God-given capacities they possess (moral, relational, rational, creative, etc.) to minister to fallen man. They will proclaim the gospel not only when the church is gathered (the church's corporate worship) but when it is scattered (through vocation and through the various dimensions of human society and culture). They will seek to minister not only to the common man, but also to the educated, the affluent, and the powerful. And in doing these things, in proclaiming and modeling God's gospel to His good world, they are glorifying him and enjoying him now and forever.

In the biblical *doctrine of salvation*, we learn that salvation is the Lord's. It is God's work from beginning to end (Ps 3:8; Jonah 2:9; Heb 12:2). As God elects and calls, man repents and places faith in Christ. Man is converted as God regenerates him, renewing his inner man, and imparting eternal life to him. Together, conversion and regeneration shed light upon the fact that a saved man now is united with Christ. This salvation is wrought by Christ's work on the cross, whereby man may be justified and sanctified. Salvation is by grace alone, through faith alone, in Christ alone, for the glory of God alone. The doctrine of salvation is full-orbed, and we must work hard to form evangelism and discipleship practices that recognize all of the salvific process. Of the many implications that this doctrine holds for our ministry practice, here are two of the most significant.

One implication is that *we must call men to repent and not merely to give mental assent to the gospel.* On the international mission field, this means that our testimonies, story-sets, and discipleship material do not excise the notion of repentance out of the gospel (under the guise of contextualization). This means that men must turn their backs on false saviors; they must repudiate tribal gods and witch doctors, reject their belief that the Qur'an is God's revelation and that Muhammad is his prophet, and cease to worship in spirit temples and ancestral shrines. In our home context, it means that men must turn their back on the worship of sex, money, and power. They must not give ultimate allegiance to things that are not ultimate, whether their idolatry is centered on a nation, a political party, a job, or a hobby.

Another implication is that *we must beware of "magical" or "mechanistic" views of salvation.* We must make clear that salvation is not mere mental assent, mere verbal profession of faith, or mere repetition of a prayer of salvation. If a person holds to such a reductionist view of salvation, he will have a wrong goal: the maximum number of people who have prayed a prayer or made a verbal profession. Further, he likely will have given false assurance of salvation to men who are not saved, and a false testimony to the church and the broader community. Finally, he will likely create methods of evangelism that are reductionist to the extreme and harmful to the progress of the gospel and the planting of healthy churches.

In the biblical *doctrine of the church*, we learn that the church is the people of God (1 Pet 2:9-10), the body of Christ (1 Cor 12:27; Eph 1:20-23), and the temple of the Spirit (1 Pet 2:5). It is one, holy, universal, and apostolic. A healthy local church is marked by the right preaching of the gospel, right administration of the ordinances, and a commitment to discipleship and discipline. It is composed of regenerate members who are committed to one another (1 Cor 1:2). These members practice their spiritual gifts (Rom 12:3-8) and bear fruit together (Gal 5:16-26) in spiritual interdependence for the furtherance of the gospel and God's program, for extending his kingdom centers on the local church.

One implication of this doctrine is that our convention will want to be careful not to allow its institutions and agencies to override the primacy of the local church. Seminaries, mission boards, and agencies are not mentioned in the Scriptures. They are man-made, and exist solely for the purpose of furthering the ministry of our churches. Good parachurch organizations exist to serve the local church. Bad parachurch organizations usurp the place of the local church. *Another implication is that we should be careful who we count as a church "member."* Southern Baptists count 16 million people as members of their churches, yet millions of them are non-attenders. Some of them cannot even be found. We must restore meaningful membership. Baptist churches have sacrificed the center of their ecclesiology if many of the members of their churches do not even evidence certain minimal marks of regeneration (such as a desire to worship with the church of which they are a "member").[30] *A third*

---

[30] See Paige Patterson's remarks on ecclesiological renewal in "My Vision of the Twenty-First Century SBC," *Review and Expositor* 88 (1991), 37-55, and John Hammett's argument that regenerate membership is the center of Baptist ecclesiology in Hammett, *Biblical Foundations for Baptist Churches* (Grand Rapids: Kregel, 2005), 81-108. Particularly helpful are Mark Dever's numerous treatments of ecclesiological issues (including meaningful membership) which evidence

implication is that we should be careful what we count as a "church." Our international workers in particular must wrestle with this issue.[31] When giving account to the convention, they must be scrupulous in reporting how many churches they have planted. The convention, in turn, must make clear that their CP and Lottie Moon giving is not premised upon a certain number of churches planted annually.

The *doctrine of the end times* has personal, national, and cosmic aspects. In the Scriptures, we find a *personal* aspect, as they teach us that it is appointed to man once to die, and then the judgment. After death, he will receive either reward or condemnation (Luke 16:19-31). We also find a *national* aspect, as we learn that the end will not come until the Messiah has won for himself worshippers from among every tribe, tongue, people, and nation (Rev 5, 7). This ingathering of the nations is not an appendix tacked on to the main body of Christian doctrine; rather, it is at the heart of God's redemptive plan. Finally, the Scriptures also tell us of a *cosmic* aspect of the end times, as Peter tells us to "look for new heavens and a new earth in which righteousness dwells" (2 Pet 3:13, NKJV). In this new universe, there will be no pain or tears as we live amidst the glory of the Triune God (Rev 21, 22).

Personal eschatology is both comforting and unsettling. It is a comfort, indeed a great joy, to know that we will dwell with our Lord eternally.

---

theological depth and breadth, as well as guidance on handling the practical aspects of those issues. See Mark Dever, *Nine Marks of a Healthy Church* (Wheaton: Crossway, 2004), and Mark Dever and Paul Alexander, *The Deliberate Church* (Wheaton: Crossway, 2005). Finally, see "On Regenerate Church Membership and Church Member Restoration," (June 2008), a resolution from the June 2008 SBC. www.sbc.net/resolutions/amResolution.asp?ID=1189.

[31] Multiple challenges present themselves on the mission field. How does one know when a group of believers counts as a church? When does a Bible study become a church? An excellent treatment of these questions is J. Atkinson, "House Church: A Biblical, Historical, and Practical Analysis of Selected Aspects of Wolfgang Simson's Ecclesiology from a Southern Baptist Perspective." Th. M. thesis, Southeastern Baptist Theological Seminary, 2006.

It is a difficult and unsettling doctrine, however, because we know that there are countless millions who have never heard the gospel and whose destiny apart from Christ is torment. This doctrine is indeed so unsettling that many have either rejected this biblical doctrine or dismissed it from their minds in order to ease the conscience. However, we must not reject or dismiss it, but rather take it to heart, allowing it to drive us to build Great Commission churches who will take the gospel to our neighbors, our communities, our nation, and indeed to all the nations.

A Mission Centered on the Gospel

Paul warns the Corinthians about the danger of factional battles in the church. In our opinion, this also applies to seminary communities, agencies and institutions, and indeed to the whole of our convention. Sometimes, the battles we fight are necessary and we wage them in an appropriate manner. But sometimes the battles are unnecessary and/or they are waged inappropriately. Often, unnecessary battles are waged because a group of people are excited about a particular idea, movement, or tradition. They begin to condescend or castigate, and seek to exclude anybody who doesn't share their ideas, emphasis, jargon, or agenda. The idea, movement, or tradition becomes a virtual test of orthodoxy.[32]

Perhaps no person, church, network, or denomination is exempt from such a temptation, and Baptists are no exception. Sometimes we wage unnecessary wars and sometimes this stems from a doctrine of "separation" (sometimes known as the doctrine of non-fellowship). This doctrine is based upon such passages of Scripture as Amos 3:3: "Can two walk together except they be agreed?" For some, this doctrine means merely that we should separate ourselves from worldliness. For others, it means that we should separate ourselves from those who do not separate themselves from worldliness. Still others, however, would disallow

---

[32] We owe this point to John Frame. See his booklet published by Reformed Theological Seminary: *Studying Theology as a Servant of Jesus*, 18.

fellowship (and sometimes friendship) with those who differ from them in any matter of theology (*e.g.*, the particulars of one's position on the rapture), physical life (*e.g.*, preference in apparel or music), or social life (*e.g.*, one's friendship with a controversial person or preacher). The result is a flattening of all theological and practical categories as if they are of equal weight and importance. For a time, I (Bruce Ashford) walked in Independent Baptist circles where such "third degree separation" is practiced. Although I admire many of these men and am thankful for what I have learned from them, this doctrine is one of the primary reasons I left those circles.

Within the Southern Baptist Convention, there have been more than a few controversies since the Conservative Resurgence. There have been public disagreements over worship styles, contextualization, Calvinism, apparel, spiritual gifts, etc. These disagreements have sometimes become major battles. One thing that is needed is a way of determining which issues are worth fighting over and which are not, as well as how certain disagreements affect our ability to cooperate with one another at various levels.

Al Mohler has proposed that the hospital emergency room provides an apt analogy for how we might make such determinations.[33] We have applauded this model on numerous occasions. Those who are reading this chapter might have had opportunity to see the goings-on of the "triage" unit of an emergency room. In triage, the doctors and nurses determine the priority of the diseases and injuries that will be treated. Shotgun wounds are treated before ankle sprains, and seizures before bunions. This is because certain diseases and injuries strike at the heart of one's well-being, while others are less life-threatening.

---

[33] See R. Albert Mohler Jr., "Has Theology a Future in the Southern Baptist Convention? Toward a Renewed Theological Framework," in *Beyond the Impasse?* ed. Robison B. James and David S. Dockery (Nashville: Broadman & Holman, 1992), 91–117, and R. Albert Mohler Jr., "The Pastor as Theologian," in *A Theology for the Church*, ed. Daniel L. Akin (Nashville: B&H, 2007), 930-932.

Pastors, theologians and missionaries would benefit from the same sort of triage. When deciding with whom we will partner and in what way, and when deciding which battles need to be fought and in what way, it is helpful to distinguish which doctrines are more primary and which are less so. Primary doctrines are those which are most essential to Christian faith. Without believing such doctrines as the Trinity, the Incarnation, and salvation by grace through faith alone, one's belief is not Christian.

Secondary doctrines are those over which born-again believers may often disagree, but which do not strike as closely at the heart of the faith. Two examples are the meaning and mode of baptism, and gender roles in the church. Disagreement on these doctrines does significantly affect the way in which churches and believers relate to one another. For example, although Presbyterians and Baptists may evangelize together and form close friendships, a Baptist and a Presbyterian could not plant a church together precisely because of their differences on church government and on the meaning and mode of baptism. Some secondary doctrines bear more heavily on primary doctrines than others.

Apart from primary and secondary doctrines, there are those which we can call tertiary. These are doctrines over which Christians may disagree and yet keep the closest of fellowship between networks, between churches, and between individual Christians. An example of a tertiary doctrine would be the timing of the rapture.

This does not mean that we avoid controversy at all costs. As one theologian (in his better days) pointed out, lack of controversy is either a sign of theological death or theological maturity.[34] We hope to avoid the former and strive for the latter. Nor does this mean that we view secondary or tertiary doctrines as insignificant. "A structure of theological triage," Mohler writes, "does not imply that Christians

---

[34] Clark Pinnock, "A New Reformation: A Challenge to Southern Baptists," (New Orleans: NOBTS, 1968), 3.

may take any biblical truth with less than full seriousness. We are charged to embrace and to teach the comprehensive truthfulness of the Christian faith as revealed in the Holy Scriptures. There are no insignificant doctrines revealed in the Bible, but there is an essential foundation of truth that undergirds the entire system of biblical truth."[35] It does, however, mean that we can have close fellowship with those who differ from us on tertiary issues but decreasing levels of fellowship when we disagree on secondary issues. The upshot of this whole discussion is that we must avoid the liberal extreme of refusing to admit that there are such things as primary doctrines, as well as the fundamentalist extreme of elevating tertiary issues to the status of primary importance.

Numerous spats center on method and practice. In such cases, it is wise to ask whether the practice at hand is based upon biblical command, apostolic precedent, or local tradition.[36] If it is based upon biblical command, then there is no question that it must be obeyed. If it is based on apostolic precedent, then it demands our attention but nonetheless is not a biblical injunction. We pay close and careful attention to apostolic practices, but some of those practices were contextual (such as taking missionary trips in wooden boats without electricity) and may be modified for today. If it is based on local (non-universal) traditions that have been handed down from believers in times past, we may respect those traditions, and seek to understand why they were formed and whether they might be helpful for us today, but we are not beholden to them.

One of the most lively and long-running of Baptist controversies centers on the issue of Calvinism. Entire forests have been chopped down to

---

[35] Mohler, "A Call for Theological Triage and Christian Maturity," www.albertmohler.com/commentary_read.php?cdate=2004-05-20.

[36] By "apostolic precedent," we mean those practice of the apostles that are described in the New Testament. Some apostolic precedent is to be imitated (e.g. church planting) while other apostolic practices are neutral and context-specific, not necessarily applying to us today (*e.g.*, writing on parchment with large letters).

provide paper for Baptist pens to argue this issue. On the one hand, there are some Calvinists who would not work together for the gospel with a non-Calvinist, because a non-Calvinist "does not truly preach the gospel." On the other hand, there are some non-Calvinists who caricature all Calvinists as hyper-Calvinists. Nearly everybody in Baptist life has an opinion on this issue, and many are willing to dispense jokes, caricatures, and sometimes even slander toward their opponents. It is our opinion that the areas of disagreement between Southern Baptist Calvinists and non-Calvinists are usually not even secondary, but tertiary. Calvinists should be able to recognize that non-Calvinists are preaching "the gospel" even if they disagree on the particulars. Non-Calvinists should not dismiss all Calvinists as hyper-Calvinists because they are not. Historically, Southern Baptists have partnered together in spite of differences on this issue, precisely because it is not primary.

Distinguishing between essentials and non-essentials, and managing to keep fellowship and partnership without compromise, is not easy. We must pray for God's wisdom in doing so. "We need to recognize," writes David Dockery, "that in essentials of the Christian faith, there is no place for compromise. Faith and truth are primary issues, and we stand firm in those areas. Sometimes we confuse primary and secondary issues. In secondary issues and third-level and fourth-level issues, we need mostly love and grace as we learn to disagree agreeably. We want to learn to love one another in spite of differences and to learn from those with whom we differ."[37] But distinguish we must. We cannot allow ourselves to be sidetracked, or worse, shipwrecked, because of unnecessarily heated or extended argument over secondary and tertiary issues. For the sake of the billions who have never heard the gospel, we must rid ourselves of fundamentalist infighting that distracts from, and contradicts, the proclamation of the gospel.

[37] Dockery, *Southern Baptist Consensus and Renewal*, 144.

Conclusion

Through four centuries of history, Baptists have displayed a remarkable continuity in doctrine and practice. With historic Christianity, we have confessed that God is Triune, that his Son is fully God and fully man, that salvation comes by grace alone through faith alone, and that the Scriptures are the very words of God.[38] In addition, we have held that the church is regenerate in its membership, autonomous under the headship of Christ, and free from state control. These last three distinctives relate to the doctrine of the church. Baptists have always been serious about the Church and specifically about the local church. It is through his churches that Christ disciples his children, directs his mission to the lost, demonstrates his glory to a watching world, and extends his kingdom. It is our great prayer that the churches of the SBC will consciously, carefully, and consistently heed the Great Commission.

The great crisis of the SBC in the late 20th Century was that biblical revelation itself was being attacked. We met that challenge and will continue to do so. The challenge of the 21st century, however, is not only to hold the ground won in the Conservative Resurgence, but to foster a resurgence in Great Commission obedience. Evangelical Baptist theology goes hand-in-hand with mission. There is an inherent connection between them. Without this connection, we lose God's blessing and its attendant spiritual power.

---

[38] Ibid., 58-98. Dockery cites Francis Wayland who, in 1861, wrote: "I do not believe that any denomination of Christians exists, which, for so long a period as the Baptist, has maintained so invariably the truth of their early confessions....The theological tenets of the Baptists, both in England and America, may be briefly stated as follows: they are emphatically the doctrines of the Reformation, and they have been held with singular unanimity and consistency." Francis Wayland, *The Principles and Practices of Baptist Churches* (London: J. Heaton and Son, 1861), 15-16.

Appendices

Annotated Bibliography
Todd Stewart, Ph.D.

Author's Note

Alvin Reid serves as Professor of Evangelism occupying the Bailey Smith Chair of Evangelism at Southeastern Baptist Theological Seminary, Wake Forest, North Carolina. Reid has taught at Southeastern since 1995.

My first knowledge of Alvin Reid came while a Master of Divinity student at New Orleans Baptist Theological Seminary. I had the privilege of taking a course on the History of Revivals and Awakenings. Although this course did not require any of Reid's writings as textbooks, the course prompted a deep interest in the subject of Spiritual Awakenings, Revivals, and Movements of God. Following graduation from New Orleans Seminary in 1998, I wanted to keep reading and stay sharp on the fascinating things I had learned in seminary. I picked up a copy of Reid's book, *Firefall: How God Has Shaped History Through Revivals*. Although this book is co-written by Reid and Malcolm McDow, it was Reid's writings in part II of the book that fascinated me the most. I enjoyed the history of the First and Second Great Awakenings, the Laymen's Prayer Revival, the Welsh Revival, the Jesus Movement, and others seasons of renewal. By the year 2000, I felt God leading me to continue my academic and ministerial studies. From my home in Mississippi, I called Dr. Reid to ask if he would serve as my academic mentor. After learning my background and interests, he stated, "Todd, if you can get accepted into the Ph.D. program, I will be more than happy to serve as your mentor." This began a relationship that has shaped my life tremendously. I studied under Alvin Reid from 2001-2008. He guided me through courses, mentorship meetings, comprehensive exams, prospectus submissions, and writing the dissertation. I am honored to present this Annotated Bibliography of Alvin Reid's writings. For it is through his writings that he first influenced my life. It is true that God has used Alvin Reid's preaching, lectures, and mentoring to influence the world. But, it is equally true that God has used his pen. While every effort has been made to identify all of Reid's writings, this Annotated Bibliography should not be considered exhaustive.

Books: Authored or Edited

Reid, Alvin L. *As You Go: Creating A Missional Culture of Gospel Centered Students*. Colorado Springs: NavPress, 2013.

> Reid covers important areas related to evangelism such as missional living, spiritual awakening, and student ministry. Reid offers the reminder to youth ministers and parents that students are missionaries. He challenges churches and youth ministers to move away from the entertainment driven, sin management model of student ministry and challenge teens toward missional living.

—————. *Evangelism Handbook: Biblical, Spiritual, Intentional, and Missional.* Nashville: B&H, 2009.

In this work, Reid presents his most thorough and exhaustive writings on evangelism covering over 450 pages. This volume is a revision and major expansion of his earlier text, *Introduction to Evangelism.* Reid has organized this volume to explore the Biblical, Spiritual, Intentional, and Missional aspects of evangelism. Topics include: A Movement not a Method, Evangelism of Jesus and Paul, Evangelism in Acts, Theology of Evangelism, the Work of the Holy Spirit, the Power of Prayer, Character, Spiritual Disciplines, Personal Evangelism, Church Evangelism, Worship Evangelism, Church Planting, Reaching the Unchurched, Reaching Children and Families, and others. *Evangelism Handbook* replaces Reid's *Introduction to Evangelism* as a standard college and seminary textbook.

—————— and Mark Liederback. *The Convergent Church: Missional Worshippers in an Emerging Culture.* Grand Rapids: Kregel, 2009.

This volume is co-written with Mark Liederbach, an ethics professor at Southeastern Seminary. Reid and Liederbach combine the strengths of conventional Christianity with the best contributions of the emerging church to envision a "convergent" church. With people leaving the church daily and churches closing the doors, this book helps explain why this happens and the solution to it. Reid and Liederbach argue that the church must get away from the "come and see" model and move to a "go and tell" model. They also see the need for missional worship. This is worship where doctrinal conviction and cultural relevance converge.

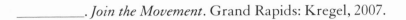

_____. *Join the Movement*. Grand Rapids: Kregel, 2007.

> This text is a revision and expansion of Reid's earlier work, Light the Fire, which was written primarily for a youth audience. Join the Movement repackages much of the same material for college students and those of the Millennial generation. Reid makes the case in this volume for Christianity being a movement rather than an institution. As one looks at the Bible and the History of Christianity, both present great movements of God. Reid challenges students to lead, join, or get out of the way.

_____. *What God Can Do*. Columbia, SC: South Carolina Baptist Convention, 2006.

_____. *Raising the Bar: Ministry to Youth in the New Millennium*. Grand Rapids: Kregel, 2004.

> This work, written to church leaders, pastors, youth leaders, and parents, serves as a call for churches and families to deepen and strengthen their ministries toward young people. Reid challenges his readers to move beyond an approach to youth ministry that is built upon "fun and games." Drawing from the young people whom God used in the Great Awakenings and the Jesus Movement, Reid notes that God has often used youth to change the world. This book serves as a call to get serious and grow up.

_____. *Radically Unchurched: Who They Are and How to Reach Them*. Grand Rapids: Kregel, 2002.

> A moving and passionate book that challenges Christians to get out of their comfort zones and reach the radically

unchurched. Reid reminds his readers that the radically unchurched come from a postmodern, pluralistic, urban world. Reid argues that young people can and should be equipped to reach the world around them. Reid notes that evangelism methods such as Servanthood Evangelism, Church Planting, Drama Evangelism, Personal Testimonies, and Worship Evangelism can all be effect in reaching the unchurched.

_____ . *It's All Good.* Wake Forest, NC: Inquest Ministries, 2002.

This work is a Bible study guide through the New Testament book of Philippians. It comes in both a leader guide and a student guide. Reid covers the book of Philippians in sixteen distinct sessions. This Bible Study guide is produced by Inquest Ministries, Wake Forest, North Carolina and is best utilized for Sunday School, small group, or personal study.

_____ . *Light the Fire: Raising up a Generation to Live Radically for Jesus Christ.* Enumclaw, WA: Winepress Publishing, 2001.

This short volume reviews the way that God has used young people to spark revival, evangelism, and mission movements. Reid presents the lives of Jonathan Edwards, George Whitfield, John Wesley, Evan Roberts, and Samuel Mills as examples from history. Reid notes that modern day youth, such as Cassie Bernall and Rachel Scott of Columbine High School, have been used by God to spark renewal. Finally, Reid covers events such as college revivals, the Jesus Movement, Coffeehouse Ministries, Explo' 72, Passion Conferences, See You At the Pole, and First Priority groups as modern youth movements.

_____ and David Wheeler. *Servanthood Evangelism Manual*. Atlanta: North American Mission Board, 2000.

> *Servanthood Evangelism Manual* offers effective and biblical witnessing strategies based on acts of service. This guidebook offers a detailed explanation of servanthood evangelism, practical applications for churches or small groups, and project instructions, as well as follow-up ideas. Over 100 simple, practical ideas are presented in this work. This is a product of the North American Mission Board.

_____ and Daniel B. Forshee. *The Net Mentor Handbook*. Atlanta: North American Mission Board, 2000.

> Written with Daniel Forshee, this volume serves as the primary "textbook" for *The Net*, an evangelism training curriculum produced by the North American Mission Board. *The Net* method of evangelism utilizes an individual's personal testimony in presenting the gospel. *The Net Mentor Handbook* provides eight training lessons coving topics like: Identifying the Lost, The Prayer Life of the Witness, Being a Lifestyle Witness, Drawing the Net, Decision and Follow-up.

_____ . *Introduction to Evangelism*. Nashville: B&H, 1998.

> Released in 1998, this work became a standard evangelism textbook in Christian colleges and seminaries. Reid covers a plethora of topics including New Testament Evangelism, the Evangelism of Jesus, Revivals of History, Theology of Evangelism, Praying Friends to Christ, the work of the Holy Spirit in Evangelism, Telling your

Story, Evangelism to Children, the use of the Internet in Evangelism, Church Growth, and many other topics.

_____ and Malcolm McDow. *Firefall: How God has Shaped History through Revivals*. Nashville: Broadman and Holman, 1997. Reprint, Pleasant Word, 2002.

> This volume, co-written with Malcolm McDow, presents a history of revival and spiritual awakening from the Old Testament until the present day. Reid authored part II of the book which covers revivals in the modern era, 1600 until today. Reid presents inspiring chapters on the First Great Awakening, Second Great Awakening, Layman's Prayer Revival, and Revival in our Times.

_____ and John Avant and Malcolm McDow. *Revival: Brownwood, Fort Worth, Wheaton and Beyond*. Nashville: Broadman and Holman, January 1996.

> This book was co-authored with Malcolm McDow and John Avant. It tells the story of a revival that spread through churches, college campuses, and seminary campuses in 1995. The revival began on January 22, 1995 at Coggin Avenue Baptist Church, Brownwood, Texas, and eventually spread through the campuses of Howard Payne University, Southwestern Baptist Theological Seminary, Wheaton College, and others.

_____ and Timothy Beougher. *Evangelism for a Changing World*. Wheaton: Harold Shaw, 1995.

> Roy J. Fish served as Professor of Evangelism for many years at Southwestern Baptist Theological Seminary. This book, compiled by Reid and Timothy Beougher,

contains a series of essays and chapters written to honor Dr. Fish. The book is organized in four parts including: Part 1. "It's New Day": Contemporary Approaches to Ministry; Part 2. "By All Means Save Some": The Evangelistic Imperative; Part III. "Revive Us Again": Spiritual Awakening: and Part IV. Roy J. Fish: Evangelist Extraordinaire.

E-Books

The following books are available in electronic form only. Some are available for pdf.download at alvinreid.com. at no cost for personal use. Others are available through online booksellers.

Reid, Alvin. *Advance: Gospel-Centered Movements Change the World.* Cited December 29, 2010. Online: www.alvinreid.com/ebooks.

> Reid notes that movements influence so much of what people do. He argues that Christianity, at her best, is a movement spread by passionate Christ followers who live for an audience of One. At her worst, Christianity becomes stuck in institutionalism and formalism, which causes harm for the gospel. Reid challenges readers to totally "sell out" their lives to advance the movement of the gospel.

_____ . *Pursuing God: A 40 Day Guide to Personal Revival.* Cited January 14, 2013. Online: www.alvinreid.com/ebooks.

> This work is a forty day plan to guide the reader to experience personal revival. It gives scripture readings, questions for personal introspection, and space for journaling each day. Topics include worry, forgiveness, repentance, priorities, God's word, prayer, temptation,

and many others. Reid reminds his readers, "where you are in five years will be determined less by what you accomplish and more by your adoration of Christ."

_____. *Roar: The Deafening Thunder of Spiritual Awakening*. Cited December 29, 2010. Online: www.alvinreid.com/ebooks.

Reid utilizes this resource to explain and define Spiritual Awakening and Revival. He gives examples from history including the First Great Awakening, The Second Great Awakening, the Welsh Revival, and the Laymen's Prayer Revival. Reid discusses how one can experience revival in their personal life, home, church, and community. Practical guides for preparing for personal revival and planning a revival prayer vigil are included.

_____. *Stronger: A Practical Guide to Physical and Spiritual Discipline*. Cited January 14, 2013. Online: www.alrinreid.com/ebooks.

In this book, Reid confronts the obesity and gluttony epidemic in America. He specifically notes how many ministers struggle with this issue. Reid offers Biblical and practical counsel to encourage discipline in all of life. This work is filled with many testimonies from those who have gotten active and let go of the pounds.

_____. *With: A Guide to Informal Mentoring*. Cited December 29, 2010. Online: www.alvinreid.com/ebooks.

In this resource, Reid teaches the concept of informal mentoring. Just as the disciples had been "with" Jesus, Reid argues that leaders advance the kingdom of God by spending time developing younger, potential leaders. Reid models this practice in his own life and notes that so much of life is "caught rather than taught." Leaders are challenged to spend time "with" younger, future leaders as everyone should be mentoring someone.

Reid, Alvin L., and Ashley Marivittori Gorman. *Book of Matches.* 2012. May be purchased through online booksellers.

Written by Alvin Reid and a Southeastern Seminary student, this book discusses a common yet specific struggle: relationships. This work helps the reader sort out relationships with God, friends, and one's mate.

Dissertation

Reid, Alvin. "The Impact of the Jesus Movement on Evangelism among Southern Baptists." Ph.D diss., Southwestern Baptist Theological Seminary, 1991.

Reid's dissertation chronicles the Jesus Movement, a revival that took place in the United States during the late 1960s and early 1970s. Reid gives details about all the major developments of the Jesus Movement including Christian Coffeehouses, Youth Musicals, Jesus Freaks, Explo' 72, and the rapid rise of Campus Crusade for Christ. Reid specifically points out how the Jesus Movement impacted Southern Baptists, including increased baptisms, increased seminary enrollment, the development of new music, the launch of WIN Evangelism schools, and the effect on youth.

Online Resources

Reid, Alvin. "Blog." Cited 15 January 2013. Online: www.alvinreid. com/ archives/category/ blog.

Reid utilizes this blog to communicate, encourage, teach, and mentor others in evangelism and matters of faith. Reid began this blog in 2006, and he continues with regular postings. Several entries are made for each month, and all older posts are archived.

Chapters or Articles in Books

Reid, Alvin. "Get Real: Mobilizing Students to Witness." In *Mobilizing a Great Commission Church For Harvest*. Edited by Thomas Johnston. Eugene, OR: Wipf and Stock, 2011.

_____. "Time Management." In *Greenhouse Project* ed. Mike Calhoun and Mel Walker. Word of Life, 2009.

_____. "Prayer and Evangelism." In *Giving Ourselves to Prayer*, ed. Dan Crawford. PrayerShop Publishing, 2008.

_____. "Youth" and "When to Raise Questions," articles in *Evangelism Guidebook*, Baker, 2005.

_____. "Foreword." *Call2Ministry*, by Dana Mathewson. 2004.

_____. Contributor to The Real World, Sunday School Curriculum for InQuest Ministries, 2003.

_____. "Revival/Spiritual Awakening and Incarnational Evangelism." In *Being, Doing, and Telling the Gospel*, ed. Chris Schofield. Nashville: B&H, 2001.

_____. Contributor to *His Heart Our Hands: A Guide for Ministry Evangelism*. Atlanta: North American Mission Board, 2001.

_____. "Invading the Radically Unchurched Culture in America." In *Here I Stand: Articles in Honor of Paige Patterson*. Davidson Press, 2000.

_____. Editorial assistant, Bailey Smith, *Real Evangelism*. Nashville: Word, 1999. Edited and assisted rewriting the book for re-publication.

_____. "Preparation by Studying the History of Revival." *Before Revival Begins*, ed. Dan Crawford. Fort Worth: Scripta, 1996.

_____. Editorial Committee for *Evangelism and Church Growth*, edited by Elmer Towns. Ventura, CA: Regal, 1996. Also contributed the following articles: "Cults, Evangelizing Persons in;" "Finney, Charles G.;" "Gospel;" "Kerygma;" "Mass Evangelism;" "Methods, Evangelistic;" "Model Church Approach;" "Music, Evangelistic;" "Pietism;" "Prayer Revival of 1857-58;" "Sunday, Billy;" "Torrey, R.A.;" "Whitefield, George."

_____. "The Zeal of Youth: The Role of Students in the History of Spiritual Awakenings." In *Evangelism for a Changing World*, Wheaton: Harold Shaw, 1995.

_____. "Witnessing without Fear." In *Fifty Great Motivational Soul-Winning Sermons*. Atlanta: Home Mission Board, 1994.

Print Articles

Reid, Alvin L. "Evangelism is Not a Dirty Word: Making Evangelism Good New Again. *On Mission*. Special Issue, Spring 2006.

_____. "Join the Movement!" *SBC Life*. September 2005.

_____. "Things Must Change." *SBC Life*. June 2005.

_____. "Reaching the Radically Churched." *On Mission*. January/February 2004.

_____. "Radical or Recreational?" *On Mission*. June/July, 2003.

_____. "The Times They Are A-Changing." *SBC Life*. January, 2003.

_____. "Teach Your Children to Witness." *SBC Life*. September/October, 2002.

_____. "Reaching Unchurched People." *Evangelism and Church Planting Today*. Spring 2002.

_____. "Raising the Bar: Ministry to Students in the New Millennium." *Faith and Mission*. Spring 2002.

_____. "Snake Handling and Soulwinning: What the 'Crocodile Hunter' Says about Reaching Postmoderns." SBC Life, August 2001.

_____. "Reaching Postmoderns." *SBC Life*, August 2001.

_____. "Twinkies or Truth?" *Studentz.com*, Summer 2001.

_____. "Reaching a Postmodern Culture through Servant Evangelism." *The Southern Baptist Journal of Theology*. Spring 2001.

_____. "Who wrote the Bible?," "How does prayer work?," "Asa," "Jeroboam," "Matthew," "Obadiah," "Temple." Articles in the *Christian Growth Study Bible*. Grand Rapids: Zondervan, 2001.

_____. "Everything I Know about Ministry I Learned Playing High School Football." *SBC Life*, December 2000.

_____. "The Spontaneous Generation: Lessons for the Jesus Movement for Today" *Journal for the American Society of Church Growth*, Summer, 2000.

_____. "Playing Games or Pursing God?" *SBC Life*, August 2000. Reprinted in *LifeTrak for Younger Youth* 1.3, Spring 2001.

_____. "The Changeless Message for a Changing Culture." *Evangelism and Church Planting Today*. Summer 2000.

_____. "Restaurant Testimony." *Home Life*, July 2000.

_____. "A Passion for God." Sermon in *Proclaim!* Fall 2000.

_____. "Saying Grace, Being Gracious." *SBC Life*, Spring 2000. Reprinted in *Christian Single*, Summer 2000, and *Home Life*, July 2000.

_____. "Hotels for Saints or Hospitals for Sinners? Reaching the Radically Unchurched in America." *Faith and Mission*, Summer 1999.

_____. "Building a Bridge Into the Next Millenium—and Eternity." *SBC Life*, June 1999.

_____. "Evangelism Books for a Church Library." *Library Journal*, Spring 1999.

_____. "Carpe DieMillenium." *SBC Life*, April 1999.

_____. "Prayer and Evangelism." *Growing Churches*, Spring 1999.

_____. "Retro Jesus Movement." *SBC Life*, December 1998.

_____. "Wonder-Full Generation X." *Evangelism Today*, Summer 1998.

_____. "If Youth Be Served." *SBC Life*, June 1998.

_____. "What's in a Name?" *SBC Life*, April 1998.

_____. "Acts of Kindness: Servant Evangelism." *Growing Churches*, Fall 1997.

_____. "The Elmo Enigma." *SBC Life* April, 1997.

_____. "Servant Evangelism," *SBC Life* May, 1997.

_____. "Substance over Style: A Theology of Worship and Church Growth," *Journal for the American Society of Church Growth*, Spring, 1997.

_____. "Revival: A Passion for God," *A Single Pursuit*, Spring 1997.

_____. "From Northampton to New Delhi: Spiritual Awakenings and the History of Missions." EMS Publications, 1997.

_____. "Jonathan and Sarah Edwards," *Home Life*, 1997.

_____. "A Passion for God: The Biblical Basis for Prayer and Fasting,"*Evangelism Today*, September 1996.

_____. "Leading a New Year's Eve Watch Night Service," *Evangelism Today*, December 1996.

_____. "Observing 'Mass' in the Southern Baptist Convention," *SBC Life*, October 1996.

_____. "George Whitefield: Peerless Itinerant," *Equipping Evangelists*, August 1995.

_____. "The Barnabas Principle," *Growing Churches*, Summer 1995.

_____. "The Impact of the Jesus Movement on Evangelism in the Southern Baptist Convention," *Baptist History and Heritage*, Spring 1995.

_____. "Biblical Motivation for Contemporary Evangelism," *Growing Churches*, Winter 1995.

_____. "Feeding the Spring: How to Maintain a Focus on Evangelism," *Growing Churches*, Spring 1995.

_____. "Equipping People to Witness Through the Sunday School," Sunday *Sunday School Leadership Large Church Edition*, September 1994.

_____. "Who You ARE: The Key to Leadership," *Growing Churches*, Summer 1994.

_____. *Beginning Steps*. Home Mission Board, 1994. Co-author of the follow-up booklet.

_____. "Putting the 'How-to' with the 'Must-Do," *Growing Churches*, Summer 1993. Reprinted in *Evangelism Today*, produced by the Evangelism Section of the Home Mission Board, Summer 1994.

_____. "Indiana Hosts Soul-Winning Conference." *Indiana Baptist*, 4 June 1991, 12.

_____. "Evangelism Events Planned in State." *Indiana Baptist*, 20 November 1990.

_____. "Total Church Life: Strategy for the Nineties." *Indiana Baptist*, 6 November 1990.

_____. "Gospel of Hope." Eight articles total under this theme (seven devotionals and a literary piece) based on 1 Peter 1:1-2:3 for *encounter!*, devotional magazine for young people, week of June 10, 1990.

_____. "Proclamation and Witness." Article for the *Biblical Illustrator*, Summer 1990.

_____. "Youth Conference Opportunity Can Bring Life to Churches." *Indiana Baptist*, 5 June 1990.

_____. "Hypocrisy." Sermon illustration for *Proclaim*, April, 1990.

_____. "Temptation." Sermon illustration for *Proclaim*, April, 1990.

_____. "Joshua -- A Blessing from God." *Home Life*. February 1990, 21-22. Reprinted in *Indiana Baptist*, 27 March 1990.

_____. "Here's Hope Revivals Kick Off Yearlong Evangelism Emphasis." *Indiana Baptist*, 27 March 1990.

_____. "Wise Investments." *Mature Living*, August 1989.

_____. "History of Awakenings Shows Impact of Concerted Effort." *Indiana Baptist*, August 1989.

_____. "Prayer Essential for Revival." *Indiana Baptist*, September 1989.

_____. "CWT Offers Witness Training." *Indiana Baptist*, 12 December 1989.

_____. "Supportive Love of God." *Letter to the Editor, Baptist Standard*, 17 August 1988.

_____. "Self-Fulfillment: Egocentrism Versus Exocentrism." The Student Forum (Publication of the Theological Fellowship of Southwestern Baptist Theological Seminary) 9 November 1988.

Online Publications

Five articles for Church Central, online publication, on youth ministry, 2003.

Articles written for Hometown Companion regularly, 2003-04.

Editorial consultant and regular contributor to *First Priority emagazine*, http://www.lpea.org. Articles include "Teach Your Children Well," Summer 2001; "Get Real: The Character of the Witness,"December 2000, "Playing Games or Pursuing God? Student Ministry in the New

Millennium (adaptation of article in SBC Life above), August 2000; "Reaching the Radically Unchurched in America," January 2000; others were written, as well.

Regular contributor to *Total Life Now* emagazine, www.TotalLifeNow. com. Articles include "Light the Fire," July 2001; "The Coming Great Generation," March 2001; "Pastoral Leadership for Evangelism: Richard Baxter," January 2001; "Technoevangelism: Using the New Technology to Share Christ," December 2000; "The Power of Evangelism in the Welsh Revival," October 2000; "A Perspective on Youth Ministry," September 2000.

_____. "What Has Trigonometry to Do with Theology?" *Inquest Ministries Article of the Month*, September 2004.

_____. "The Generation of Hope." *Inquest Ministries Article of the Month*, www.inquest.org. June 2001.

_____. "A Fresh Fire for Church Growth: Preaching on Spiritual Awakening,"Personal Evangelism Online Emagazine, 1999.

_____. "Living in the World What We Sing in the Church," Personal Evangelism Online Emagazine, 1999.

_____. "Refocussing a Church on Evangelism." Personal Evangelism Online Emagazine, 1999.

Book Reviews

Review of Ronald J. Sider, *Good News and Good Works*, Baker, in *Journal of the Evangelical Theological Society*, Spring 2001.

Review of Thom Rainer, *The Bridger Generation*, B&H, in *Faith and Mission*, Fall 1998.

Review of *Purpose Driven Youth Ministry*, Zondervan, in *Faith and Mission*, Fall 1998.

Review of Kevin Graham Ford, *Jesus for a New Generation*, IVP, 1995, in *Strategies for Today's Leader*, Spring 1998.

Review of Hank Hannagraaf, *Counterfeit Revival*, Word, 1997. In *Faith and Mission*, Spring, 1997.

Review of *Worship Evangelism* by Sally Morganthaler. Zondervan. In *Faith and Mission*, Fall, 1996.

Review of *The Spark That Ignites*, by Robert E. Coleman (Minneapolis: World Wide Publications, 1989). In *Search* (Winter 1992).

Review of *Theirs Is the Kingdom:Celebrating the Gospel in Urban America*, by Robert Lupton (San Fransisco: Harper and Row, 1989). In *Search* (Winter 1992).

Review of *Mastering Outreach and Evangelism*, by Calvin Ratz, Frank Tillapaugh, and Myron Augsburger (Portland: Multnomah, 1991). In *Criswell Theological Review* (Spring 1992).

Review of *George Whitefield: God's Anointed Servant in the Great Revival of the Eighteenth Century*, by Arnold A. Dallimore (Westchester, IL: Crossway Books, 1990). In *Criswell Theological Review* (Fall 1991).

Review of *Growing an Evangelistic Sunday School*, by Ken Hemphill and R. Wayne Jones. Nashville: Broadman Press, 1989. In *Search* (Fall 1991).

Review of *America's Only Hope*, by Anthony T. Evans (Chicago: Moody Press, 1990). In *Criswell Theological Review* (Spring 1991).

Review of *Rise and Shine: A Wake-up Call*, by Charles R. Swindoll. Portland: Multnomah, 1989. In *Criswell Theological Review* (Fall 1990).

Review of *Lost!*, by James M. Surgener. Nashville: Broadman, 1988. In *Search* (Summer 1990).

Review of *Witnessing Without Fear,* by Bill Bright. San Bernadino: Here's Life, 1987. In *Search* (Spring 1990).

Review of *The Master Plan of Discipleship,* by Robert E. Coleman. Old Tappan: Fleming H. Revell, 1987. In *Search* (Spring 1990).

Review of *Reclaiming Inactive Church Members*, by Mark S. Jones. Nashville: Broadman, 1988. In *Search* (Spring 1990).

Review of *God the Evangelist*, by David F. Wells. Grand Rapids: William B. Eerdmans, 1987. In *Search* (Winter 1990).

Review of *Power Evangelism*, by John Wimber with Kevin Springer (San Francisco: Harper & Row, 1989).

Review of *Evangelism Encounter*, by Dick Sisson. Wheaton: Victor Books, 1988. In *Criswell Theological Review* (Fall 1989).

Review of *The Doctrine of Prayer*, by T. W. Hunt. Nashville: Convention Press, 1986. In *Criswell Theological Review* (Fall 1989).

Person Index

Scripture Index

Genesis

3:9 *108*
12:1-4 *115*

2 Samuel

23:2 *185*

Esther

2:15 *102*
4:13-14 *102*

Psalms

3:8 *208*
19:7 *184*
20:1 *38*
54:1 *38*

115:1 *74*
119:105 *185*

Proverbs

18:10 *38*
27:17 *12*
30:5-6 *184*

Isaiah

6 *5, 115, 117*
6:1-3 *205*
6:8 *117*
26:8 *103*
43:7 *204*

Amos

3:3 *211*

Subject Index

A

B

Baptism *62-66, 68, 148, 213, 228*

Belief *73, 85, 134, 192, 196-197, 202, 205, 208, 213*

Bible *7, 12, 22, 56, 73, 85, 91-92, 101, 122-124, 137, 147-150, 152, 184-185, 191, 194, 196, 199-200, 204, 206, 210, 214, 222-223, 231*

Bible Belt *196, 199*

Biblical *17, 27, 29, 34, 44, 46, 70, 73, 83-85, 107-112, 124, 126-128, 130-134, 138, 140, 143, 145, 159-164, 169, 172, 175, 184-186, 188-189, 192-196, 198, 202-204, 206-211, 214, 216, 220-221, 224, 227, 233-235*

Blessing *5, 25, 42, 49, 115, 177, 189, 216, 235*

Boldness *132, 137, 154*

Brownwood Revival *18, 225*

Building *18, 27, 70, 84, 95, 97, 151, 161, 173, 198, 203, 232*

Burden *6, 38*

C

Calvinist *205, 215*

Campus *51, 56-57, 62-63, 93-95, 160, 170, 194, 200, 225, 228*

Centennial Celebration *55*

Character *5-7, 27, 36, 38-40, 42, 45, 94, 110, 115, 144, 167-168, 184, 194, 221, 236*

Charles E. Fuller Institute of Evangelism & Growth *154*

Child *x, 17, 19-20, 27-28, 61, 78, 87-88, 116, 122, 149, 160, 162, 171-172, 216, 221, 224, 231, 236*

Choice *11, 20, 24, 66, 117-118*

Christ *ix, 7-15, 22, 34, 36-40, 42-45, 47, 49, 57, 62, 69-74, 77-78, 80, 84, 87, 89, 91-95, 99, 101, 103, 107, 109-110, 112, 114-115, 119-121, 123, 125-128, 130, 132, 136-141, 143-146, 148, 150-156, 160-170, 176, 178-179, 185, 190-191, 199-200, 204-206, 208-209, 211, 216, 223-224, 226, 228, 236*

Christendom *4, 118, 119*

Christian *x, xi, 7, 11-13, 15, 23-24, 27, 38-43, 45, 49, 52-53, 55-57, 61-62, 66, 69-70, 72, 79-81, 84-88, 99, 106-109, 111-112, 118-119, 135, 143-146, 148, 150-156, 158-159, 165-167, 171, 174-175, 184-186, 191, 195-199, 202-203, 205-206, 210, 213-216, 222, 224, 228, 231-232, 242-243*

D

Death *19, 24-25, 40, 102, 110, 123, 136, 210, 213*

Decision *10, 19, 21, 81-82, 139-140, 191, 224*

Denomination *xiv, 13-14, 55, 62-64, 67-68, 72-73, 79, 81-82, 120, 144, 211, 216*

Devotion *53, 93, 235*

Disciple *7, 10, 14-15, 20, 27, 35-36, 38-42, 45, 110, 113-114, 117, 124, 132, 136, 144, 149, 156, 158-159, 161, 163, 165-166, 169, 176, 189, 192, 194-195, 216, 227*

Discipleship *ix, 8-10, 12, 20, 136, 175, 192, 203, 205, 208, 209, 238*

Divorce *22-23, 25*

DNA *68, 110, 186, 193*

Doctrine *5-7, 10, 85-86, 131, 149, 184-185, 200-201, 203-214, 216, 239*

Downtown *121, 160, 166*

E

e3 Partners *171-172, 176, 193*

Easter *83*

Easy-believism *175*

EE *68, 154*

Encouragement *x, 13, 47, 71, 91, 98, 176*

Enemy *18, 24, 29, 38-39, 43*

Ephesus *22-24, 149*

Eschatological *41*

Eschatology *210*

Eternal *36-37, 40, 42-43, 45, 84, 92, 108, 121, 123, 136, 140, 208, 210*

Ethic *110, 114, 195, 205, 221*

Evangelicals *4, 111-112, 122, 136, 199*

Evangelism *viii, ix, x, xi, xiv, 3-5, 8-10, 12, 38, 44, 47, 61-74, 83-84, 87, 111, 118, 129-134, 136-141, 143, 145, 147, 149, 152-156, 160-161, 168-170, 175-176, 178, 201, 203, 205, 208-209, 219-221, 223-225, 228-239, 241-243*

Evangelist *viii, ix, 9, 48, 56, 130-131, 133-134, 136-139, 141-156, 163, 203, 226, 233, 238*

Evangelistic *viii, 10, 44, 63-64, 66-73, 84, 87, 108-110, 126, 129-133, 137-140, 152, 154, 169-172, 174-179, 188, 194, 201, 226, 230, 238*

Extra-biblical *204*

F

Facebook *91, 95, 100*

Faculty *183*

Faith/faithful i*x, 6-8, 11, 14, 18, 33, 38-39, 44, 46, 53, 55, 70-71, 74, 97, 117, 124, 126-128, 130, 132, 136, 138-139, 144-145, 149, 151-153, 160, 166, 169-170, 177-179, 190, 192-193, 196, 198-199, 201-205, 208, 213-216, 228, 231-232, 237, 241*

FAITH *68*

Fall, The *184, 204, 207*

Family i*x, 17-20, 24, 28, 39, 61, 87, 95, 198*

Fasting *102-103, 118, 233*

Father (God) *35-43, 109-110, 113, 115-117, 140, 160, 167, 187, 205*

Fear *8, 85, 120, 150, 158, 230, 238*

Fellowship *11, 34, 86, 211-215, 236*

Festschrift i*x, x, xiii*

Festival *70, 103, 160*

Follow-up *82, 131, 224, 234*

Forgiveness *6, 114, 123, 140, 167, 226*

G

Gift of Evangelism *viii, 141, 147*

Gift of Evangelist *142-147, 149-151, 153-156*

Global Harvest Ministries *154*

Glory *5, 12, 15, 41-43, 45, 63, 74, 103, 118, 128, 160, 171, 177, 186, 189, 198, 204-205, 208, 210, 216*

God *x, 5-10, 13, 15, 17-27, 34-36, 38-40, 43-47, 50-52, 57, 59, 62-63, 67-69, 71-72, 74, 80, 84, 87, 89, 91-92, 94-95, 98-103, 106-128, 131, 133-135, 137-138, 144-146, 148-151, 154, 158-165, 167-168, 170-172, 175-179, 184-194, 198-200, 202-205, 207-210, 215-216, 219-220, 222-223, 225-228, 232-233, 235-236, 238*

God's plan *17, 116, 121, 131, 177, 210*

God's Word *19, 22, 185, 200, 226*

J

Jerusalem *123, 128, 133, 148, 155, 161*

Jesus *vii, ix, 7, 15, 18, 20, 22-24, 26, 29, 34-46, 62, 69-72, 74, 78, 81, 91-92, 99, 107-110, 112-119, 121-123, 126-128, 130, 132, 134, 136, 139, 144-145, 148, 151-153, 155-156, 159-161, 164-167, 177, 185, 189-190, 194, 200, 204-205, 211, 221, 223-224, 227-228, 237*

Jesus Movement *vii, ix, 61-67, 70-72, 74, 220, 222-223, 228, 232, 234*

Jew *102, 165-166*

Jewish *102-103, 133, 149, 165-166, 206*

K

Kingdom *18, 33-36, 41-44, 46, 87, 98, 102, 106, 110, 112-113, 116, 122-126, 128, 141, 150-151, 154, 159, 165, 178, 186-187, 190, 192, 199, 209, 216, 227, 237*

L

Lamb *24-25, 189-190*

Lampstand *22-23*

Language *24, 85, 96, 119, 185, 193, 195-198, 201*

Lay person *144, 171*

Leader *8, 12-14, 28, 41, 48, 50, 55, 58, 66, 72, 81, 83, 94, 98, 109, 112-113, 119-121, 142, 146, 150-151, 153-156, 163-164, 169, 171, 174-177, 222-223, 227, 237*

Leadership *vii, x, 1, 34, 49-50, 93, 98, 110, 150-151, 153-154, 174-176, 179, 234, 236*

Liberty Baptist Theological Seminary *160, 243*

Liberty University *160*

LifeWay *147, 158, 194, 201, 242*

Local associations *14, 201-202*

Lord *x, xiv, 4-8, 10-12, 14-15, 24, 34, 39, 56, 62, 68, 70, 74, 103, 118, 130, 132, 134-135, 146, 152, 156, 184, 188-191, 201, 204-205, 208, 210*

N

NAMB *68, 162*

Neighborhood *69, 87, 120, 161-163, 197*

NET *68, 224*

New Testament *34, 44, 115, 131-132, 136, 138-139, 142-143, 147-148, 150-151, 206, 214, 223-224*

Non-Calvinist *215*

North Greenville University *xii, xiii, 150, 264, 265*

O

Obedience *xiv, 5-8, 10-12, 37, 40, 44, 115, 117, 134-135, 153, 164, 190, 216*

P

Parachurch *62, 209*

Passion Movement *103*

Pastor *ix, xiv, 4, 13-14, 17, 22, 24, 80, 83, 85, 96, 98, 100, 109, 120-121, 130, 144, 146, 148-152, 154, 163, 196-197, 201, 203, 206, 212-213, 222, 236, 241-243*

Pentecostal *67*

Philosophy of evangelism *viii, 129, 140*

Poor *80, 122, 126, 200-201*

Post-Christian *195*

Poverty *24, 80*

Pragmatism *138, 205*

Pray *4, 13-14, 18-19, 27, 33-46, 51, 56, 78, 93-94, 98-99, 101, 118, 121, 137, 146, 148, 173, 176, 179, 200, 208, 215, 224*

Prayer *vii, 13-15, 18, 33-56, 58-59, 67, 92-93, 96, 99, 102-103, 134, 175-176, 188, 193, 197, 202, 208, 216, 219, 221, 224-227, 229-233, 235, 239, 242*

Preach *9, 33, 63, 73, 81, 85, 101, 120, 127, 132, 139, 148, 188, 190, 192-193, 196, 202, 206-207, 209, 215, 220, 237, 241*

Preacher *5, 21, 93, 121, 196, 212*

Proclamation *9-10, 57, 109, 112, 122-124, 126-127, 133, 137-139, 163, 170, 172, 203, 215, 235*

Q

Qur'an *208*

R

Racism *24*

raison d'etre *186*

Redemption *8, 44, 107, 109, 177, 179, 186-187*

Refugee *19*

Regeneration *208-209*

Relational *36, 106, 207*

Relationships *13, 65, 70, 84, 87, 95, 106, 163, 168, 170, 207, 228*

Religion *49-50, 205*

Repent *23, 26-27, 136-137, 139, 140, 208*

Repentance *26, 69, 123, 170, 208, 226*

Resurgence *xiv, 5, 11, 15, 64, 69, 72-72, 77, 84, 86, 89, 92, 94, 184-185, 202, 212, 216*

Revelation *40, 186, 202, 204, 208, 216*

Revival *vii, xiv, 6, 18, 33-34, 43-45, 47-51, 53, 55, 57, 59, 62-63, 65, 92-95, 148, 200, 219-220, 223-230, 233, 235-238*

Revive *34, 44-45, 89, 226*

Ritual *36*

S

Sacrifice *8, 19, 21, 25, 71, 123, 156, 163, 167, 209*

Salvation *18, 57, 73, 92-93, 108-109, 131, 135-137, 139-140, 185, 188, 190-191, 204, 206, 208, 213, 216*

Sanctification *40, 42*

Sanhedrin *178*

Satan *39, 185*

Savior *10, 15, 34, 37, 39, 70, 107, 168, 187, 208*

Scripture *36, 73, 91, 101, 111, 113, 123, 125-126, 133, 138, 140, 147, 149, 153-155, 164, 184-189, 192-193, 202-206, 209-211, 214, 216, 226*

Seed *17, 199*

Seeker-sensitive *84*

Seminary *ix, x, xi, xiv, 3, 61, 65-66, 71, 73, 112, 129, 141, 152, 154, 160, 170, 183, 185, 202, 210-211, 219, 221, 225, 228, 236, 241-243*

Sender *109-112, 115, 117, 119*

Sermon *81, 142, 195, 197, 202, 206, 230, 232, 235*

Servant *10, 100, 102, 182, 211, 223-224, 231, 233, 238, 243*

Sex *208*

Sin *43, 62, 80, 114-115, 123, 125, 127, 133, 135-137, 139-140, 155, 167, 185-187, 190, 220, 232*

Socio-cultural *185, 195, 199*

South Asia *170, 192*

South India *178*

Southeastern Baptist Theological Seminary *x, 66, 129, 141, 170, 183, 185, 202, 210, 219, 241-243*

Southern Baptist Convention (SBC) *viii, 15, 63-69, 71-74, 170, 183-184, 186, 189, 194-195, 202, 209-210, 212, 216, 230-234*

Southwestern Baptist Theological Seminary *xi, xii, xiii, xvi, 61, 73, 225, 228, 235, 263, 264, 265*

Spirit temples *208*

Spiritual awakening *vii, 31, 33-34, 43-47, 49, 61-62, 64-66, 219-220, 225-227, 229-230, 233, 237, 242*

Sports *11, 15*

State conventions *14, 72-73, 201-202, 242*

Story *5, 11, 25, 27, 48, 50, 52, 55, 58, 72, 86, 87, 92, 95, 101, 103, 109, 113, 116, 121-122, 208, 224-225*

Suburbanites *79*

Suburbs *80, 196, 210*

Sunday School *4, 86, 112, 185, 223, 229, 234, 238*

T

Teenager *92, 94, 96, 101, 103*

Temptation *39, 45, 133, 205, 211, 226, 235*

Tempted *21, 193*

Testimonies *50, 208, 223, 227*

Testimony *24, 39, 43, 190, 206, 208, 224, 232*

Tradition *ix, 68, 106, 109, 165-166, 184, 211, 214*

Transitions *18, 37, 48, 86*

Tribal *197, 208*

Tribal gods *208*

Triennial Convention *189*

Triune *108, 186, 210, 216*

Truth *5, 6, 9-11, 14, 19, 22, 36, 40, 45, 48, 71, 73, 84, 92, 111, 115-117, 158, 160-161, 163, 167, 186, 190, 194-195, 204-206, 214-216, 231*

Turkey *23*

U

Unbeliever *39, 72, 131, 136-139, 141, 144, 149*

Unchurched *viii, 77-89, 151-152, 197, 221-223, 230-232, 236*

Unity *41, 151*

Unreached *14, 174, 177-178, 188, 191-193*

UPG *174*

Urban *53, 79, 115, 199, 222, 237*

Urgency *39, 136, 161, 170*

V

Valor *19-20, 24-25, 27, 29*

Vision *viii, x, 55, 59, 74, 113, 121, 163, 174-177, 183, 189, 209*

Vocabulary *196, 198*

Vocation *15, 198, 201, 207*

Volunteer *56-59, 160*

W

Wagner Leadership Institute *154*

Wife (wives) *ix, x, 3, 19, 21-22, 25-26, 29, 78, 87, 118*

Wikipedia *105*

WIN *65-66, 228*

Wisdom *39, 98, 112, 118, 137, 147, 189, 215*

Witch doctors *208*

Witness *8-10, 35-36, 38-41, 43, 61-62, 65-66, 70, 116, 123, 137-138, 143-146, 148, 153, 156, 184, 187, 202, 224, 229, 231, 234-235, 238*

Witnessing *8, 70, 131, 153, 166, 224, 230, 238*

World War *19, 58, 73*

Y

YMCA *56, 57*

Youth *ix, 50, 58, 62, 64, 66, 70-72, 200, 220, 222-223, 228-230, 232-233, 235-237*

Contributors

Daniel L. Akin (PhD, University of Texas at Arlington), President and Professor of Preaching and Theology, Southeastern Baptist Theological Seminary.

Bruce Riley Ashford (PhD, Southeastern Baptist Theological Seminary), Provost, Associate Professor of Theology and Culture, Fellow for the Bush Center for Faith and Culture, Southeastern Baptist Theological Seminary.

John Avant (PhD, Southwestern Baptist Theological Seminary), Senior Pastor, First Baptist Concord, Knoxville, TN.

Roy Fish (PhD, Southwestern Baptist Theological Seminary), Distinguished Professor Emeritus of Evangelism and Former L.R. Scarborough Chair of Fire, Southwestern Baptist Theological Seminary.

Tommy Kiker (PhD, Southeastern Baptist Theological Seminary), Assistant Professor of Pastoral Ministry and James Draper Chair of Pastoral Ministry, Southwestern Baptist Theological Seminary.

Matt Lawson (MDiv, Southeastern Baptist Theological Seminary), High School Pastor, First Baptist Church, Woodstock, GA.

Bobby R. Lewis (PhD, Southeastern Baptist Theological Seminary), Senior Pastor, Salem Baptist Church, Dobson, NC.

Larry Steven McDonald (PhD, Southeastern Baptist Theological Seminary; DMin, Reformed Theological Seminary), Professor of Christian Spirituality, Dean and Director of Doctor of Ministry Studies, T. Walter Brashier Graduate School of Christian Ministry, North Greenville University.

Doug Munton (PhD, Southwestern Baptist Theological Seminary), Senior Pastor, First Baptist Church, O'Fallon, IL.

Matt Queen (PhD, Southeastern Baptist Theological Seminary), Assistant Professor of Evangelism, Associate Dean for Doctoral Programs, Roy Fish School of Evangelism and Missions, Southwestern Baptist Theological Seminary.

Thom S. Rainer (PhD, Southern Baptist Theological Seminary), President and CEO of LifeWay Christian Resources.

George G. Robinson (DMiss, Western Seminary), Assistant Professor of Missions and Evangelism, The Richard and Gina Headrick Chair of World Missions, Southeastern Baptist Theological Seminary.

J. Chris Schofield (PhD, Southeastern Baptist Theological Seminary), Director of the Office of Prayer for Evangelization and Spiritual Awakening, Baptist State Convention of North Carolina.

Ed Stetzer (PhD, Southern Baptist Theological Seminary; DMin, Beeson Divinity School), President of LifeWay Research and Missiologist in Residence, LifeWay Christian Resources.

Todd Stewart (PhD, Southeastern Baptist Theological Seminary), Senior Pastor, Lee Road Baptist Church, Taylors, SC and Adjunct Professor of Evangelism, T. Walter Brashier Graduate School of Christian Ministry, North Greenville University.

David A. Wheeler (PhD, Southwestern Baptist Theological Seminary), Professor of Evangelism, Associate Director of the Center for Ministry Training, Associate Director for the Center for Church Planting, and Director of Applied and Servant Evangelism Ministries, Liberty Baptist Theological Seminary.